Jewish Girls Gone Wild

"Linda Pressman brings her humor and keen eye for detail to this 1970s coming-of-age story set in Arizona. It's a tale about finding your place in an ever-changing world, something all of us can relate to." – Windy Lynn Harris, author of *Writing & Selling Short Stories & Personal Essays: The Essential Guide to Getting Your Work Published*

"I adore [Pressman's] wit, [her] turns of phrase, and [her] observational humor…. There were so many individual sentences, paragraphs, and whole sections in here that I just loved – descriptions that perfectly brought back to life a moment from my own 70s youth that I'd long forgotten; character portrayals that nailed a person in a few sentences; dialogue that's truly authentic; and just so much cringe of coming of age. I'm wheeling out the highest of praise here…" – Theo Nestor, author of *Writing is My Drink*, and *How to Sleep Alone in a King-Sized Bed*

"The road from Skokie to Scottsdale is filled with love, life lessons and so many sisters. Linda Pressman perfectly captures what it's like to be an outsider in a new town, in a story only she can tell. You'll laugh, you'll cry, you'll plotz -- in all the best ways."
– Amy Silverman, author of *My Heart Can't Even Believe It: A Story of Science, Love and Down Syndrome*

Praise for
Looking Up

"A memoir that is truly memorable." – *Writer's Digest*

"Humor and tragedy blend seamlessly in this memoir of childhood upbringing and family trauma. A memoir whose heart pays considerable homage to its subjects." - *Kirkus Reviews*

"...Pressman is a talented writer and this book is a testament to her parents' truly indomitable will." - *Publishers Weekly*

"*Looking Up* is hilarious, beautiful, painful and powerful. Pressman is a gifted writer." - Frannie Sheridan, Writer and Performer of *Confessions of a Jewish Shiksa…Dancing on Hitler's Grave,* and winner of The Gabriel Award on NPR.

"…funny, wacky, and heartbreaking…a story offering a unique perspective on the Holocaust, one generation removed from the war." - Cindy Sher, Editor, *JUF News* and Writer, *OY!Chicago*

"*Looking Up: A Memoir of Sisters, Survivors and Skokie* is horrifying, tender and irreverent. This book about a family of nine figuring out life's complexities is like no other memoir I've read on the Holocaust." - Sandra Hurtes, author of *On My Way to Someplace Else* and *Rescue: A Memoir*

Grand Prize Winner
Writer's Digest 20th Annual Self-Published Book Contest

Jewish Girls Gone Wild

A Memoir of
Skokie, Scottsdale, and the Seventies

LINDA PRESSMAN

Printed in the United States of America

First edition January 2022

ISBN-13: 9781725922235 Paperback
ISBN-13: 9798787594362 Hardcover

Library of Congress Control Number: 2021914258

Cover design: Izabela Designs

Website: lindajpressman.com

Facebook: Linda Pressman, Author page

Twitter: @barmitzvahzilla

Email: lindajpressman@gmail.com

or linda@lindajpressman.com

Jewish Girls Gone Wild is a work of nonfiction. It is a story of growing
up told from the author's perspective as a teenager. It may not reflect
that of other family members or other participants in the events in the
book, and the title is intended to reflect solely on the author. In various
places in the book humor has been used and, in those places, the
narrative should be considered humorous rather than literal. Names have
been changed and some composite characteristics may have been
utilized to protect the privacy of the individuals involved.

Table of Contents

In memory of my mother, Helene Burt
In memory of my father, Harry Burt

Jewish Girls Gone Wild

Opening
Wifeless

Across the street from us, Ethel Shapiro is dying.

As the months disappear after our cross-country move, turning 1973 into 1974, and then into 1975, so does our neighbor, piece by piece. When she emerges from her house, her husband Mickey pulls his car right up to the door on their great looping driveway in order to minimize her steps, carrying her off to one remedy or another. Her paisley dresses, which once fit, now hang on her like curtains and she wears a mysterious, dramatic turban on her head and huge Jackie Onassis sunglasses.

I'm fourteen, so I don't really know yet what dying looks like and no one talks about it, as if by mentioning the word cancer they will call it into being. Ethel's illness goes unremarked, just that suddenly she and Mickey can't be here or there, at this neighborhood poker party or that one. There's some shrugging, some awkward silences.

Ethel had been an essential part of our neighborhood, one-half of one of the boisterous Jewish couples living on our Arizona street, forming a poker-playing social group. When we first met them after our move from Chicago, she appeared vibrant and healthy, bounding off with Mickey to all the parties, her hair back-combed to the ceiling, wearing those pretty paisley dresses and practical pumps.

At the poker parties everyone understood their place in the social fabric. It was 1973, after all. Each couple was a husband and a wife, no monkey business, no girlfriends, no boyfriends. There was no past in which they weren't together and no future in which one was missing. No one is allowed to get divorced or die, to be single or a widow or a widower or a sex-crazed divorcée or a sex-crazed widow, sex-crazed being a term reserved somehow for women. Some allowance could potentially be made for a man who found himself suddenly single – men, after all, would soon be snatched up. But definitely no women. There was an overriding belief that single women steal husbands.

Ethel caused some consternation among the other ladies when it became known that she'd been married before. More than that, she didn't even try to hide this fact, to prevaricate, to pretend that her life began with Mickey. She even admitted to having a son from her early marriage. No one, absolutely no one, had been married before, or at least admitted it, not in 1973. She was saved from being ostracized only by this second marriage.

The neighborhood couples, which included my parents, Harry and Helen, all matched up very neatly, two by two by two, a Jewish Noah's Ark on a one-block long street in the middle of the Arizona desert, all drawn to buy houses there by a billboard advertising the neighborhood out front with the builder's name, Mitch Cohen. My parents are odd in a way no one mentions – they are Eastern European Holocaust Survivors passing for a regular American couple, both from the shifting boundaries of pre-war Poland. Their preferred language is Yiddish, and their preferred company is our family, all left back in Chicago, in Skokie, and all from unspeakable pasts. It's clunky for my parents, hanging out with these American Jews in our new neighborhood, all of whom were safely in the U.S. generations before the war, safe here with their American accents, with their curiosity over my parents' accents. My parents bristle when asked where they're from. If pressed, they say they are French.

Ethel was dying slowly, but my dad died quickly in the spring of 1975, beating her by less than two months, heart attacks being quicker than cancer. She comes to his funeral in March. I see her exit the house hanging onto Mickey's arm for support from my position in the limo at our house across the street. We didn't know that we'd be at that same mortuary, at that same cemetery, by early May, all of us gathered there for her this time.

Then my mother is alone, and Mickey is alone, a widow and a widower, sitting in their identical houses on their identical lots, staring out of their identical living room windows at each other across the street. Although my mother dates, although she works, although she gets matched up over and over again, the thought of Mickey seems to be on a continuous reel looping through her brain. A man, conveniently widowed right across the street. A man who, of course, needs a woman. A man, sitting in the gloom of his house day after day, wifeless.

I have a picture of my mother from later that year. She is cute and perky, only forty-five-years old. Her hair is a mass of blowing ash blonde fuzz. She's wearing a polyester pant suit with wide lapels, a shell necklace shows through the open collar of her shirt, and she's holding a smart pocketbook. She is squinting into the sun, sunglasses in her hands.

Then I notice a few other things about the picture. She's across the street, in front of Mickey Shapiro's house, in the spot where he once pulled up to get Ethel. And my mother is not just over there, but familiar enough to have a picture taken over there, like she lives there.

The picture has a giant date scrawled on the bottom – September 17, 1975. Six months after my father died, four months after Ethel died.

The two of them rejoin the neighborhood poker parties together, my mother the pretend Ethel, Mickey the pretend Harry. It's the 1970s, after all, and everyone has to be a couple.

One
A Different Kind of Heat

There are families who fly across the country on vacations and there are families who drive across the country on vacations and I, permanently ensconced in the rear-facing seat in my parents' Ford Country Squire station wagon, am part of a family that drives.

In 1970, coinciding perhaps, with the purchase of this car, my dad suddenly got the wild and crazy idea that he should pack up his younger set of daughters, the youngest four of seven, and take a vacation, his first after nineteen years in America. Not that he needed a vacation. Of course not. Vacations were for lazy Americans. My dad, the Holocaust Survivor, the Polish Immigrant via Siberia, via Tashkent, and via the kosher meat-packing industry of New York, wasn't like those weak American men. He could outwork them, out-lift them, and now he had the wonderful opportunity to prove he could out-drive them. And so he did, first to Toronto one year, to Florida the next, and then all the way across the country to California the third year. We stop in Arizona on our way and suddenly his mind is made up. In 1973 he packs up the cars and we move.

Did he have visions in his head of the good life? Of lounging poolside year-round in Scottsdale calling his brothers in Chicago on our outside extension, asking them how they were enjoying the snowstorms? Of timing his calls precisely for the middle of those snowstorms in order to drive his point home? Did he expect the brothers to visit, and then visit again, and then again, until they bought matching houses on our new street, until he recreated Skokie in Scottsdale, a Jewish American shtetl, this time in Arizona?

Most likely, yes.

I'm in the way back of the back of the station wagon, in the backward seat, which means I'm always facing what we've just driven away from instead of what we're driving towards. I need to have one row of seats and my little sister Mindy has to have the other, in the middle, far enough away from each other so neither of us will kill the other fighting during the drive.

It wasn't always like this between us. Since our family is arranged like a mini sorority house, in a permanent state of hazing, it's the older sisters, Francene, Lauren, and Brenda, against the younger ones, the twins, Denise and Sherry, and me and Mindy. I'd always found my relationship with Mindy very satisfying, for me anyway. I had bossed her around and tormented her. I'd been her mini-mom in a family where each older sister was the mini-mom of the sister below, and I was stuck with the twins above me. Two mini-moms. She obeyed me, at least better than I obeyed the twins. One day Mindy ruined this set up by standing up for herself and clobbering me. I was still somewhat flummoxed that she'd objected to being my personal servant. Things gradually became volatile. I couldn't be happy until I'd restored the status quo and she wasn't going back.

So I'm essentially alone in the back of the car until Dad agrees to stop each day.

I have a rich life here in the back back of the station wagon, my little all-window cabana. I wave at all the truckers. I draw pictures of the Model T-like fronts of their trucks. I ponder their cargo. I draw, I write, I notice the landscape, flat plains leading to flat topped mountains in New Mexico and finally to pointy brown mountains in Arizona. The one time we had continued onto California I had watched as the mountains continued changing, turning green, until everything turned blue at the ocean. I sing the appropriate anthems – *America the Beautiful* and the *Star-Spangled Banner* – singing about waves of grain when I see waves of grain, and purple mountains majesty when there are actually purple mountains majesty right in front of me.

For the move, we're a two-car caravan containing my parents and six of their seven daughters. The oldest sister, Francine, who is married, will follow within the year. Mindy and I, being the lowliest of the low, the youngest of the young, are permanently stuck with our parents in the station wagon. I am thirteen, skinny, sickly, with braces and pimples. Mindy is nine, cherubic-looking, with curly hair that our mother sometimes massacres into a ragged, uneven pixie. Behind us, lost somewhere way down the skinny Interstate, a dot on the horizon, is the other car, the Impala, the teen car, which contains my sisters Brenda and Lauren, eighteen and nineteen, the twins, who are fifteen, and our dog, Rusty. Theirs is the party car, with music pouring out of the windows along with cigarette smoke. When we stop, they have just a few seconds to turn down the radio and crank the windows wide to get rid of the billowing cigarette smoke, to pretend to dad that their ride is as boring and uneventful as ours. He doesn't know they smoke.

"Herschel, What's the rush?" my mother complains in the front seat, using my father's Yiddish name. She holds a map upside down along with the Holiday Inn travel guide, which lists all the Holiday Inns in the country. We only stay at Holiday Inns.

My dad is not exactly driving across the country so much as he's careening across the country. There are either no speed limits in 1973, or none my dad obeys. I watch as he approaches and then passes all the cars, as he expertly maneuvers our station wagon like it's a Maserati, leaving the Impala puffing behind.

I'd like him to drive slowly so I could ponder everything we're leaving behind. I need time to reflect on this move, to be pensive, to mull. The streets of my Skokie childhood line up in my memory, along with my best friends, the boy I thought I'd marry, our house – certainly the most wonderful house ever – the gangs of roving kids my age or my sisters' ages, scattered all throughout the neighborhood. A neighborhood like a giant *mishpocha* – everyone knew our business and we knew everyone's business. This was normal and good and expected. I need my dad to slow down. I need to write it all down and imprint everything on my brain, from my teachers' names and the names of all the neighbors to the details of the Bar and Bat Mitzvahs I'd attended, ripped away halfway through my thirteenth year. My grandparents, my cousins, my aunts, my uncles.

But my dad doesn't linger, and he never drives slowly.

For him, getting anywhere is invariably a race. There can be only one victor and it's going to be him. Every day he starts out planning to beat all the traffic heading west out of the hotel, out of the tiny cities we stay in, heading out on the Interstate.

In the waning days of July, a gigantic moving truck had pulled up in front of our house in Skokie, throwing shadows on everything around it. Everything was to be moved from the house into the truck except us, the cars, and the dog. Dad had scientifically calculated how long it would take this behemoth to get to Arizona. He uses his own statistics – he once made it to Arizona in a record-breaking two days – for him just a quick race around a portion of the globe, so for the truck he calculates a very slow four days. He gives the truck a two-day head start. Then we hand over the keys to our house to the strangers who now bewilderingly live there, go stay in our aunt and uncle's house down the street based on these calculations.

We leave on August 3rd, and somewhere along the way, Dad zooms past the truck.

Of course, it would have made more sense to drive alongside the truck on our westward journey, to mimic the truck, chugging painstakingly up the hills and then barreling down the other sides. But my dad only has an on and an off switch, there is no control for speed. If he's driving, he's driving fast because he's in a constant race to prove himself the equal and better than everyone and everything, so it's necessary that even the professional truck driver, nameless and nearly faceless as we pass in a blur, knows this too.

***

We're on the road and we know that our party is made of two cars full of us and a barking dog, but in the world inside our dad's head, where authorities must be cheated first or they'll steal us blind, there are not eight of us and a barking dog. We are, instead, four people, no dog. My dad has figured out somewhere along the way that hotel rooms are charged per occupant *for the same exact room!* So, of course, we are always the least number of people with the greatest number of beds, the ones who don't exist crouching down in the parking lot inside the cars with the dog while my dad checks in. Although we officially have no dog, the dog doesn't know this. He barks excitedly. We hush him up, like he understands English. Ultimately, we hide him, muffle his barks, we bribe him with food, and we take him on walks far away from the hotel office.

We make our way across the giant map of the country, overtaking our moving truck which left two days before us. The trip is now familiar. Illinois, Missouri, Oklahoma, the Texas panhandle, New Mexico and, finally, Arizona. Dad wins the race down the highway. We beat everyone – the moving truck, my sisters in the Impala, the house being built.

He can't help himself. He can't help but try again and again to beat his own best time, running a permanent race against himself, against the weather, against the roadway, against other cars, and against fate. We can't stop, can't stay for a while, can't rest by the pool for another day, even though we'll beat our moving truck to Arizona by days, even though our house won't be ready to move into for a week and we'll have to stay in another Holiday Inn, this one in Scottsdale. So we beat the truck somewhere in the panhandle of Oklahoma or the panhandle of Texas – who knew there were so many panhandles? He zooms past it going one hundred miles per hour, his comfortable driving speed. My dad had timed our drive wrong, estimating that giving the truck a two-day start would be sufficient for all the vehicles to pull up, synchronized, at the exact same moment at our new house. But we get to Scottsdale days before the truck, the house isn't ready anyway, and we retreat to the Holiday Inn Scottsdale.

"Get up, you bums!"

Dad is standing in the doorway to the connecting room at dawn the next day waking us all up so that we can sneak out of the hotel, drive like crazy to our next destination, and then do it all over again the next day.

Dad drives and drives and drives. For some reason, perhaps wanting to rest up before we begin our descent into Phoenix, we stop in Gallup, New Mexico. This town suits all of Dad's purposes. It's tiny so he can be the big city slicker from Chicago instead of the greenhorn with an accent from Poland, and there is a Holiday Inn sign blinking greenly from the side of the road. This is all he needs to be happy.

We're far enough away from home that I've had my time to get pensive there in the way back of the station wagon. I'm thirteen and I'm already lamenting my lost childhood. I'm filled with foreboding about the future, worrying about whether I'll make friends in Arizona and marrying myself off at eighteen, like my oldest sister. Looking around gives me no comfort. Every single thing looks wrong. There are flat expanses of land in all directions instead of the congestion of the Skokie streets and strange chopped off, squared off, mountains instead of the comfort of the flat prairie plains. I'm trying my best to feel like a Manifest Destiny-type pioneer, the car my stagecoach, but, really, I'm just terrified by what awaits me in Arizona. I'm buoyed up by the fact that kids lined the streets like paparazzi when new kids moved into our neighborhood back home, and then by what happens when we get to Gallup, New Mexico.

I do the usual. I run into the room Mindy and I are stuck sharing with our parents, quickly change into my skirted bathing suit. I slap a rubber bathing cap on my head and then zoom full tilt out towards the pool.

But there's something different going on this one night in Gallup, the motel at the intersection of several Interstates, people meeting by chance here that one night, on their way east or west. That one night there's a roving band of transient children there, like the Land of Misfit Toys on the western edge of New Mexico. My sisters, Denise and Sherry get swept off into a group of teenagers, instantly popular, smoke rising from the center of their huddle, and, once I dry off, I'm gathered into a ragtag group of tweens.

We have nothing in common except this one perfect night, this perfect breeze, our identical motel rooms, our parents, distracted, already mentally at the end of the road, whichever direction. Or maybe I'm the only one thinking this or mulling much of anything over at all. The others are smoking and philosophizing as only thirteen-year-olds can, smoking in a way I know that shows they've done it in front of a mirror because I have, blowing fancy smoke rings and great big dragon-like exhalations from their nostrils. In other words, they're smoking and I'm coughing but I'm not willing to admit I'm asthmatic because I've decided that asthma is something

I'm leaving behind in Chicago.

This gang is led by a boyish girl who absorbs me into the roving pack, leading us in an endless circle – to the pool, then loping through the parking lot, careening through the lobby. I'm aware I only fit in with these kids by virtue of being the right age and at the right Holiday Inn in the right city on the right Interstate on the right night. Nothing else in the world matters.

This is my first foray into the world at large, outside of my Skokie habitat, like I'm some kind of rare species raised in captivity. They're a pretty wild bunch. I think if I'm not careful in a few crazy hours I could end up devirginized. I'm aware of my differences. I have some idea from my hometown that everyone in the world is Jewish, but here I am, and if this is a harbinger of something, anything, I'll take it. Everything is a clue, a talisman. Is this what I'm going to find at our new home? Are swearing, smoking, ragamuffin kids like these going to be my new best friends in Scottsdale? Is this it? My sign from God? A born optimist, I'll take any sign and I'll take any friends.

In the morning they're gone and we're gone, some of us heading east and some heading west, and I never see them again. It turns out that night really is a harbinger of things to come – my sisters off smoking with their set of cool kids and me running with the hooligans. The writing is on the wall – our family is going to bust wide open and split into a million tiny pieces – smoking, coughing, wild pieces. It turns out that our Jewish family can't move from Skokie and stay intact.

***

Only my parents, my little sister, and I have seen the place we are to live, no one else was with us on our couple of buying trips. That's why it's so bad when Dad drives triumphantly down from the mountains of Flagstaff ready to show off this place, this desert oasis, to the rest of his scoffing daughters with a grand flourish, complete with pool that he's bought them. That'll shut them up. He drives triumphantly, though once we get off the freeway it's a hell of a drive. Suddenly he can't speed, which really cramps his style. He takes the Interstate as far as he can then heads east. He is still triumphant as we pass nothing but block fences facing the road, no houses, and I'm thinking, *oh, c'mon, show your faces*, because in Chicago the fronts of the houses face the road. Of course, they don't turn around and even if they did, they'd be 1960s low-slung slump block houses, puny, and if my sisters saw them, they'd screech to a halt in the middle of the road, turn around, and head back to Chicago.

We continue heading east, past convenience stores, past rutted roads, past fellow drivers in trucks with cowboy hats hauling bales of hay, our mouths circles of astonishment. Horse trailers, feed stores, all illuminated in the bright, dazzling sunshine. We are definitely not in Chicago anymore. Even my heart is sinking, and I was there for the house hunting trips. Dad makes a final triumphant turn from the larger street, suitably named Cactus, onto a smaller road and then, at Cortez, he whips the car in one final triumphant arc all the way around the house, which clearly is not ready for us. There is no fence and no landscaping. The house is a beige rectangle, apparently grown from the dirt. Since the fence is missing, Dad is able to circle the house and pull up behind it,

14

where he's expecting to see a gleaming blue pool, the ultimate triumph to show his daughters a thing or two. It's impossible to see where we are exactly because of the twisting tornado of dust kicked up by the two cars. But we're not in a pool.

Or at least not completely. Dad parks, gets out of the car and sees that he's almost driven off the dirt embankment into the gigantic dirt hole of the unfinished pool, the front wheels teetering on the edge. No cement, no cool decking, no lawn chairs, no blue water, no Mexican tile. Just a pit, really, and a sad, sad house. We cringe at this, knowing Dad has literally moved all of us from Chicago based on the promise of the clear, blue pool that was supposed to greet him.

It's an inauspicious beginning.

I hear my sister Denise yelling through the open windows of the Impala parked behind us.

"I'm not staying in this goddamned hellhole!"

Sherry agrees, "No way!"

In this one instance, I am grateful that my father is nearly deaf from childhood Scarlet Fever – he can't hear them. Mindy and I look at each other. Is she thinking what I'm thinking? That we have previewed Arizona for the rest of the family, we've been their eyes and ears, we chose this place for them. They entrusted their fate to a thirteen-year-old and a nine-year-old.

Dad backs the car up, furious. The Impala follows us as we screech out towards our hotel.

By that night, when we're sitting in the Coco's Restaurant by the hotel, Dad has calmed down. Food calms him down. Food he understands. Maybe a Schnapps.

15

Of course, he'd prefer it if he never had to eat a restaurant meal in his lifetime. The memories of starving during the war, of just how hard he had to work to earn money to get food, are still fresh in his mind. Throwing money away on a restaurant meal, on tips? No. He would rather my mother dance attendance on him for the rest of his life, as she's already done, providing impeccable five-course meals. What for he needs to eat somewhere else instead of good, home cooked food by Chasia, my mother and his slave?

It's *Amerikanish* nonsense, when all a man needs, ultimately, is a hunk of black bread and an onion? That's all they had in the Old Country, after all. What for does he need all this *mishegoss*, waiting and a waiter – who wants to wait? - and table manners and confusing forks and spoons and hot sauce delivered to the table that one time he mistakes for a nice tomato soup and then, when his mouth almost bursts into flames, declares *this* is the end of eating out?

But, of course, we go, because we're stuck in the hotel and a Holiday Inn it must be, no kitchenette nonsense for my father. Since it takes him about fifteen or twenty years in this country to allow himself to enjoy such a strange *goyische* thing – the restaurant meal – he's certainly going to enjoy it when he finally gets there.

It's not just a meal. Oh no. It's symbolic. This is it, finally. He has arrived. There's the child, then Herschel, not the more Americanized Harry, running around his Polish farm being treated like dirt by all the Poles in town, chewing on that hunk of black bread and an onion, and then, flipping forward very quickly, through endless blood, sweat, and tears, trains to Siberia, snow and more snow, bullets, a dead sister, a dead nephew, our laundry in Chicago, money, real estate, and the birth of one disappointing daughter after another, here he stands at his pinnacle – the king at the head of the table at Coco's Restaurant at the Holiday Inn in Scottsdale, Arizona.

"Stop *schnorring*!" He glares at me and Mindy, warning us as we polish off the tiny basket of club crackers on the table. We will eat anything free on the table.

He's certainly going to enjoy this meal. There will be no gobbling. Time will slow to a crawl so Dad can relish this moment. He needs a slow pace, a glacial pace, icebergs arranging themselves before him, for Paleolithic time to end and Mesolithic time to begin.

Dad will eat. Of course he will. He is certainly going to enjoy his time at the restaurant. There will be a big steak and steak knives, and there will be butter. There will be coffee, and there will be a stinky cigar. There will be conversation – just him talking. This is not just a table to my dad, this is his ship of dreams, the golden land – he reclines in glory, in freedom. Having walked into this restaurant, a walk of two decades, no one is going to wedge him out. They'll have to close it to get him to leave.

The waitress reappears, says, "Can I interest you folks in any dessert this evening?" perhaps trying to bring the meal to an end.

My dad just scowls. He looks at the dessert menu even though he has no intention of ever, in his life, ordering a dessert. That would be highway robbery. He orders coffee, lights up a cigar, which is the perfect dessert. He leans back and back and even farther back and contemplates his world, mulling over the distance between a small farm in Poland and

17

the Coco's Restaurant in Scottsdale, Arizona, at the distance between Siberia and this new home in Arizona. He nods his head at his decision to move west. Clearly this is already the good life.

When he's mused, sipped, chomped, leaned, relaxed, smoked, and waxed poetic, finally, he is done. He pays the bill, and we walk out, the lights turning out behind us.

Two
Uprooted

A t one end of the highway is our Skokie house. There's a downstairs with linoleum flooring and a gigantic bar and a laundry room where my mother sews endless reams of curtains for our windows and then sews them again, all while talking in various Yiddish dialects on the telephone, the cord for which has been yanked down there from its spot on the kitchen wall. There's an upstairs with the three bedrooms which somehow hold the nine of us, the three oldest sisters in one, my parents in another, and the four youngest sisters in the last bedroom, at least until the twins kick me and Mindy down to the basement to experience their teen years more fully. There's different-colored carpeting in each room, and a bathroom with fuzzy floral wallpaper and a chandelier. Plenty of people have a chandelier in the dining room, not so many in the bathroom. This is a point of pride for my mother. Every tour of the house includes this bathroom.

There's the main floor with the kitchen, dining room and living room, with plastic-covered furniture, heavy marble tables, a piano, and barrel-shaded lamps. There is a foyer that gets larger and larger over the years, as my mother has it tiled and retiled, extending it, finally, so far that it undulates all the way to the staircase. Somehow, even though our living room is decorated in 1950s French Provincial, intended to resemble Marie Antoinette's drawing room, there is a shiny wood hi-fi because the seven of us can't live without playing Beatles records, and I can't live without my Monkees 45s, walking dreamily around the marble table while I imagine marrying Davy Jones.

There are staircases – two – a front door on the side of the house trimmed out in black railing, a small grassy lot with a dilapidated, dangerous swing set unsecured to the ground so that every time we swung it would lift off the ground, higher and higher and higher. I thought it'd be kind of fun to go flying off into space if it ever became completely untethered, but really, I just would have catapulted to my death. There are trees and thick shrubberies that our neighbor plants to keep us out, but which we bore through to find whatever they're hiding – an above-ground pool, a new dog, children. There is an alley with garbage trucks rumbling by and silver garbage cans and a whole different-looking neighborhood when viewed from the back, the houses unrecognizable, some yards sprouting garages over the years.

The house we leave behind is brick with wood trim and large picture windows and the street is dotted with similar houses, like little postage stamps, each one magically spilling out children our age when it's time for school each morning and when it's time to play each evening. The streets we leave behind are tree-lined, hedge-lined, fire hydrant-lined, neighborhood kid-lined, jump rope-lined, banana seat bicycle-lined.

To me, we're just an average family of seven sisters and two Holocaust Survivor parents – laundryman father and industrious homemaker mother – squeezed into a three-bedroom house. My mother, apparently in an attempt to avoid all thinking about her war years, stayed busy in the laundry room sewing, or cooking over cauldron-sized pots in the kitchen, a phone tucked between her shoulder and her ear. When she hangs up the phone, which she does briefly here and there just to come up for air, she talks about the thing nearest to her mind every waking moment of her life, an ongoing narrative filling our lives and our brains and the nooks and crannies of this house – the War. Not just any war. In our house there only was one war, WWII. There was only one forest, only one bad guy, the Nazis, and there's only one story worth telling.

This was the war that had catapulted my parents out of their home villages in Poland and Lithuania, sent my dad to Siberia and Tashkent, sent her to the Forest – and there's only one forest – and landed them both in DP Camps after the war, there to meet and fall in love. Or, if not exactly fall in love, at least to decide to get married. Like many of the war refugees, they had a gut feeling about how best to spit on Hitler's grave, and the best way was by getting married and having children. The war is the thing that catapults them to American shores. The war is what turns them into a quintessential 1950s married couple in a suburb, reproducing themselves three and a half times. That's our war.

In the Old Country, the yardstick against which we

21

measured everything we did, no one ever moved anywhere. If you were fortunate enough to have a house, you stayed in that house. Before the war, my mother lived in a house with her parents, brother, sister, grandfather, and her aunt and uncle, along with her baby cousin. That was who lived in their house – everyone. No one ever moved because where would you move? The Jews of Krivich lived closely together and they didn't leave until the Nazis marched in. After that, some never left, dying there.

Arriving from the freezing cold of Eastern Europe, the devastation of war, from living in Displaced Person camps, from war years lived in the forest, in Siberia, my parents are thrilled with Chicago. The idea that they could stay somewhere, could be citizens, could own things – Jews could own things! – like land and a house, never ceased to astonish them. Also, Chicago was so much warmer than Siberia – who knew?

But after thirteen years in Skokie, thirteen years in suburbia, thirteen years passing for a regular American couple with accents, my parents start to notice people moving up out of Skokie, to better suburbs, like Northbrook or Highland Park. They had become Americanized enough to recognize the writing on the wall, that those who stay put do so because they're stuck there. The American dream and the American house get bigger and bigger over time.

My dad must be a big shot. He can't just be left behind in Skokie, in their starter house – who knew there was a starter house that wasn't also a finisher house? – while all the *shlemiels* are moving up to something better. Each weekend we pile up in the station wagon and go look at model homes. We ooh and aah at dormers, at homes on hills. Mindy and I choose our favorite house based solely on the velocity with which we can roll down the hilly front lawns. I am thrilled that we will be rich and own a mansion.

But then my dad discovered California.

What's it like to a guy who is sure that Chicago is a heat wave compared to Siberia to suddenly discover that California exists, that Arizona exists? Because when Eastern Europe spits him out, when he gets flung across the ocean by Hitler, by the USSR, by world events beyond his control, how can he not stay where he lands? Yet, there it is, beyond dispute. An ocean, mountains, lush green vistas, and mild temperatures.

The west beckons to my dad like it's finally going to be the dream of America that he thought of as a boy in Poland, the America where the streets are paved in gold, and so he drives out of Chicago, our station wagon his covered wagon, to the other end of that highway, where another house awaits us, a Scottsdale house, circa 1973. An Arizona house.

Dad has his convoluted, multilayered reasons for why we need to move to Arizona. First there's the glaring problem of me, the dying asthmatic child. I'm not aware that I'm dying, but everyone around me seems to believe this. My five older sisters seem willing to let me die so we don't have to move, but my parents seem to be opposed to that. All I'm aware of is that my life changes dramatically after becoming asthmatic, with me now spending half the school year gasping for breath in our basement, unable to make it up the stairs or, having made it up the stairs, gasping for breath up there and unable to make it back down. Most of the time I stay down there, where all my needs are met, my subterranean hospital room. After all, there is a bathroom, a fold-out couch I share with Mindy as our bedroom, there are a bunch of TV sets – almost a museum of TV sets – lining the wall, some working and some not, which my father Dad had accepted in trade from his customers. He is always willing to barter laundry for a TV set. Sometimes, with careful adjustment of the antennae, we could even get a picture. Unfortunately, sometimes Mindy was the antenna. Of course, living life sick in the basement meant I lacked other things that I might need to have a full life, like school or boys or bikes, or nature, so maybe having an asthmatic child, a possibly dying child, was a compelling reason to move.

Do I evoke memories of my father's dead sister Faige when he sits beside me and watches me struggle for breath each day? Does he think that each breath will be my last? Our road trips had started out as hospitals on wheels for me, my lungs a barometer of where I might be able to live out a full life. Dad certainly preferred California. California had a lot of panache, a lot of style. My parents even had some Holocaust Survivor friends in Los Angeles, a big plus for them, being able to talk about the war nonstop. But it was in Arizona that I took my first full breath of air in two years, hopping right out of the car and directly into the hotel pool. Breathing.

There are other things chasing us down that highway. Like my father's heart attack in 1972, or the fact that he is obeying his doctor's orders at his own convenience, popping Nitroglycerine capsules whenever he overdoes it. Even if it is his health which forces our move, would he admit that?

"What heart attack?" He thunders, anytime anyone

mentions that he'd been hospitalized. Yet there's a definite feeling that he doesn't want to die like a dog in the laundry. He wants to be free of it, knowing that it is tenacious – the laundry isn't going anywhere, he has to move far away to escape it.

He liquidates, selling things that are logical to sell, like our house and the business, but also things that are illogical to sell and which could have made us millionaires, like the apartment building we owned in West Rogers Park containing sixteen rent-paying apartments. My dad gets rid of that too. He leaves it all behind, the two brothers, the two sisters, the brothers-in-law, the sisters-in-law, the nieces, the nephews. The graves of my grandparents.

Why would a Jewish man with seven daughters move away from Chicago and out to primitive cowboy Scottsdale, circa 1973? Why would he move to a place where people referred to synagogues as churches and asked me, routinely, if we were "those same Jews who killed Jesus?" Maybe he figured that, having married the first off so easily, at eighteen-years-old, the other six of us would be launched with no effort, twenty-year-old Jewish boys showing up on our doorstep one by one to claim us as we each turned eighteen.

But could anything have forced my father, that immovable ox, to do anything he didn't want to do? No doctor's orders, no sickly child, would have made him hit the road if he hadn't wanted to. I'm sure it's the road that beckoned him, the empty highway, the freeway, the interstate, the idea of going somewhere no one had been. He had a need to break free, to fly. Of course, he expected his brothers and their families to follow him, but first he was going to fly.

25

We end up with a flat brick of a house thrown on the desert floor. It's a shoebox of a house, about a mile long, or appearing so anyway. A sideways house set at an angle on our lot, with a sideways double garage with false windows facing the street giving the impression of even more house there but there's not. Bedrooms that, instead of going up a staircase like in Chicago, go out in one direction and out in the other direction, like a train, everyone circling back and ending up back in the kitchen, exhausted from our journey. It takes some getting used to, the left and right of it, the east and west of it. We're used to walking in houses and climbing up or down, but here there's flat terrain only. There are only two stairs in the entire house - the one going down into our sunken living room and the one coming back up out of it. We've been raised looking askance at ranch homes, as they're called in Chicago. And now, what do you know, we live in one.

Our house is on a corner acre, with a huge expanse of flat, brown, dusty dirt between it and the street. It's basically a corner of dry Arizona land, plowed over and over again by the construction, so that when we move in the front yard is rutted brown dirt in a huge triangle from the front of the angled house to the street. What we acknowledge to be our backyard – really just the swimming pool – is surrounded by a very short-looking-but-allegedly six-foot-tall block wall. Beyond that wall is another rutted brown dirt triangle extending to our property line.

Inside the house there's a family room with plywood designed to look like wood paneling but which really just looks like sheets of plywood painted to look like that. There's a built-in bar with smoky glass, and there's a beehive fireplace in the corner. There's the kitchen, separated from the family room by a row of spindles on a room divider. There are dark brown cabinets, one of which I burn down making popcorn that December, the house saved only by one of my older sister's quick thinking with a bag of flour. There's an intercom that never really works.

There are Harvest Gold appliances and Harvest Gold Formica countertops and somehow matching shiny Harvest Gold floral wallpaper on the walls. There's an electric coil stove which is my mother's pride and joy, scorning the gas stove of Skokie as old-fashioned, the oven's pilot light she used to have to light, with its flame that chased her arm out every time. There's a tiny closet of a pantry, but, still, it's three times as big as the broom closet we used for food in Skokie. There are four bedrooms down one hall and one tiny hot bedroom at the other side of the house, an isolation room for whichever sister can't get along with the others, sent there to sweat her differences out.

The shiny wallpaper doesn't stop in the kitchen. Mom brings home gigantic books of wallpaper samples and soon finds the most obnoxious ones with which to cover the house. A loud red and blue floral goes in my bedroom, one with glaring yellow suns for the twins' room, and lime green tic tac toe checkerboards for the next room, which is lobbed between whichever sisters who move in the house and out of the house over the years. In a moment of Mod 1970s hysteria, she picks wild patterned metal mini blinds out of other sample books for all the windows.

There is an intercom that never works, though it's fun

27

just to say we have it, like we're rich and using it to call live-in maids. We'd much rather use our regular communication system of screaming and yelling down the hall to each other. There's a hall bathroom with two great angled medicine cabinets, one on each side, a huge mirror, double sinks, and a linen closet filled with threadbare towels and dingy gray sheets. Mom has moved our linen closet intact. There is a tub that has to double as a chair for the sisters not at the sink, and on which various sisters can sit and harangue the others – to finish at the sink, to get out of the bathroom. It is just assumed that there is no privacy. This bathroom is for all of us and, later, for our grandparents and all of us, their disembodied dentures floating in cups for the night.

Down the hall and in my parents' room there is their bathroom with their double sinks, a scale with broken springs, and a few precarious steps down into their sunken shower. There's a walk-in closet with a light switch that is installed backwards so the up is off and the down is on, and which smells of the mothballs used to preserve my mother's prized mink stole. There is a suite of bedroom furniture with matching nightstands, a headboard, and a long dresser with double mirrors. There's an alcove that has a sliding glass door to the pool and there they've dumped more of the Skokie living room furniture there, including a pair of curvy chairs with velvet cushions. They never sit there.

There's a sunken living room for Mom's fancy couches, from which she finally removes the plastic, just in time for our dog to become incontinent, there's a dining room for her ponderous chandelier, and a foyer which must be tiled, my mother agonizing over the choice. After all, she is the

28

queen of foyer tile, having turned our Skokie foyer into a wild, bending meadow of tile flowers. Finally, and mystifyingly, she chooses an ominous black eight-inch tile to welcome guests to our home, like they're dropping into a pit of despair upon walking in the door. This is the first thing she eventually rips out.

We immediately battle over the bedrooms, even though we now have five of them. What fun it had been, bragging to everyone who would listen back in Chicago about how we were moving into a veritable mansion with five bedrooms, about how we'll never have space problems again. We move in and, like some primordial science experiment, the new square footage is instantly eaten up, taken up, filled up. We are crammed in once again.

The Allied moving van finally pulls up after panting its way across the country. The movers unload everything needed to make this house a home. There's our itchy tweed couch, Dad's de rigueur recliner, our smoked glass coffee table, our barrel-shaded lamps, Mom's prized chandelier, and the contents of our linen closet intact – my mother never throws out a towel. And one more thing. There's a set of washing machines from our Chicago laundry, the set my dad just couldn't part with, like he's carrying them along to make a new home, the machines his hearth fire. We are home.

Three
Just Like in Chicago

This is how we get to our house in 1973 if we're driving in from Phoenix out to our part of town, an area somewhat resembling the surface of the moon, with dusty dirt and rocks and, off in the distance, some looming brown mountains. Unlike the moon, there are low slung houses scattered here and there, but there's no knowing that till we get there.

First, we have to figure out how we're getting over the mountains. There are only a few choices. There's the flat road, there's the curvy one, and there's the wonderfully-named Dreamy Draw, which is one lane in each direction, snaking over a mountain range of undulating, yes, brown dirt hills.

Assuming we take Dreamy Draw, it dumps us off at the end, in a little commercial area and then we make a right turn. It's important to look around and enjoy the sights of civilization, because that is absolutely the last we will see of it for a while, unless we count Capstone Cathedral, the triangular, church with its pointy green tip, a few miles down the road. An oddity certainly. It's our last view of grocery stores, of a tiny movie theater, a drug store, some restaurants. We definitely need to make sure we have gas before pulling away from this tiny bit of civilization before turning. There's not another gas station for miles. From this point on, we could run out of gas on our way to get gas.

Then we drive and drive. We see flat houses planted on the side of the road, burning up in the sunshine, along with vast expanses with nothing but scrub bushes, tumbleweeds, and crooked trees. This is the Sonoran Desert, after all, not the Sahara, the Arabian, or the Painted. There's just light brown dirt stretching out in all directions, punctuated by scrub bushes and a dead cactus here and there.

Finally, there will be a four-way stop sign and a golf course looming into view on the corner a few miles up. We make a left. There will be three streets of houses, then a big swathe of desert, and then finally, popping up like a mirage, with nothing to the north of it and nothing to the west of it, and, of course, the emptiness to the south of it we just passed, is our street, Cortez. Named after the Spanish conqueror of the Mexican Aztecs. We make another left. There are only sixteen houses to choose from and ours is conveniently the first on the left.

There are certain things that my father simply must have in our new home, all intended to mirror the absolute perfection of our house in Skokie, including a wood-paneled family room, a bar, even if our new one is really just a converted closet with a smoky, veined mirror, because where else would Dad keep his ornamental collection of gigantic Canadian Club Whiskey bottles? When designing the house with the builder my parents had looked quizzically at all the choices. The only thing they could imagine in the world was the perfection of what we were leaving behind, made infinitely better by a double garage, by sunny skies, and by the swimming pool, which alone justifies our entire move. So they said, "We want the house to look like our house in Skokie."

When it comes time to meet with the pool contractor

in order to pick out a design for the pool, again my parents are befuddled. This time they can't tell them to make it just like in Skokie. In Skokie, the best we'd had was a daring two-foot-tall above-ground pool for a few years, until the patched and repatched holes in it connect into one giant blob of a hole, and it has to be thrown out.

They don't know from oval, square, oblong, they know nothing about depth, built-in benches, diving boards, slides. They had no carefree childhood memories to look back on, to wistfully lament how nice it would have been for my mom to have had a pool while she was running from the Nazis, or for my dad when he was transported to Siberia. As Holocaust Survivors, one from Lithuania and one from Poland, my parents are certainly your go-to people for information about how to survive a war in a freezing forest with no coat and no shoes, and they're your go-to people for information about how to milk a frozen cow in Siberia. But a pool? They don't exactly have the life experience for this task.

"There's something to pick? We want a pool," they say, "with water."

Pressed further, they say they want a blue pool. In the ground, not above ground like all the *schlimazels* back in the Midwest. That's it, they nod their heads in unison. A pool with blue water in the ground.

Finally, they look at the model home with all its bells and whistles, then they look at the pool there, and they say, 'We'll have one like that."

So we end up with one like that. A large serving tray in the ground, rectangular, with handles on either end. A diving board. With steps that we walk in to enter, and a slightly sloping bottom until suddenly there's a massive drop off, a Loch Ness-type unfathomable drop, until it reaches the depth required for the diving board. There's blue water and cool decking and a tight little block wall fence hemming in just the pool section of the yard and leaving the rest of the acre alone, untouched except for a border eventually to be outlined with Oleanders. Everyone had bushes outlining their yards in Chicago and what's good enough for Chicago is good enough for Arizona. Hundreds of Oleanders later, they have their hedge.

But what to do with all that land, a commercial acre's amount of land, stretching out into space? In Chicago the natural answer would be a lawn, but we're not in the Midwest anymore so grass isn't just going to sprout up spontaneously forming a convenient football field for us. We are thwarted. We're unable to replicate our Skokie house on the outside since what grows naturally here seems to be a combination of scrub bushes, dead cacti, and beer cans from old keggers.

We learn quickly that the natural unkempt desert is clearly out of the question. We're allowed our "desert landscaping" of course but it must look like a prettified version of the real thing. The real desert is considered too deserty for the front yard of homes. It needs to be tamed. We must landscape the natural version into a pretty postcard version of itself.

Later that month an Italian guy named Gus drives by, sees the mess of our front yard, and rings the doorbell. He's curly-haired and wears a gold horn on a chain around his neck showing through the open neck of his shirt. He offers to do our landscaping. He's not exactly a landscaper, more like a hardworking guy scraping together odd jobs. He has a work truck parked outside but surprisingly few tools, just a shovel really, and he works alone – even though we have a raw acre and he's taking it from a pile of dirt to something else.

My dad loves a self-made man, so this is his obvious choice for a landscaper. He loves to bypass the thieves who would steal him blind at the real companies, loves the idea of hiring someone right off the street, so he loves Gus, even if he's not Jewish. After all, we're in Arizona now. He doesn't expect Jews. He also maybe doesn't expect Italian landscapers, but what does he know from landscapers? He admires the machismo of Gus doing everything himself, of not needing any help. My father can relate to this.

Gus draws up some preliminary plans and shows them to my dad. Gravel and gravel and different colored gravel, along with palm trees and cacti, kind of like we live in a turtle terrarium.

Dad says, "No lawn like in Chicago?" Of course.

"An acre lawn?" Gus says. "You know how much water that'll take to keep it alive? And the sod will be very expensive to lay. It doesn't just grow here like back east. Do you want to be chained to a lawnmower?"

Gus seems to understand the essence of my father, that my dad will be his own boss. He will not be a slave to anything, not to another person and certainly not to a lawnmower and a lawn again, just like in Chicago. He frowns at any mention of money. He liked the idea of having some land but had planned on the land taking care of itself, maybe growing its own landscaping.

He compromises. He agrees to a gigantic triangular front yard of gravel. Instead of looking like our front yard in Chicago it ends up looking like our alley in Chicago, a whole yard of rocks. Rocks which, in Chicago, would have been called rubble, but in Arizona they are called granite and are purchased and picked by color. Apache Brown, Desert Gold, Pink Coral, Rainbow Mist.

First Gus somehow levels the land, laying black plastic over the dirt to prevent anything from spontaneously growing, with a few holes left open here and there for a palm tree or two, or a cactus. A sea of landscaping rocks is spread on the black plastic. A baby saguaro cactus is placed – very carefully – in one spot, just a foot-tall hump that will take decades to grow into the multiple-armed thing we think a cactus should look like. There's a prickly pear cactus, and a palm tree that grows at a forty-five degree-angle. There is a green Palo Verde tree that will bloom, its seeds scattering all over the yard, making slim, green Palo Verde babies pop up here and there, like grass.

Gus goes all out, even laying paving stones to form a walkway from the front door to the garage with rocks so slim that they tilt and sway and are barely big enough for one person to stand on. He put in bushes inside the front portico and outside too – because Dad just can't get away from the Midwestern ideal of box hedges – and then rings the property with oleanders on the south, east, and west – only pink and white oleanders – and all mixed up so that when they bloom there is no symmetry. Then he's done.

My father surveys his kingdom. He looks at things two

35

ways, through his own eyes and through the eyes of the potential Chicago visitors, namely his brothers and their wives, his sisters, and their husbands. His new Arizona self understands the need for gravel and fully understands desert landscaping. The Arizona self understands that the norm in this new community is to have exactly what he's got – a beaten back desert. However, the miniature uncles and aunts who live inside his brain don't quite see it that way. They see ugly gravel, incomprehensible gravel – in a front yard. He can hear them now, the mortification, the comment, "*Nu*, Herschel, you couldn't get grass?"

So he consults with Gus, who is now practically household staff, and Gus mulls it over and finally says, "How would you like a river?"

My dad doesn't like to look dumb but he's clearly out of his league on this discussion. He knows laundries, he knows apartment buildings, and he knows how to drive like a madman from Chicago to California, Arizona – back and forth, back and forth – but a river? How is Gus going to manage to put in a river? He looks around, perhaps looking for a tributary of the Volga, the Dnieper, maybe the Danube, but only sees desert for miles around us. He imagines the unimaginable – excavation, rerouting another river to run through this exact front yard thousands of miles away. The cost.

He shakes his head. "Nah. We don't need no river. We got a pool in the backyard. That's enough for swimming."

Gus looks like he doesn't understand for a minute, then he says, "Oh I don't mean a real river, Mr. Burt…"

"Call me Harry."

"– Harry. I mean river rocks. They're the color of a river. You take them and you make them look like they're a twisting river running right here in the front yard. It can help to break up the gravel in a yard this size."

"It costs more than regular rock?" River, shmiver, to my dad it's all about money.

Gus nods, "Well, they are much bigger rocks..."

"I don't think so, Gus. We don't need to get so fancy shmancy."

"Some hills then? So we can put the palm trees behind them like an oasis?"

Once again, my father, "It costs more, Gus?"

"Two hills were an option in the basic package."

The gloom disappears from my father's face. "We're back in business, Gus! We're simple people, Gus. Italians, Jews. We understand each other." And my dad amiably slaps his hand across Gus's back to go for a walk to see his kingdom.

We end up with peachy-colored rock blanketing most of the acre. Plopped down in the center of the front yard, neatly spaced in the vast expanse of stone are two brown volcanic rock hills undulating out of the peachy blandness around them, a palm tree on each, a cactus on one. The landscaping comes to a dead halt wherever it can't be viewed by passersby or visitors, a few feeble pebbles just beyond our driveway where half the acre stands unused, the wild and untamed desert beyond our pool wall. After all, who needs such a big yard when we didn't such a big yard in Skokie?

Gus works for a long time on our landscaping. He works from

when the weather is still boiling hot to when it's not. I see him when I go off to school each day on the school bus and he's still there when it drops me off again, our own personal day laborer.

Eventually, the job is done and Gus packs up his shovel and drives away in his work truck, considerably more worn for its time on our job. He reappears about year and a half later when Dad calls him for some additional work. He's had a while to mull over that gigantic expanse of front yard in the time we've lived in Arizona. He's had a chance to see what others have done with their gigantic expanses. He's also noticed that it's annoying having all the cars pull up to the side of the house — what's the use of getting double doors going into his fancy Arizona house, the pool straight through, out the back, if everyone pulls up to the side of the house and goes in through the garage?

So Gus cuts a horseshoe-shaped swathe in the granite and clears it away, he lines the edges with rocks and fills in the middle with fine gravel, driveway gravel, so cars can park there on the boomeranging curve. All of us, learning to drive, or drinking and driving, or angry and driving, will run over the jagged rocks.

And then Gus is finally gone for good and the yard stays like he left it for the next forty years, untouched, untended, a botanical wasteland, trees either dying from neglect or sprouting like weeds along the curb when Mom gets distracted for a few decades. Seeds fly off the Palo Verde, landing and growing where they will. She refuses to pull out any seedlings.

Right then Dad looks out on his kingdom. All is well.

Four

Arizona Shtetl

My mother and I are standing in the doorway of our new home in Scottsdale, waves of 120-degree heat rolling in the house, the sound of cicadas in the trees. It's August 1973 and we just moved in here a week ago, leaving our tri-level home in Skokie behind, along with the tree-lined streets set up like grids at right angles, as far as the eye can see, marching all the way to Lake Michigan in one direction and out into Illinois farmland in the other. We now live in this flat shoebox of a house on a street of what will one day be sixteen houses, one street only, inching out into a one-mile square of desert in North Phoenix, with whirling brown dirt kicked up by dust devils, and scrawny round scrub bushes dotting our acre.

But this morning there is some excitement, a moving truck shows up next door. Our new neighbors, Adele and Herman Kaplan, come over to introduce themselves to us, leaving their children, Ileen and Robby, behind.

The Kaplans are very friendly. Friendly, like they come over right away, before they unpack. They're a lock-stepping couple, they talk at the exact same moment, interrupting each other's sentences, finishing each other's sentences, each other's thoughts, rounding out each other's punch lines, though they just may not know they are punch lines. Mom and I stand in the doorway nodding and smiling until our faces are frozen.

The Kaplan's common belief, which we learn the minute we meet them, is that Adele Could Have Done Much Better Than Herman. This is no secret. Adele, indeed, tells us this in front of Herman.

"I could have done much better than Herman."

Herman nods his head in agreement, "Of course she could have! Look at her! Isn't she beautiful? She's too good for me and I know it!"

Adele continues – well, they both continue, she with the main narrative and Herman running a side commentary agreeing and expanding on her statements.

"My family," Adele says, wearing tennis whites and full makeup, full jewelry, each finger with a ring on it, "is very rich. VERY rich, if you know what I mean? And they wanted me to marry rich, or at least a professional."

"Of course they did! One thousand percent true! Her family was rich and mine – forget it!" Herman said, shaking his head in disgust at himself.

Herman continues, "She could have married a lawyer maybe, a doctor. She could have had a doctor! Look, she could've gotten any guy she wanted. I'm just some no good *schlemiel*. She's too good for me. I agree with that one thousand percent!"

Adele continues. "But I fell in love with Herman, even though he just does window coverings for a living."

And Herman nods and says, "All types of window coverings. Curtains, shades, venetian blinds, even something for your sliding glass doors. I'll be happy to bring over my sample book. How's next Tuesday?"

Adele goes on, "It hasn't always been an easy life." She

wags her finger at me and I nod like I know. Because I'm thirteen and all.

Herman agrees. "But I've always given her a roof over her head, and we have two beautiful kids. Ilene, oooweee, is she smart! And looks just like Adele! Her spitting image, like twins, so beautiful!"

And then Adele lowers her voice a bit and says, "And we have our son, Robby. He's a little slow."

"A little slow," agrees Herman, "Like you say in Yiddish, a *bissel klug*."

"Of course my family blames Robby on Herman. They say he never would have come out like he did if Herman had been smarter. That you just can't mix brains like that, they say. One smart and one not so smart."

"It's true," Herman nods, "I'm not so smart! Adele is my gem, so beautiful and smart!"

Then suddenly, "Hey, look, here's Robby now!"

I stop my head on its back and forth swivel from Herman back to Adele, back and forth again and again, their suddenly drafted eighth grade marriage counselor, and look at Robby, who's loping over from their dirt front yard to our own, in pants that are too short and a striped dress shirt even though it's really too hot to even wear clothes, much less long-sleeved clothes. He's a skinny, pale, kid with an elongated, somewhat crooked face. His hair is sticking up and looks like it's been cut at home, unevenly, and slept on badly. He brushes straight past introductions because he has one interest only, tools. Do we have any? Can he see them, touch them, play with them, maybe borrow them from us? Are they power tools? Are they in our garage? And he begins loping around

41

the house.

Adele and Herman shush Robby, and immediately exit stage left, waving goodbye as they each grab hold of one of Robby's arms and walk quickly away, saying, "No, no, Robby, the Burts can't let you play with their tools. Robby, please don't ask the Burts to play with their tools again. Do you understand us, Robby?" Until, finally, having crossed the property line dividing their home from ours and believing that there is, perhaps, a concrete wall between us, they are shouting.

"ROBBY, YOU WILL NOT ASK THE BURTS TO SEE THEIR TOOLS AGAIN AND DON'T LET US CATCH YOU OVER THERE LOOKING FOR THEM!"

Our friendliest neighbor turns out to be Robby Kaplan, who kind of comes to live in our house, or our garage, anyway.

That's the neighbor to our left.

Our other nearby neighbor, right across the street, takes their time showing up. All the houses are new, the neighborhood is new, just a lone street carved out of this square mile of desert in Scottsdale, a planet moving from uninhabitable to habitable, houses under construction up and down the block, and empty lots, and a barricade at the end leading to the wild desert.

First the house stands empty, the model we'd viewed when visiting from Chicago. An identical floor plan but different exterior elevation. Arches, a circular driveway, everything top notch, model perfect. The houses on the block have all been sold, so it's not the model anymore and it just sits there humming day after day, waiting for the family that will move in. Our builder tells us it's a family of all boys. I light up. Seven boys? I don't know the word *bashert* at that time, but I feel it, standing there hearing those words. I get positively teary-eyed that I no longer will have to worry about my impending spinsterhood, even though I'm thirteen. The universe has provided a mate. Just think of it, seven brothers for seven sisters – neatly ignoring that one of my sisters is married already – seven grooms for seven brides, and yes, Seven Brides for Seven Brothers. I am swept up in the romance, thirteen and already trying to marry myself off.

As the weeks wind on, that number starts shifting downward. Seven to six, which is okay because I have a married sister, then six to five. I sigh, thinking it's unfortunate, but I guess one of my sisters just won't be able to get married. It hops right past that, though to five, then four, then what shows up.

They move in their house, and I am immediately dismayed by one thing, one indicative sign, parked like a blinking arrow in their driveway – their brand-new Lincoln Continental Town Car. I suddenly know everything I need to know about them. We are not a Lincoln Town Car family over here on the immigrant side of the street. We don't drive luxury cars with scary grilles that come thundering up behind slower drivers on the road and push everyone else aside. We don't drive pretentious cars that serve as our calling cards, telling everyone we've made it, mostly because we're in a permanent state of making it, never quite there. Our family has simpler automobile imagery, including our Ford station wagon, the Chevy Impala my older sisters drove to Arizona, and a Chevy Silverado truck that comes with the business Dad ends up buying. Their car alone tells me they are about as different from us as possible. The weddings are off.

We have low standards for what constitutes a quality father here in 1973. The excuses made for our father generally ran along the lines of, "He earns a good living," and, "Your father works hard," both of which I believe are intended to explain why he's completely uninvolved in the life of the family.

Our world view is that our father is representative of all men, difficult to deal with when he gets home from work until he drinks a Budweiser or two. He's angry if anyone talks to him during his solitary dinner which is two hours after ours, our mother running around to serve him, summoned by the ringing of his fork against his beer glass. Our expectations are already lower than low. We would never expect a father to know where dishes are kept or the birthdays of their children. I have a suspicion that some days my father barely remember our names. We keep growing and looking different, he tells us, and, yes, he works so much.

But Mickey Shapiro, the new neighbor, is pretty much off the charts on the bad dad scale. It seemed that he had gotten early retirement from some job in New York and given a retirement package that included a new car every few years, this new house, and a membership to the nearby Century Golf Club, the only one which admits Jews in 1973. He dresses the part of an early retiree living a life of 1970s leisure with his checkered Sansabelt polyester pants and white golf shoes and shirt, his gut falling over the waistband and his muttonchop sideburns creeping down his cheeks. We hear him yelling a lot over there, peering around suspiciously at our house, our comings and goings, yet he and his wife Ethel are immediately absorbed into the Jewish social life of the block. He automatically belongs and is automatically tolerated. Nothing matters, not his boorishness, not his rudeness. He is Jewish and he lives on Cortez Drive. He automatically belongs.

The Shapiros have a dog, Lucky, but he's not like our dog. He's a rangy, loping, yelping figure of a dog, mostly a spotty Dalmatian but he sniffs the air in a Rin Tin Tin manner, a crazy dog. He guards the house. Not that there is anything to guard from – our street sits alone on this little piece of planet, no one nearby, unless he is actually guarding against us. He's an informant-type of dog, alerting Mickey to all the shenanigans going on in the neighborhood and, as luck would have it, all the shenanigans are happening over on our side of the street.

Our dog is a little different than this dog. Rusty is overweight, non-athletic, gay but not out, or we wouldn't be trying desperately to mate him with a girl. He's encumbered by a fur coat more suited to the Siberian tundra rather than the Arizona desert. He's a worried dog. If an intruder broke in, the dog would leap into my arms, and I'd have to bark and snarl to scare the intruder off while he cowered. Both Mickey Shapiro and his dog seem to know this.

While Lucky growls and slobbers behind Mickey's backyard gate, fantasizing about turning my dog into a delicious leg o' lamb, Rusty and I go for long, meandering walks in our new desert habitat. I guess in the overall hubbub of the move no one had considered how the dog would adapt to Arizona. He couldn't exactly unzip his heavy Shetland fur coat and neatly step out of it, revealing a lean, spry dog suited to desert temperatures. He's so, so eager to go outside, leaping to run to the door when I open it, and then a blast of Arizona heat hits him and I can just feel his brain recoiling, his slow dog brain flipping back through his memory cards containing winter and snow and springtime and rain and blossoms on trees and Robin Red Breasts and red fire hydrants and worms and green grass that just grows naturally from the ground without having to be planted. Where'd all that go?

Unlike the dog, I can wear less clothes, wear flip flops and shorts. I'm not even aware yet of how the desert can kill. Also, I need to go for a walk because I need to check on the houses under construction, which is my job right now. My dog is unfortunately my best friend so he must pull up his proverbial bootstraps and come with me.

We're a pensive pair, or at least I am. I can't really speak for the dog. I spend a lot of time wandering around the houses under construction. I get familiar with the building methods, at first surprised that my original knowledge of how to build a house, provided by The Three Little Pigs (Bricks, good, Straw and sticks, no good) doesn't seem to matter around here. There are no Chicago bricks in Arizona, or basements, or upper stories. Every home is a ranch, all the exteriors shmeared in an adobe-looking stucco, even if they're built of sticks, Styrofoam, and chicken wire underneath.

Our houses are not quite that bad. They're built out of gray cinder blocks with no insulation. Then comes the stucco which makes all the houses look like they will last hundreds of years. The roofs are flat, the fireplaces are beehive, the living rooms are sunken, the doors are hollow.

There are hazards along the way, like the holes some

animal has burrowed. Like cacti reaching out to grab me. Like the scrub bushes that have pulled up their roots and become dangerous, brambly, rolling tumbleweeds. There is the harbinger of doom lying in my path every day, telling me that time is short – a ten-foot-long dead cactus, worn down to its wooden skeleton. Rusty and I stand for a moment looking at it, a requiem. We skirt around it and head back.

Five
Polish Cowboy

No sooner had we put our bags down in the Holiday Inn, no sooner had Mindy and I thrust our brunette heads into bathing caps and barreled our way to our first belly flops in the motel's sunshiny pool, than my dad was stomping out of the hotel, his arm looped around the shoulders of a realtor enlisted to find him a new business.

"Listen, you don't know, but I built a business from scratch in Chicago. From nothing. From nothing I built a business and support my family – seven daughters you know? I know business! Laundry, shmaundry, sure, I can run a laundry. I brought two big machines with me just in case. I can run anything!"

With twenty-five thousand dollars from the sale of this business burning a hole in his pocket, along with the cash he got for our apartment building in West Roger's Park, he set about finding a new business. They started – where else? – with laundries. After all, he knows the business inside and out, which, to a normal human being, is a good thing and a good idea, to go into a business you know. This doesn't account for the fact that he wanted to leave all that behind in Chicago, along with heart attacks and sick daughters, and the hustling required to get third-rate nursing home laundry accounts. He was prosperous now – he didn't have to kiss anyone's you-know-what anymore.

Dad *chops* and *klops* his way through the businesses for sale in Phoenix in the summer of 1973, he and the realtor moving through all the categories. They look so long that by the time he buys something, we're out of the hotel and into our house, Mindy and I barreling into our own pool now. It's not like Phoenix is overflowing with business listings just waiting for my dad to come along and make magic. Sure, there are laundries and laundromats. There are also businesses so foreign to him that they are automatically off the list, like feed stores and saddleries, restaurants. My father will never completely understand restaurants.

Inside our house, Dad is a cyclone moving through the rooms, a whir of restless pent-up energy. Time is money, after all. How many times did we hear him say that? Should he buy this, should he buy that? Maybe he should go into dry cleaning? Maybe buy a moving company? Maybe this, maybe that, maybe this other thing? He and Mom pour over the Arizona Republic and the green-colored Phoenix Gazette newspapers day and night looking for businesses for sale – some way to lasso him out of the house, out of our hair.

Finally, they go see the least likely prospect of them all, a produce store called Farmers Produce Market, in south Scottsdale.

This is the perfect storm. The owner, Gene, and his friend Lou, the chief loiterer, just happened to both be hanging around that day, flirting with the two cashiers. My dad immediately has to prove that he's not some yokel with a Polish accent, he's a man's man, the king of the hill, the Jewish

Archie Bunker. They immediately voice their doubts that he can run this kind of business. A food store is different than a laundry, they say, maybe it's not a good idea. Dad bristles. Of course he can run a business! Any business! Not just a laundry! How different can a produce market be from a laundry, after all? He's no greenhorn!

He buys the store. The ownership changes but, somehow, these men come with the store, my dad's new best friends. It turns out that my dad doesn't just buy a store, he buys a lifestyle.

Gene, the former owner, hangs around, part of a network of philandering divorced men roaming through Scottsdale who not only cheated on their ex-wives but aren't even faithful to their post-divorce girlfriends. He says he'll hang around for a while to train my dad, but one day I listen to our produce man's muttering and hear that Gene is having an affair with one of the two cashiers who came with the store.

Lou, the third wheel on Dad's triad, also hangs out at our store, an impossibly lecherous, short Italian guy who constantly leans on the checkout stands complaining and moaning about his ex-wife, who hates him, and the Catholic Church, which won't allow him an annulment so he could just move on. I am apparently his confidante even though I am only thirteen.

These are my father's new buddies. They've been cut off from their families and swing through Scottsdale bars and nightclubs each night and soon, the party after the party each day at Farmers Produce Market is exactly that. My dad has to keep up with them, has to go out after work and go to the clubs.

My father has traded his brothers in Chicago and all his family, all of whom are loyal, for Lou and Gene, who are not. They are the ones teaching Dad the ropes of the business.

They teach my dad about pricing – about marking up and loss leaders. With two cash registers going all day with lines of customers snaking throughout the store – my father is exultant. This is the life! My dad compulsively checks the cash registers to pull out money all day long. At the end of the day he shuffles it in his hands, rich.

Once he's working and counting this cash, my father gets even more expansive. A truck was included with the purchase of store and he adopts it as his own. This doesn't really raise an eyebrow since it leaves more cars for the rest of the drivers in our household. But it does raise an eyebrow when his wardrobe begins to change. The pants are the same, the shirts the same, socks still black. One day he leaves the house wearing cowboy boots, the next day he adds a bolo tie. He doesn't go so far as to adopt a cowboy hat for his head. Perhaps even he realizes that wearing one would be taking this masquerade a little too far.

My dad becomes an Arizona Cowboy. He doesn't appear to see any conflict with this new identity and his old, that of a Polish Holocaust Survivor. He also may not have been fully aware of the practical life that spawned the cowboys – the roping and riding and ranches. He sees men swaggering around this primitive 1973 Scottsdale that he's hauled us off to, swaggering around in cowboy hats, boots, and bolo ties, driving trucks, and it's these things he adopts. The appearance of a cowboy. I wonder, is my dad just a master at camouflage?

Is he wearing what the locals wear in order to blend in, a learned wartime skill?

He's still familiar as Chicago Dad. He's impossible to talk to, penny-pinching, driven towards making enough money – a wall of money – to keep poverty and Poland and the World War II on one side and himself on the other. He zooms off to the store in the Silver Silverado each day, the wheels whirring in the dirt.

I'm walking to my bedroom one day and hear the never-heard-before sound of football coming from our family room.

"Will someone change the channel?" I yell out. "That is so loud!" I understand there's football on TV but in all my life there has never been football on *our* TV once. The idea that someone might have put football on TV intentionally and for the purpose of watching the game is so out of the realm of possibility in our family that this isn't a consideration. The only possibility is that a sister sat down in front of the TV, started watching, walked away and the unthinkable happened, a football game came on.

"Dad's watching." My sister Mindy yells back. My dad could never yell back because he is half deaf and whatever is left of his hearing is filled with the sounds of, yes, football.

This is another new, strange, and terrible Arizona Dad phenomenon. I don't think I fully appreciated how much I liked having my father not like sports until he suddenly does, and then it's too late. In the past, this sports thing, the American obsession with the kicking or throwing of a ball here or there down a field, this caring about a trivial game, so much less important than freezing, surviving, than Siberia, was always bewildering to him.

"What kind of bullshit is this?" he would say when glimpsing a game. He was busy making a living. When he finally sat down in his favorite chair at the end of each day, TV had a certain set purpose. It was for entertainment or news. He couldn't wrap his mind around the idea that this, this grown man game of chasing balls, of hitting balls, that this mattered. Everything was compared in importance to the war. Was this important compared to the war? No. To starvation? No. To a dead sister buried in Tashkent? Double no.

So when the first game ever appears intentionally on our TV in Arizona and is left on instead of the station being immediately changed, I think maybe it's an anomaly, a mistake. It'll pass. Maybe he's just trying to get along with his new friends, Lou and Gene, since we seem to have purchased them along with our store.

But it stays on and Dad is strangely enthralled with it, with the spontaneity of it, with the live and die of it, with the no-canned-laughter of it. Of course, he prefers Archie Bunker for entertainment, but in this he gets to *be* Archie Bunker, he gets to yell at the players from our family room, he gets to fight with the referees and the coaches from the safety of his recliner.

When I add up these changes, the sports thing with the TV blasting and the din of the yelling, both from my dad and the sports fans in the bleachers, along with the vision of my father in a bolo tie and cowboy boots climbing into a Chevy Silverado truck each morning, I understand. Things have changed and they're not going back.

One day, while it's still August and 110 degrees, Dad decides to start a new fitness routine, riding off on a bicycle on a hot Sunday for an all-day ride. We cannot stop him. Mom watches him ride off into the shimmering distance like it's the last she'll ever see of him, and we all glue ourselves to the windows for hours, expecting the worst. Finally, he returns, red-faced, nearly sun-stroked, a big success.

"See?" he says, "No one thinks I can ride? Only you kids can ride? I was riding in Germany after the war – you don't know nothing."

What we do know is no one can stop him from doing anything he wants to do.

At our store, our family is on public display, my father the jovial proprietor, like a politician, shaking hands with the men and kissing the babies of all the customers. And we are the jovial proprietor's daughters, obediently reciting our birth order number to complete strangers. There was no public face of our family in Chicago, no one wanted to meet the laundryman's daughters.

My father, of course, has friends now, and that's something different. He never had friends in Chicago, only brothers and brothers-in-law. Gene, along with his sidekick, Lou, are now part of our daily existence, like two perverted, disheveled uncles, leering at us up and down, then down and up. Having sold the store to our family, having trained Dad already in the intricacies of owning a produce market, I wonder, isn't it time for them to move on?

Dad alters because of his contact with these two men, he changes from a frumpy, Studs Terkel-type of Chicagoan into a something slicker, something not so easy to peg. He wears cologne at the store. He goes out drinking. There's that Polish Cowboy thing. He'd never been a perfect husband, I knew that. I knew that in the world of parent lotteries I was amazingly fortunate to get the winning hand I got, my mother. Back in Chicago, my parents had done their share of fighting. When he'd pushed her too far back then, eventually my mother would pull herself together, maybe after he'd been out carousing all night with his employees, whom he called the "Puerto Ricans." She would confront him.

"And where were you all night, Herschel?" She'd sneer, her eyes narrowing.

I remember cringing because I knew nothing good could come of that. Dad always won every argument because the winner was always the one who cared less. How much could she fight with him when she had a terrifying vision in her mind of being alone with her seven baby orphans and no roof over her head, maybe back in the forest in Eastern Europe? The fact that none of us were babies or infants or toddlers, or even little anymore, didn't matter. In her mind it was always the forest.

Dad would yell back, "No one tells me what to do! I'm the man of the house! You push me and I'll leave, just like *that!*" He snaps in her face. And that would end the fight until the next time, my mother kept docile by the women around her, the aunts, her mother, her mother-in-law, her sister.

But in Arizona, Helen Reddy is on the radio singing "I Am Woman, Hear Me Roar" and it suddenly becomes my mother's battle hymn. She finds her voice, especially in response to Dad's new flagrant cheating, with mysterious women calling our house and asking for him by name. Something has been freed up inside her. Not being watched by the complacent aunts, not being told constantly, "Sha, he's a man, let him have his way, he'll come back." Instead we've moved, she can't hear them telling her this from Chicago, and she believes the words of the song. My mother roars.

As a matter of fact, there's a lot of roaring suddenly. Mom's constant yelling at Dad to take it easy, don't lift the box of oranges, don't lift the box of bananas, all while he jumps in and out and in and out of the bed of our pickup truck. She yells for him not to smoke cigars, to obey his doctor, to slow down, to stay home, not go out with the two divorced *schlimazels*.

But there is one big change. Now, when Dad yells, "I'm the king of the house! You don't tell me nothing!" she yells back and says, "If you're such a big shot you can leave."

I hear this changed tenor in their fighting, certain that they are going to get divorced, based on the sheer number and the escalation of the fights going on between them, and the number and escalation of the women calling the house for him, and escalation of her fury and tears and screaming, and the escalation of his slamming doors as he leaves the house over and over, to go out with the new friends he'd suddenly acquired. Because suddenly he's part of this posse and my dad is hell-bent on proving he can keep up. No wife is going to stop him. No children can stop him either.

Six
The Land of Iceberg Lettuce

Danny, our produce guy, pulls me aside one day.

"Linda, I'm going to tell you a secret. Look here." He waves at one of the refrigerated cases. "You see how clean the mirrors are back there? That's because I washed them with lemons."

He declares this to me definitively, triumphantly, with a firm shake of his head. And what do you know, but the next thing I know, I am scrubbing the mirror at the back of the units with lemons. There will be no appealing to the parents.

This is my life now mainly because there are a lot of jobs to be done at Farmer's Produce Market. Some of them already have people in the positions, people we inherit when we buy the business, like Danny the produce guy, and the two cashiers. That leaves me wandering the floor of the store. No glamorous jobs left over. I'm a reluctant indentured servant, my term of service probably until I can escape to college.

This is a new world for me. I didn't know that "produce guys" existed before we bought the store, these specialists in green aprons who know when it's time to put out a new box of bananas, who know how to arrange towering displays of cantaloupes to their best advantage, who have

57

encyclopedic knowledge of every fruit and vegetable known to humans. Danny is this breed of produce guy. In his fifties, short and thin with a radio announcer booming voice and a jowly face, he undertakes my training.

He has not stumbled into this job by accident, rather, he is a Produce Man by trade and has his own code of ethics which he carries forth mightily at Farmer's Produce Market, despite the challenges. It's a personal affront to him when the fruits and vegetables aren't in place, looking their best. He is willing to share his knowledge of every fruit and vegetable in existence and seriously discuss their merits with customers. He doesn't like any of the monkey business going on between the former owner and one of the cashiers, and he doesn't like the former owner. He is a faithful married man with a "Missus" at home who has no name at all, just "the Missus." Danny cares about only one thing, the produce, and that it's all displayed to its best advantage. For some reason, he decides to train me.

When I'm really stupid and untrained I am allowed only to unload produce onto display cases. Danny parks himself nearby and casts a critical eye upon me, sighing and belaboring this endless, thankless training. He admonishes me gruffly as I stack the produce, jumping in to save it from never being bought due to my haphazard stacking. I'm taught to put the ripe bananas out first and save the green ones for later. I'm taught to put strawberries in boxes with the red ones at the top and bottom and the green ones in the middle, that trickery is part of retail. There is an exhausting amount of information to teach a stupid kid like me — a veritable University of Produce here in our store.

There are non-Produce-related tasks, like bagging, at

which I'm particularly adept. There's cutting the gigantic cylinders of Colby Longhorn cheese into one-pound pieces, then heating up the cellophane machine and wrapping each one, weighing and pricing them. There's all the other minutiae of running our store, the searching for cigarette brands among a wall of packs, the weighing of produce on the broken, antique scales that come with the store, there's the refilling of the paper bags, of the plastic bags, of the cooler.

There's the truly mundane stuff, all left to me as the lowliest of laborers, like turning on the light switches for all the wet produce display cases and then spraying them down to keep everything glistening. We don't have an automatic rain shower system and apparently the produce needs to be wet. I wonder, do people want to buy their produce dripping wet? I'd never noticed this before myself. The times I'd gone shopping with my mother in Skokie all the produce was locked up tight, pre-selected, in cellophane packages, not running wild like in our store. No shopper in Chicago was allowed to inspect anything, only to peer suspiciously at the Styrofoam bottom and the clear-wrapped top. Danny runs me through my paces every time I show up at the store. There will be no appealing to the parents.

Clearly the most interesting thing I do is stock the cooler. For this we have a one-size-fits-all coat hanging on a peg. I put it on and walk into the eerie, silent, muffled world of the cooler. On one side are cases of milk and anything else that needs refrigeration, on the other side are the glass doors that the customers will open to get the milk, the cheese, the yogurt. I can see them, but they can't see me, here in the gloom of the interior, here in the gloom of the job, although sometimes my ghostly hands flash by.

Back in the University of Produce, Danny is sighing heavily while leaning on a wide broom.

"Linda, think about it. You're going to have to be able to tell these folks when a pineapple is ripe. They're going to expect you to know, have you thought about that? Here, pull these center leaves and I'll show you. Then meet me over at the watermelons and I'll teach you about those brown spots on the fruit." I glare at my sister, grabbing a smoke by the second register.

Later I move up and suddenly I'm the cashier – the silly, underage, cashier. And then I'm free from Danny, ringing the customers up.

Right away, it's apparent that we are out of our depth. We have bought a produce market, a place where people who really care about their produce come to shop – the forerunner of the organic grocer – but we are not of that world. We're from the land of iceberg lettuce and processed cheese slices and soda pop delivered straight to our garage by our pop man in Chicago. Before we buy our store, the only vegetables I've heard of are celery, carrots, onions and potatoes, Jewish vegetables, things Mom makes unrecognizable in some soup or another and which come floating to the surface, great globs, in our bowls. My mother ran an Eastern European kitchen, one in which vegetables have their lives beaten out of them before serving.

Additionally, there's nothing natural or organic about us as a family, though that's what we're purporting to sell. To me, fruit is apples and oranges and bananas. I have no idea there are different types of apples or oranges. I've never seen a plantain.

But once we own the store, we have to get exotic. All the world is in there – mangoes, Kiwi fruit, papaya, persimmons, casaba, squash, red leaf lettuce, parsnips, eggplants, pine nuts, plantains, and pinto beans, a far cry from our standard Eastern European diet of fat and then more fat. I stand there dumbfounded, thinking maybe all of this is plastic fruit until Danny pulls out his Produce Man knife, always handy in his apron pocket, and slices them open for me, showing me how they're all peeled, the seeds in each, and forcing me to take a bite or two. I feign interest because I am very polite, and he is very serious. But really, I'm hoping I don't need to know all this. Why would anyone shop for a Persimmon?

In other words, I still prefer bananas.

There are inherent problems with using daughters as indentured servants in a family-owned business. First, our dad's unwillingness to pay us leads at least me to take my wages from the cash register drawer. According to my parents, my rate of pay as a child should be basically zero. They're feeding me, aren't they? Do I have a roof over my head? I take more than zero. I figure I should get minimum wage circa 1973, 1974 and so I meticulously pay myself, calculating the hours between my arrival at the store and the end of each workday, when my sister and I total out the register, turn off the lights on each display case, and slide the huge piece of plate glass that constitutes our door back into its place, both of us on the other side of it.

The second reason my father probably shouldn't use his daughters as indentured servants is because we are more slovenly than real employees, more likely to flirt with teenaged male customers, to sell beer to our high school friends, and smoke cigarettes while lounging like bums on the second register island. After all, we were never hired, we can't be fired, and we may not fully understand the relationship of how our actions at the store relate to our success as a family.

Even though Dad must know we can't live on air alone, that our cars won't run without gas, that it costs more to live in 1974 in Scottsdale than it did, say, in 1937 Poland, he watches the cash register like a hawk. The cash register is the visual embodiment of his heart beating in his chest.

He has an Old Country relationship with money, which I can now see up close. He cozies up to the cash registers. He checks both cash drawers. Without warning, he'll swoop in and grab all the money, better to hide it from potential thieves, furtively stuffing it all into a brown paper bag and hiding it in the trash can beneath the registers, which seems like an ingenious idea until someone throws it out one day with the garbage.

"Move!"

My dad peremptorily comes behind the check stand, ordering me out of the way. He opens the register. The money he retrieves is a pile of odd bills – ones and fives and tens and some twenties. In Dad's hands, however, it's all magically transformed into hundreds, and then he counts them, flipping through the bills like a Las Vegas poker dealer, never missing one, never making a mistake. It is mesmerizing. He is exultant at the totals when the store is doing well but gloomy and irritable when the bills fly by too quickly, the stack too small. Pretty soon he can tell by the heft of the bills in his hand, by its thickness, if it was a good day or a bad day.

He's a one-man security camera, guard-dog, and lie detector test, the IRS and the FBI all rolled into one. When he gets home each night, he adds up the store money, dollar by dollar, check by check, with an antique oversized adding machine, its lever sticking out on top. He comes up short every time.

We are supposed to both admire Dad's finesse with the money and not see it at all – there is to be no mention of the money because this, *this money*? This money doesn't even really exist. It's all accounted for already, *dummkopf*. This chunk of hundreds for the mortgage, and this chunk of hundreds for the pool that fueled our enthusiasm about moving to Arizona, and this chunk of hundreds for our cars and gas and food – at the last he gives us a glare. Seven daughters eat too much food.

Because overall, we need to remember one very important fact. When Dad balances his piles of money against the piles of food we eat each day, all seven of us gobbling and gobbling away at the pile of money like termites, we know that his complaints are well-founded. At home we're eating him out of house and home, and at the store we're eating all the profits.

Our store is located on a bleak stretch of Scottsdale Road at the southern tip of Scottsdale, the building a former convenience market. Across the street to the south gleams a full-service and full-sized supermarket. Even we can't imagine why on earth anyone would walk in our store when they could go there and satisfy all their grocery and produce needs in one place.

My father is obsessed with this supermarket. He is the David to the Goliath of food stores at the southern tip of Scottsdale Road, doing mighty battle with them, while they don't even know we exist. He sends a couple of us over there on a reconnaissance mission, to spy out their produce pricing. My sister and I walk through the produce section with a clipboard writing down the prices. When an employee approaches and asks what we're doing, we're at least good at lying. We say we're doing an economics project for a class. Like we would ever do homework.

"Push, Linda!" Denise yells at me.

I disagree. "No, pull, don't push!"

Denise and I are standing outside the store, trying to open the behemoth plate glass sliding doors, which requires serious force, pushing and pulling. Once they're open for the day, they stay open. Customers can't be expected to heave ho every time they enter or exit. Inside we get the side effects of a permanently open door – insects, heat, cold.

The store itself is shaped like a rectangular box. Basically, a box of produce. A path from the front door straight back to the back room is right in front of the entrance, with a door on the right into the cooler. Turning away from the cooler, there's a quick jog by the bathroom, and then the long back room itself, a room which shows the lie to the front of the store – it's dark, dreary, and dirty.

To the right of the entrance we have two cash register

stands with real working conveyer belts but only sometimes-working cash registers. There are antique-by-accident produce scales at each stand, a pretty cool foot pedal for the conveyer belts, and a wall of cigarettes behind the first. I live in dread of a customer wanting cigarettes since, when they do, I must fruitlessly search to find the desired brand. There's a long wall of coolers in which we keep the milk and cheese, and in front of it are a couple of square display tables which are piled high with fresh baked tortillas and natural breads and snack bars. On the rest of the walls of the stores are coolers holding vegetables, and in the middle more display tables with fruits and other vegetables. I take a quick tour of the entire place every day when I get to work to make note of changes in pricing. These are the days before bar coding, before calculators – I'm the computer register, calculating price and exact sales tax in my head.

And why do our customers go to the extra work of saving their produce purchases for our tiny store? I think maybe it's because they don't quite fit in either, the odds and ends of people who have landed in Phoenix by accident in 1973, 1974. They somehow glean that we don't fit in so perfectly either and they flock to us.

There's our favorite East Indian couple with their tiny daughter named Priti, which I think is the English word Pretty, wondering at the pressure of the name. What if she doesn't grow up pretty? The Mexican farmers show up, their rickety pickup trucks piled high with produce, wheeling and dealing with my father. I'm sensitive towards people with accents, protective. Every immigrant is my father, my mother, one generation away from me. My dad is happy to see them. He will buy anything, good or bad produce, as long as it is cheap.

Mormon customers pour in, seeming very interested to have stumbled into a whole store filled with real, living, breathing Israelites from the Bible. Hebrews, right there in front of them! I stand there in my jeans and t-shirt, my lank brown hair curled in two stiff wings next to my ears, pimples dotting my face. I don't look exactly like the latest greatest version of the people of the Bible.

It's from them that I learn I am allegedly a Chosen Person. I've never heard this before, not having attended Hebrew School. I'm interested in this concept because before this time my entire Jewish education has consisted of horror stories from the Holocaust popping out of my mother's mouth unexpectedly, any time, any day. It's a constant tape on rewind there, she, frozen in the scenes of greatest horror of her life. I have been raised safe, in 1960s and 1970s suburbia, and find this bewildering. Why does my mother insist the Jews are never safe, that a Hitler will rise again? The tape plays over and over in her head, ultimately comprising my Jewish upbringing. It had always felt that if Jews were "chosen" for anything, it was to be killed and ostracized and destroyed as a people.

If "chosen" is suddenly a good thing, well, tell me more.

Our back room soon contains quite a collection of material. We have Books of Mormon small ones and big ones, several Good News Bibles from the reborn Christians, there are pamphlets from the 7th Day Adventists, who confusingly keep predicting that the world is going to end, even as those

66

dates roll by with the world never ending. There are brochures from Jehovah's Witnesses. There is a certain type of customer service we are required to maintain at the store when encountering our proselytizing customers. This involves listening to religious testimony politely but does not involve converting. I figure they have the best of intentions – to save us from what they are sure is hell fire. That's pretty nice of them.

There are the teens wanting beer. There's the guy who has a crush on me who is losing his sight, wanting me to be the last thing he ever sees. There's the guy who's inherited a chain of local movie theaters along with his string of blonde girlfriends. There are the elderly customers who can't hear me, the blind who trust me to count their money, the people who are like family. There are blunt old ladies who tell me when I start gaining weight, sending me into our grungy little bathroom crying all night, and there are the customers who bring in gigantic bags of change to pay for their order and count it right there on the counter, a line snaking off in the distance behind them.

Sometimes at the end of a workday, dad fires up the pickup truck and asks who wants to ride in the back – Mindy or me? I consider this a great treat so, being older, I get to be the cargo when it's time to go home.

From my position in the bed of the truck, I can watch the world go by sideways, just a peripheral view. First there are the lights of the other businesses near our store, then there's the narrowing of Scottsdale Road in Old Town where my father must slow down. Then, when we zoom past Chaparral Road heading towards Shea, the truck is engulfed in darkness, the night air gets colder. The truck bumps along and I watch the stars.

Even with the camouflage of Dad's new cowboy persona and Mom's new tennis attire, the tiny Phoenix Jewish community finds us. I overhear the tentative conversations, one brave Yiddish word tossed randomly into a sentence and which, if lobbed back, is our secret code to recognize one another. Surely, only a Jew will understand these words. If they're not lobbed back, no harm done, just a quizzical look. I do it too. I might be ringing up a purchase and spot a Jewish last name on a customer's check. When they ask where we moved from, instead of saying Chicago, my generic reply, I say Skokie, which, it turns out, is a code word for Jewish. And, boom, a connection.

Pretty soon we have all our ragtag companions, and we are thrown together in a tiny island of Jewish people in the middle of the Christian ocean of Arizona - for Bar Mitzvahs, for weddings. My parents have run as far from their Jewishness as they can, thousands of miles. They've searched for a house as far as they can away from the Jewish world. They've turned their backs on all of it – only to find it waiting for them in Arizona.

There are the Rosens, he a lawyer and she a judge, with their numerous identical curly, dark-haired children all attending private schools, and inhabiting a mansion with two staircases – one at the front of the house and one in the back, for servants. To me, this is way better than having a swimming pool. There are the Koens, with their two slightly creepy kids, a teenage girl and a smarmy boy who stalks my little sister.

There's Cantor Kushner, an immigrant like my parents, possibly Transylvanian, which, up until now, I didn't even know was a real place. He's pasty-faced, with a thick accent and greasy black hair in a widow's peak, like Bela Lugosi. His wife Arlene is the beauty of the pair. Dark-skinned and buxom, she moves along beside her husband like a clipper ship, always in full sail.

My mother, who should have had a lot in common with Arlene Kushner, since they are both foreign-born, despises her instead, in a way only a woman born in 1930 can hate another woman, especially when that woman claims to have been born in 1931. She senses Arlene's phoniness, her conceit, and most of all, she despises the way Arlene adores her husband, the way her life revolves around that vain peacock of a man. Mom had given that act up a long time ago. She has been worn to the quick by her marriage to Dad, beat up by it. There's no worshipping left, no gratitude and adoration, like she sees shining out of Arlene's docile eyes.

To me, there is nothing admirable about the Cantor or his wife. I know I'm supposed to admire him because he's the Cantor, and I am in awe about actually knowing anyone in Jewish religious life because this has never happened in our family before, but I don't. They are parvenus – and I think this knowing we're one step from the Old Country ourselves, with my father going through the money he saved for decades faster than it can be replenished. The Kushner are different than us. Wheedling, aspirational, and fawning to those richer than them, they are snobbish towards anyone poorer. They strike a difficult balance with our family – should they scorn us or worship us? I imagine the evidence of the produce store versus the house on an acre warring in their minds.

The problem is that we are not seen as the social equal of everyone else. We are not the children of an attorney, a doctor, or a judge. We are not the children of a Cantor and his adoring wife. We fall a little lower than that on the social scale – we are the produce store owner's children, almost serfs. The Rosen kids treat us as they must treat hired help, with a type of condescension, like we're amusingly blue collar and working class, not even entrepreneurial because a produce market just doesn't make the grade. There's something I can't quite pinpoint. Like maybe I should be in the kitchen at these parties, preparing and serving the fruit and vegetable platters instead of out mingling with the guests, like we're tradespeople whom their parents have deigned to befriend.

I'm so used to people seeing my potential and imagining my great future that when I realize this is occurring, I'm shocked. I wonder, am I wrong? Is this it for me? Am I going to stay a produce girl for life?

Seven

The Official Tour

My father is perched outside on one of our plastic-strapped lawn chairs. He's found just the perfect day to call his brothers in Chicago. The news says it's freezing there and it's gorgeous in Arizona, an ideal time to call. He schleps one of the extension phones to the outside extension, plugs it in. He pulls the chair up beside the phone with the pool in the background, as if somehow his brothers will see him, will know where he's calling from. When he's planted there, poolside, a bit of dappled shade upon him, he makes the long-distance call.

I hear only his side.

"Sid!" I hear, as he greets his brother. "You're enjoying the weather there? You like the snowstorms?"

He listens. I'm sure my uncle is disclaiming any affinity for snowstorms.

"You like it so cold? Ha! I know what it's like, so cold! Me, I'm outside next to my swimming pool, Sid. With a phone outside too." Does he think his brother has answered the phone while sitting outside in the snowstorm?

He nods his head for emphasis. "You should be here.

71

What? You gotta be there in the snow like a *shlimazel*, killing yourself every day, freezing? You come out. Bring Ida, she'll see."

The call ends but he's not done. He has to call Meyer, his other brother, and the same conversation ensues. When he's done, he's also done sunbathing.

He has no interest in sitting outside poolside.

There is a feeling of expectancy after our move to Arizona. There's the hustle and bustle of it, the swimming pool of it, Dad chomping at the bit to buy a business, any business, of it. There's also the fact that we fully expect our uncles to move their families out to Arizona right after us. We're the children of the oldest brother in the family. Our family myth tells us that our dad's brothers follow him in all things. He emigrated, they emigrated. He worked in the meat packing industry in New York, they worked in the meat packing industry in New York. He moved to Chicago then bought a house in Skokie, they moved to Chicago then bought homes in Skokie. He bought a laundry, they bought laundries.

So of course if we move to Arizona, they will have to move to Arizona.

Would my father have even moved if he'd thought for one second that they wouldn't follow him? How could he stand to be apart from them, the brothers so similar and who had traveled so far together? And could my uncles stand to live in a Chicago that was missing my dad, knowing he was just there – over those mountain ranges, at the end of those prairies, past those panhandles, around that final bend?

Dad demands that they come see Arizona for a visit,

preferably in the winter, when they'll get on the plane in Chicago at thirty-two degrees and get off in Phoenix at eighty-two degrees. Of course, their exploratory visit is timed differently than this. They visit when it's hot, when Arizona has burned to an even crisp, when our shoebox-shaped houses look smashed flatter than usual, collapsing under the heat, and when our gravel front yard is even more obviously a pathetic substitute for a lawn.

They get off the plane, a lock stepping group of four, standing in their coats. There's Dad's two brothers, Meyer and Sidney, and the brothers' wives, Rose and Ida. These are the brothers of his heart, the brothers with whom he withstood Siberia and the death of their sister. The brothers of Typhoid Fever, the brothers of the Displaced Persons camp, the brothers of the Black Market in Germany. They're dressed for fall and it is fall, but fall in Arizona is actually summer, so it's still one hundred degrees. Waves of heat undulate off the pavement. They can't click their metal seatbelts, can't touch the metal door handles of the car. Dad immediately gets flustered by Phoenix failing to impress them, by Phoenix failing him just when he needs it to be at its most impressive. Even he can't argue what's obvious to everyone, that Phoenix is melting.

So he takes them on the official tour. Up Camelback Mountain to park in the lovers' cul de sac at the top where no parking is allowed, to ooh and ah over the view, then around the other side to have them crane their necks and narrow their eyes to find the Praying Monk, a jutting piece of stone that looks like a monk kneeling in prayer.

Aunt Ida sniffs. She says, "Nu, Herschel, even the

mountains are Christian?"

He takes them to Rawhide because he thinks maybe a western show with a staged shootout will make Arizona irresistible. He shows them shopping centers squat on the ground and a sky above as big and blue as a dream. Mountains just standing there in the middle of town, free to look. We send them off on their own two-day adventure to the Grand Canyon, then take them to Slide Rock in Sedona and show them the great orange mountains there. He ends with the *coup de resistance,* a customized tour of our store when it's busy.

He doesn't realize that, in order to move this in their minds from an unthinkable horror to simply unthinkable, he needs to show them a Jewish community. The JCC, some synagogues, kosher butchers, a kosher bakery. Dad would have done better with a Jewish tour of Phoenix. His brothers and their wives have children at home to marry off, after all, Bar Mitzvahs to throw. One brother and his wife keep kosher. Unfortunately, my dad has purposely ignored anything related to such a thing as Jewish Phoenix. We move and, other than buying from a Jewish builder, we've hidden from the formal Jewish community except when they find us by accident at our store. Even then we've got one foot in and one foot out. We're out in the sticks, away from this fledgling community until later – decades later – the Jewish community moves en masse out of downtown Phoenix and clomps up, synagogues eventually encircling our house.

They take pictures. Of cacti. Of cowboys. Of downtown Scottsdale, the West's Most Western Town, since it's quite different from Skokie, the World's Largest Village. Dad says this would obviously be a great trade – a town instead of a village.

My aunts sniff with disapproval at our house. They say in unison, "A ranch?" which is a bad thing. No one in Skokie wants to live in a ranch. No stairs! They check the closets for the missing stairs going up, the missing stairs going down, but they're just closets. They go on Mom's elaborate winding tour of the house, then stand expectantly in the front hall. Where's the rest of the house? Where's the second floor? They don't care if we walked a mile in one direction and a mile in another. None of that counts if there's no upstairs, no basement.

"What, Chasia," Aunt Ida says, using my mother's Yiddish name. "It's a ranch? Where do you put the girls?"

My mom gets defensive. "In five bedrooms and twenty-five-hundred square feet, that's where I put them. Who needs a basement?"

Then my aunt turns to my dad. "And no lawn, Herschel? Where do the children play?"

He's ready for this one. He's been rehearsing for months.

"They play in the pool!"

They go outside and Dad shows them the pool, bounces on the diving board, then shows them the rest of the acre spread out beyond our tiny walled-in pool section, his back forty. He shows them his oleanders, his mounds of gravel – the pretend mountains in our front yard – all the building going on up and down our street, and, by the way, which lot do they want to buy? There's an open lot *here* and *there* and *there*. He's ready to take them to the sales office and sign them up. My aunts shake their heads. They aren't moving anywhere. He has just gone too far this time, they whisper to my uncles.

75

Aunt Ida, her lips pursed, nods at the pool, she agrees it's quite a pool, a lovely pool, but no promises.

"Anyway," she says, "we can get a pool in Chicago."

My uncle laughs nervously.

This is a problem because Dad, of course, is not going back to Chicago. Why would anyone stay in Chicago? He can't fathom the reasons. Look again! He waves expansively at our acre, at the pool, at the mountains in the distance, like he owns them. He finishes with a flourish towards me. "And look at especially how Linda is not sick anymore!" and I look up, shocked to suddenly be the object of attention. And then, because I'm not allowed to ever contradict my father, I pretend to be thriving.

Though we can't seem to get Dad's brothers to move, other acquaintances and family members do show up. Like our uncle Abe and his second wife, a former nun, whom he married only after he'd searched the entire Jewish world for a wife after my aunt died. Another uncle shows up with a shiny, new wife, running from his grown children, until my cousins track him down and lasso him back to Chicago. A family from our Skokie neighborhood, the Saltzmans, pack up and settle a half mile north of our house.

And, of course, it's so cold in Chicago, my grandparents show up for the winter.

I'm standing in our hall bath trying to brush my teeth, but things look a little more crowded than usual on the counter. I'm trying to figure it out when suddenly I notice the problem. There are two clear glasses standing there containing two full sets of teeth. I recoil in horror.

My grandparents have arrived in Arizona.

A few months after we get to Arizona, when the dust has settled, the boxes have been unpacked, and our life has assumed its new cadence, they show up.

Was this planned? Because no one told me about it. They are to come out to Arizona from November through March each year, squeezing into our house, claiming one bedroom, displacing one sister, and instantly assigning eight people to one full bathroom.

There are two main types of activities that go on in the bathroom once our grandparents arrive, the teen-based activities and the elderly-based activities.

The teen-based activities basically involve popping pimples, putting on makeup, and primping up and up and up for nights out. The elderly-based activities involve washing their disembodied teeth and then placing them in those cups standing by, to soak for the night, and my grandmother nearsightedly tweezing chin hairs since she doesn't want to look like a goat. For this she peers through her gigantic bifocals which, in turn, magnify her eyes, so that if I happen to walk in the bathroom at that exact minute, it looks like a tiny shrunken elf with enormous eyes is peering at me out of the mirror.

This Bubbe of mine is unhappy, and rightfully so. She was made this way by the two great tragedies of her life. There was the day in 1941 when she saw her extended family herded by Nazis into a house in her village, a grenade thrown in after them, and, a renewal of misery, on May 29, 1969, when my mother's sister Reva died. She had gotten used to the war memories, though she never stopped looking for her dead. But after Reva dies, I don't see her smile for seven years straight. She doesn't crack a smile and is seen only glaring at the camera in any photographs, her lips tight, angry, like the person taking the picture was somehow the God who took her daughter. When she arrives for her first winter in Arizona, only four years have passed since Reva's death and, in her lifetime of mourning, this is nothing.

It took until their second winter with us, my grandfather suddenly not himself, what I think is senility, blank somehow, cheerful like a baby, jolly despite having been a formidable man his entire life. He falls, and then he falls again. Onto her one time. One hundred eighty pounds of grandfather falling forward onto one hundred pounds of grandmother, she pinned beneath him in our sunken living room as he trips up one of the two steps in the house.

And then she smiles. Is it the close proximity to this different grandfather? Is it because, in his dementia, he has lost his companion anger at losing his child and smiles into her face trapped there beneath him? Does he become his young self and she her young self, there for one moment flailing on the living room floor, forgetting time and place and age, saying things to her in Yiddish that makes her blush?

All I know is that we heave and we ho and we get him up again and then we help her to her feet, and she is different somehow. Smiling.

They make it through a few yearly trips and then, a few months after their last visit, my grandfather gets worse, falling becomes more frequent. He turns seventy-six on the

Bicentennial. My mother has a dream the night of August 25th, 1976, that he comes to visit her "to say goodbye." He hugs her while she lies in bed. She wakes up to a phone call from her brother saying that my grandfather had died that day, at that moment, miles away, in Chicago.

Once my grandparents arrive, they form a tiny island of Orthodoxy in our house, a tiny eastern European shtetl transported intact into 1973 Scottsdale. My grandmother only wears dresses, my grandfather wears suits and a fedora, like a proper Litvak. We eat anything, but they are kosher. They ship in boxes of frozen kosher meat from Chicago. We eat anything. They do Shabbos. We have no clue that Friday is any different from the other days of the week except as it regards our social lives. They have heavy Lithuanian accents and we are all American.

This Bubbe of mine is apparently aware that there's not one thing in our house that isn't *tref*, so she travels with one precious saucepan packed in her luggage. This pan will do everything she needs it to do, and she's certainly done with less. She can boil in it, broil in it, and fry in it. She can use it as a saucepan, a fry pan, even as a bowl in a pinch. Everything in the world can be cooked in this one pot. After all, she had saved the family while living in the forest during the war using a discarded German helmet as a pot, so certainly she can manage with this, cooking their meals separately each night. On Fridays, like clockwork, she bakes two regular challahs, round and burnished with a perfect braid running down the center of each, and a miniature round diabetic challah with no sugar for my grandfather.

There's a wall between their rituals and us. After all, it's a well-known fact that our mother has kept us an island of Jewish ignorance on purpose. My mother, post war, has no time for God. We are so ignorant that I'm not sure that we even know we're ignorant, we think we're knowledgeable. We don't believe in any organized religion, even our own. One of the things I do believe I'm knowledgeable about is judging my grandparents' Orthodoxy. Certainly, regular Judaism, as embodied in all the Bar and Bat Mitzvahs I've attended, is mystifying enough. Why go crazy with it? Overall, there's a feeling that, instead of my grandparents trying to pass their Judaism onto us, we're trying to pass our agnosticism onto them.

Judaism to me is whatever I think it is. If I grew up with something like bacon, it is automatically Jewish. If I didn't grow up with it, like the Hebrew Bible, then it's not. I am a mini-philosopher, deciding questions of great import with my teenage brain, like that the laws of kashrut are outdated and no longer necessary after refrigerators were invented. My family seems to think as one regarding our faith. Whatever we think is the right thing for all Jews to think, the right level of Jewishness for all Jews. If we decide that kashrut is incomprehensible, then that's what it is, for all time. If we decide we don't need to pray in a synagogue but can pray in a closet, then that's our opinion on that. We have decided.

So, of course our grandparents' Orthodoxy is all wrong. It's the 1970s. Shouldn't all women be wearing hip polyester pantsuits by now? My grandmother only wears severe dresses, hose, practical pumps. I think women should literally let their hair hang down, but hers is coifed into a

80

ginger-colored bubble, all air, no hair. All of it is incomprehensible – the tiny single pot, the shipped in frozen food, the candle lighting on Friday evenings, and her head covering, which is anything she can grab hold of, even a napkin.

Challah, we all seem to agree, is not dumb.

I spend a significant amount of time trying to convince her to let go of the old ways. I succeed only in getting her in pantsuits. It takes more than a decade.

My grandmother's Orthodoxy forms another good reason in my mind to cast off the weight of centuries. She seems so rigid about it, almost unhappy about it. As a judgmental teen, I see only that it she is following what seems to be an incomprehensible and onerous set of rules, just because she'd always been following them. At the time, I don't understand what has wiped the smile from her face, the death of my aunt and that in a very real way, she is still looking for her Holocaust dead. I'm just young enough to expect other peoples' experiences to mirror my own. If I can be happy despite the burden of the past, why couldn't she be?

But Chicago is too cold for my grandparents to stay the winter, and so we cram in the bathroom, the sisters living at home and now two grandparents. The two sets of disembodied teeth continue floating eerily in their cups.

Eight
New Girl

For some reason, once eighth grade starts, my dad decides to start driving me to school each day in his store truck, wearing his cowboy regalia. I duck down in my seat as we drive.

I see a shimmery heat mirage ahead of us in the road which looks look like water but, as we approach, turns out to be nothing, just a dip in the road. I see another wavy apparition up ahead moving along on the side of the road, something that tells me in one frozen image that I'll never fit in, not in this eighth-grade class and maybe not ever. I see one of my classmates on her way to school. Not in a car. Not on a bike. Not on foot. On a horse.

How can I fit in a place where people ride horses to school?

But there are more immediate concerns causing some irritation, like the fact that my father mispronounces the unfamiliar Spanish street names. Because I'm such an expert after taking one year of Spanish in sixth grade.

He says, "The school's on Cholla, right?" pronouncing the double Ls even though it's a Spanish word and pronounced "Choya."

I roll my eyes because I'm thirteen and because my Polish Holocaust Survivor father has bewilderingly decided to become a cowboy.

I say, "Cholla, Dad," emphasizing the correct pronunciation, like I'm suddenly so fluent that I can correct my father who speaks five languages.

We ride in silence after that. We get to the school, he stops, and I jump out.

On the first day of school, I show up, part of a stampede of eighth graders, possibly the only brunette in a teeming horde of blondes. I go to classes, I eat lunch, I go to study hall, and I know nobody. My day is filled with dead silence, although all around me there are groups of kids reuniting after the summer, all thrilled to see each other, the girls standing in circles, wearing similar outfits – different than mine – and clutching their hard notebooks to their flat chests. No one looks familiar to me and I'm not sure they'll ever look familiar to me, like I've been programmed from my early years to recognize my *mishpocha* only. I can't tell one blonde blue-eyed kid from another.

I'm a skinny, asthmatic stick and have silver braces, a funny chin that just keeps growing when the rest of me stops, and a shag haircut with a side part and swooping bangs over my interconnected, caterpillar-shaped, black eyebrows. There are clear dotty pimples all over my face like a map of the metropolitan suburbs of Chicago, a clue to where I belong. Connect the dots and an image forms of my home in Skokie.

I have only one plan for this move, basically that being the New Girl, I will immediately be popular and sought after.

There is no backup plan, no idea that this might not work. After all, for thirteen years I had watched new kids show up in Skokie and be swarmed with attention. Actually, they didn't even have to show up in person, it could just be a moving truck mysteriously pulling in front of a house on the block. That was all we needed to know that something was changing, something was shifting in our orbit, on the static screen of our world, in the status quo. Like detectives, the neighborhood kids would stake out the house, watching the movers unload, looking for clues of whether kids were moving in. Were there boxes of toys? Bicycles? A frilly canopy bed? In my assessment, the worst outcome would be boys moving in. The next would be if there were teenagers — we had enough of them. The best? A girl exactly my age. Sometimes right while we were watching, the family pulled up in their car. Depending on the age of the kids in the car, the neighborhood kids disbursed. The ones of us who were the same age stayed to fight it out.

New kids were swarmed, stalked, wooed, cossetted, adored, guarded from others who wanted to steal your new kid, and fought over. Based on proximity, the new kid could be yours because you could simply stalk them more effectively if you lived on the same block. I had managed to nab one in fifth grade when a girl moved in on my block, but I'd lost a battle over a new girl who moved in during fourth grade. She was two streets over, on Trumbull, and two of my friends who lived right there won the territorial war.

Arizona is different. There is no swarming going on. New kids move in every year, every half year. Here and gone, transient, flighty. There can be nothing more common around my new middle school than a new kid. They are to be ignored until they worm themselves into some kind of group, or some group splits open at the seams to gobble them up, making it seem like they were always there. No one *needs* the new kids. The whole school was doing perfectly fine without them.

It's survival of the fittest out here for new kids in the eighth grade at Cocopah Middle School. The school is filled with tiny, twinkling blonde cheerleaders, so beautiful, unapproachable, so perfect. Girls with skin that has never seen a Stridex pad, girls whose brilliant white teeth have never seen braces, girls whose noses will not need straightening. They have perfect boingy, bouncy legs that catapult them in mid-air, twirling and somersaulting, lifted on each other's shoulders, higher and higher, in pyramid formation up to the sky, their blonde hair glinting in the burning hot sun.

There's nothing I can do to become like these girls. No amount of hair dye, no workout regimen, no tiny skirt, will make me into one of them. They were created centuries ago, millennia ago, not in the shtetls of Poland and Russia as I was, but in the mountains of Sweden and Norway, in the rolling hills of England and Ireland, all combining to put forth the bluest eyes, the blondest hair, the most veinless legs, culminating here, in the middle of Scottsdale, Arizona.

Yet, I look optimistically around me, ready to count my Jewish brethren. Coming from Skokie, I think that just about everyone is Jewish. My world is separated like that — Jewish and its opposite, non-Jewish. Apparently, I am wrong. I get to Scottsdale and am disconcerted to discover not only that Jews are a minority and non-Jews the majority, but that the non-

Jewish world is made up of a gazillion smaller denominations, all separate factions and denominations of Christianity, all agreeing on one thing only, that they all hate Catholics. Unless they are Catholic.

Gone are the familiar names of my childhood friends, names like Dina and Shelly, Roslyn and Rona or Sheila, boys named Mark, Larry, Stuart. Names that recite Torah up on a *bimah*, that dance the *hora*, that serve in a *minyan*. Instead, I'm surrounded by names that all seem to be derivatives of the word "Christ:" Christina, Christine, Christa, Chris, Chrissy, Chrystal. There are the K names, like Kelly, Kathy, Kim, Krista, Kristen, Kirsten, Ken, Keith. All Ks, just like the Ku Klux Klan.

I have a funny, sinking feeling that I'm the only one named for a dead relative.

Attractiveness is gauged by a different measuring stick. There is a pedigree I don't have. A lot of my fellow students have older siblings who have paved their way, maybe a brother over at the high school on the football team, athleticism being a road to popularity. Some run track, others are in cheer or pom or other activities where one minute you see them and the next you don't, as they launch themselves into the air above my head. Burt girls are earth-bound.

I am amazed at the school's whiteness. I wonder why there aren't any black kids. I suspect my new city of racism. There are cowboys and there are Native Americans and, this is surprising for me, they are cowboys too. There are cow chicks, the female equivalent to a cowboy. There are tough white girls who spend all their time terrorizing the eighth-grade population. There are dorks and there are beautiful popular girls with their hair curled in wings who will never, ever accept me, not even at our thirty-year reunion. There are short, creepy bullies who observe me so closely, apparently looking for a nickname, that they start calling me "Chin." There are hippies with floppy hats and long hair. There are tall, handsome blonde-haired, chiseled-featured, Christian boys whom I immediately decide I'll marry, forgetting Skokie and the Holocaust in one fell swoop. There are smokers and girls who dye their hair and girls who bleach their hair. There are girls who are not virgins at thirteen and they are the ones who dye their hair and beat everyone up. There is a principal with a paddle in his office and teachers who hate kids and a PE teacher who believes asthma is just another excuse to try to get out of running laps.

And there is me. I realize quickly that I'll never simply make friends. The real question is, how am I going to buy them?

My neighborhood dead ends at a swathe of desert, but off in the distance, through scrub bushes and tumbleweeds, through mesquite trees and gopher holes, there is another neighborhood, the two unconnected, and that is where my first friend, Lucy Tindall, lives, who is new to Arizona too, but from Pittsburgh. Whereas I am somewhat wild-eyed in panic at being alone for even one second in the school day, Lucy is self-contained, sitting alone like she's in a bubble, or on an iceberg, spending all of her free time in study hall. She's been forcibly yanked from her true home, but mentally most of her is in Pittsburgh floating above the head of her eighteen-year-old boyfriend, not here with her parents, whose marriage is breaking into tiny fragments day by day. Lucy recounts the evidence of this to me in one of our first conversations, that they have separate bedrooms, that her mother is always conveniently ill, her father taking on time-consuming hobbies, both of them fighting nonstop. I'm dumbfounded. I'm certainly used to having parents with a troublesome marriage, but I'm not used to admitting it.

Since Lucy is floating in the air three thousand miles away, shivering in the Pittsburgh fall, she is odd, but certainly good enough. The most important thing is that I don't have to wander about school alone, sit by myself at lunch. We become friends. Now that we're friends, she wants me to come over.

All I have to do is walk through this tiny swathe of dusty desert to get to her house. She gives me simple instructions to find it, saying, "We're the ones with a vacuum cleaner for a mailbox." This is unusual, of course, and I really have no idea what I'm looking for. The only vacuum cleaner I've seen in my life is our Hoover upright which comes up to my waist, so I wander around for a while looking for a mailbox that looks like that.

It turns out that her father has retrofitted a canister-style Electrolux vacuum cleaner as a rural-style mailbox, removing the wheels and attaching a red flag. He did this, first, because he sells Electrolux vacuum cleaners, so the mailbox is now a type of sign in front of their house, hopefully leading to more sales, and second, because he's somewhat of a vacuum cleaner collector and *artiste*. He has a workshop at the house in which he turns old Electrolux canister vacuums into various *objets d'art*, like a bread box, end tables, a lamp – what can't he do with an Electrolux, he wants to know? This, I decide, is in some ways even worse than my dad being a laundryman in Chicago, with the way he hauled his two favorite commercial washing machines with us when we moved. I had to be thankful at least that he hadn't installed one of them in front of our house to become the biggest mailbox ever.

At Lucy's house we sit in her gloomy dark room, slatty light coming in through the blinds, and we do two things. First, we must worship and analyze her boyfriend in absentia, every phone call, and every word of every phone call, and second, she must vacuum while I watch. The boyfriend thing, of course, I'm used to. Parsing out male motives from words in a letter or their various mumblings on a phone call is all par for the course of being an eighth-grade girl. We're always trying to decode male behavior, discover obscure clues, and turn nothing into something.

It's the vacuuming that's a little odd because she's not vacuuming as a chore. During the course of a two-hour visit Lucy might pull out her own personal Electrolux canister vacuum, with its accordioned hose and the multiple crevice tools, repeatedly, like five or six times, in an endless attempt to vacuum up each crumb that falls, every dust mite that cascades through a beam of light, and all the dirt that landed on the floor since she last vacuumed twenty minutes before.

I come from a family where cleaning is a dreaded necessity, in which the whole army of us tackle the house with one designated chore each. I am in charge of the tile floors in the foyer, the three bathrooms, and the laundry area. I learn to clean nothing else. I definitely don't know how to vacuum.

My position is that no matter how odd Lucy is, I have to put up with her. The alternative of being alone is unacceptable and, naturally, I'm sure that if I lose her, I'll be alone. Lucy's norm becomes the norm. Vacuuming her room ten thousand times while I visit? No problem. Sitting for hours discussing the boyfriend, agreeing with whatever she says about him? I'm game. Listening to an ever-increasing litany of her personal problems, the melancholia, the litany about her parents, her father literally entwined in an Electrolux cord, the vast superiority of Pittsburgh over any other place in the world? Fine. Pretending I'm not mad at her when one day she peeks over the stall door in the girls' bathroom at school while I'm in it? I start to fray at the edges.

One day she tells me her biggest secret.

"My ears never grew. They're the size of a five-year-old's ears."

I'm not sure exactly what my reaction to this revelation is supposed to be but I guess it's the wrong one. I'm surprised, of course, that this is her secret because her ears are there plainly for anyone to see, right on the sides of her head, not exactly a secret. I express amazement – is that what she wanted? Because if I had to pick between ears that stopped growing and my Dudley Do Right jaw that keeps growing, I'd pick the pretty little ears.

The following Monday Lucy meets me at school and says, "Linda, I think we need a break from each other. We've been hanging out together a lot and I think we need a break."

And just like that, though I'd clung to her as my only friend, though I was willing to make do, even though I was willing to live in the shadow of her gloom, she wasn't willing to make do with me. I'm alone again.

I'm not the only new girl on the planet, of course. There are other new kids also wandering blindly around campus, being cast off by group after group after group. I wander for a while but eventually figure out who's new and who isn't. That's how I end up with three friends all at once, all new girls, and my boring life ends instantly. One, Nina, is from Boston and becomes my best friend of sorts. Another, Mona, is from Chicago and is half Jewish, as she tells me, my Jewish radar on red alert. The last girl, Lori, is a wild bleached blonde who can't hold a conversation long enough to provide a history or geography, so I don't know where she's from. Instead, there's just a blur of her hair as she constantly tosses her head and fake laughs, along with shirts so high and pants so low that an endless expanse of flat thirteen-year-old belly shows in the middle. As a group, they're all wilder than any friends I'd had before.

It's these girls I cling to, follow, and awkwardly try to fit in with, running at a mad dash all over campus. They become my friends, my motley crew, a wall between me and the kids who want no part of me. It never occurs to me that the litmus test for a friend is liking them. I have no idea that I have a decision to make. If they like me, I like them.

All of us having been rejected or bounced out of each social group one by one, we form our own group of misfits, Nina and Lori vying for the top spot.

Nine

Third Wheel

One day Nina hands me a picture while I'm over at her house. In it she's standing in front of a Boston mansion in the snow, bundled up in a hat, mittens, a winter coat, and boots.

She says, "This is me in front of my house where we used to live. We lost all our money, that's why we live in *this* house now."

I look around at the reality of Nina's Arizona house — a new but crumbling home built by the second-worst home builder in Arizona, located on an acre of horse property. There are some raggedy chickens squawking outside, bunnies in Nina's room in a cage, their pellets carpeting the floor, there are a few swayback, mule-like horses dotting the edges of their property, along with a few goats that live both outside the grimy sliding glass doors to the patio, eating the lawn chairs, and inside the grimy sliding glass doors, wandering into their family room to chew on the curtains for a while.

It was dirty, disordered, and disheveled, her mother good naturedly sitting at the chipped laminate kitchen table, chain smoking and mulling over the solution to the world's problems with her eldest daughter, an apparent spinster though she's only in her late twenties. I wonder, is this a family that was *just* rich – like the minute before they moved? Because there's no evidence of it, no aging finery, no dilapidated china, no crystal, no feeling of squeezing their old elegance into the squalor of their Arizona house.

Just the contrary, in fact. Everything fits just fine. Nina extolls the virtues of Corelle china to me at length. They don't appear to notice or care about grime. I, firmly ensconced in a middle-class hard-won by my Holocaust Survivor parents, have been trained from birth by my mother on how to detect crystal from glass, how to find the hidden geisha in her Japanese china, and how to identify watered silk from silk satin. I'm used to everyone in Skokie having exactly the same things we had which included a living room just for show and which was decorated like the court of Louis IXV, chandeliers, kitchen appliances that all matched, with a sink that matched too. Some of the ladies on my street went a step farther, installing thick museum-type roping and a plastic walkway to protect their living room tableau. This is the world in which I'd grown up.

I'm wowed by other stories, like when Nina says she pried off her own braces on the way to Arizona after deciding she no longer needed them. There is the story about how her hair miraculously turned blonde from its original brown and the story about how she woke up one day and her eyes had turned green though previously they had been whatever-on-earth-color mine were. She wistfully bites her lower lip and looks at me sadly, and says, "Gosh Linda, I hope that yours change color one day too!"

Based on this evidence, my theory is that she posed in front of a random mansion and claims it as her own. There are no pictures of Nina inside.

Nina's father is younger than her mother and a mailman, coming home each day in the Arizona outfit of shorts, socks, mailman shoes. He doesn't look like a man who had just been rich but who had lost all of his money somewhere on the road to Arizona.

The family consists of Nina and several brothers, all gorgeous, all pug-nosed, all blonde, all who look like her father, and all of whom barely talk to me and do not ever confirm or deny the Boston mansion story, the green-eyed story, the overnight-blonde-hair story, the prying-braces-off-the-teeth story. They are afraid of Nina, who has learned to fight in this household of boys and can hold her wiry own with them. She won't hesitate to chase the younger ones down and pin them to the ground.

Nina's got something that her mother and oldest sister don't seem to have, a type of hyperawareness of how they live, and ambition for how she'd like to live. I can feel it teeming inside her – how is she going to get herself from here to there, from this house to the inside of that mansion?

It's soon established in mine and Nina's friendship that she's in charge and I'm not. Since I'm supposed to be in a permanent state of gratitude towards Nina just for deigning to be my best friend, I'm kept busy trying to match my mood to hers, to mirror her every emotion.

Sometimes she's in a bummer of a mood, which means I need to be in a bummer of a mood. Other times she is hyper, like bouncing off the walls hyper, and I need to be bouncing off the walls with her, but not to exceed her. Exceeding her mood is very bad. She, in turn, will never mirror my mood, she is contraposed to my moods. If I dare to have a mood of my own – and I just don't after a while – she hyper-analyzes me. Why am I so happy? What do I have to be happy about? Maybe, just to bring me back down again, she throws a little tidbit out there.

"Linda, ya know, people are always asking me, 'Why do you hang out with Linda? You could be hanging out with WAAAYYY better people!' and I tell them, 'You don't know her. She is so much fun!'"

Or she says, "Linda, I was just noticing how pretty you are. You look SOOOO much better now than when I met you!" And, just like that, mission accomplished. I'm no longer having fun.

There is the good side of Nina, like the fact that excitement and controversy follow wherever she goes. Everyone knows who she is, and she is impossible to ignore. There is her particular manner of speaking, all in superlatives – Oh my God, is everyone the BEST EVER at everything they do! So talented, SOOOO beautiful, so, so, nice. SO, SO, SOOOO spiritual!

She has strong opinions. One of them is about the greatness of the musician Alice Cooper and why he should be president. I'm almost certain that Nina is the only person in the world who thinks this. Another is her resistance to the

Theory of Evolution ("show me one modern day Missing Link and I'll believe in it."), and another is that she is opposed to hitchhiking. Hence, we end up walking everywhere in the Arizona heat. We can be found trudging up the side of a road walking the three miles from my house to our closest shopping center and back again, it's just what we do. We wouldn't dream of asking for a ride for this short distance. And since we walk everywhere, we get to see the scenery up close, especially the desert between our school and the shops.

The desert doesn't start right behind the school, more like a couple of house-strewn streets away. After we pass the last of the white-pebbled rooftops, the horse corral-filled backyards, the endless expanses of slump blocked walls, there it is. There's nothing mystical about this piece of Arizona desert. It's not a white-sanded Sahara, it doesn't contain any huge saguaro cacti. It's just what I come to know as the Arizona desert circa 1974, with motocross tire treads zipping this way and that way, sagebrush bushes that grow like a ball, round and green, and the light brown dusty dirt crisscrossed with the tracks of the animals that run through there, and there are prairie dog holes. There's the path we beat walking through it, well worn by nearly a decade of middle schoolers on our way to the convenience market.

Eventually there are bulldozers.

Since Nina's in charge of our personality, of our outrages and our opinions on everything, she's thought this matter through for us. Our opinion is that the desert must be saved. The problem of how to save the desert falls to Nina, our mastermind. I'm sincerely hoping it won't be similar to her plan to convince Alice Cooper to switch his career from music to politics, spray painting "Alice Cooper for Prez" on the lockers at school.

"Should we sabotage the bulldozers or just put some signs up?" she says. "Or maybe organize a protest?"

I imagine a raggedy-looking picket line of fourteen-year-olds – no voters among us – all incensed at the gobbling up of this pristine piece of desert – a whole quarter mile of desert, smashed between a convenience market at one end and our school at the other. Outraged mainly because we were using it for other things at the time, like smoking pot and make out sessions and running from our principal right off our campus at full tilt, to hide out there.

For a long time she talks about this idea of saving the desert, considering even spray painting a slogan on the trees, but there weren't many and it did seem to conflict with our ecology stance, or we could spray paint the tractors, but even we weren't nervy enough to end up in jail.

We do nothing ultimately, except sulk in impotent rage. I get preoccupied, forget to check on it, start high school. When I think to look over there months later, the bulldozers have had their way. The desert is gone.

"Linda, do not leave me alone with him!" Nina hisses through clenched teeth shaped in a smile, indicating her boyfriend Paul on the bed. I nod. Of course I won't leave her alone. I am her loyal minion and bodyguard.

Midway through eighth grade, Nina gets a boyfriend. She chooses Paul Harris to be her boyfriend, yanking him out of complete obscurity, and things change. As a group, we're suddenly not such a bunch of misfits anymore. The language of boyfriends is one the entire school understands. Suddenly Nina is not just a new girl, her social ranking skyrockets. What no one understands is, why Paul Harris? This is a choice so confounded, so odd, so incomprehensible, that no one knows what to make of it.

It's unexpected because Paul is a short, motocross-obsessed, childlike boy, with pelts of blonde shaggy hair that hang over his ears like Shaggy on Scooby Doo. His life up until Nina picks him for her boyfriend has been spent in obscurity, basically hanging out with his best friend, the acne-prone Dan Garrett, and riding motocross bikes in the desert. In the world of appealing boyfriend opportunities at Cocopah Elementary school in 1974, there are better choices. Like boys who are somewhat socially adept or who can hold up a conversation, boys who are nominally groomed. Yet, Nina picks Paul and she raises him out of this muck to boyfriend status for the months of their relationship. I realize that this purposeful choosing of a lesser guy is similar to her choosing me for her best friend, for rising me from the muck.

I gain some importance as the conduit to information about the couple, a matter of fascination for the entire eighth grade. People pull me over to ask varying questions. "Is it true that Nina's dating Paul Harris?" and then, "How can it be true that Nina's dating Paul Harris?" and, "What is Nina thinking, dating Paul Harris?" The combined concentration and attention of the entire eighth grade is focused on them, parsing them, wondering at this mystifying choice.

She apparently has her reasons and, as far as I can tell, none of the reasons are that she particularly likes Paul. She seems to like being in control, and she is definitely in control in this situation. She seems to need to say no to a boy, and she definitely says no to Paul. I know this because over the months of their relationship there are many scenes in his bedroom where I'm their reluctant duenna, witnessing the horrifying sight of Paul madly jumping on Nina and saying, "Can't we do it yet?" Each time her answer rings out, "No!"

In all the years of our friendship I secretly think I'm the smart one and Nina's the dumb one, but she proves herself smarter than me right there at the beginning. She consolidates her power among the eighth graders by having a boyfriend and raising her status. In our small world, she becomes someone who's had a boyfriend and so becomes someone desirable to be a girlfriend.

There are many bad things about this situation as far as I'm concerned. The most obvious one is that now we have to hang out with him and his accompanying entourage, mainly his best friend and fellow motocross bike rider, Dan Garrett. So we are now hanging out with Dan Garrett. Paul's also close to his older brother, who looks like a stretched-out, Gumby version of Paul but whom I think, privately, was perhaps dropped too many times as an infant. This means I get to hang out with the brother too.

Dan Garrett and the brother hate me with a passion. Dan seems to resent being paired up with me like we're destined to pair off because our best friends are a couple. Even worse, if we pair off, Paul gets the swan and he gets the duck. He is not taking the duck. Even if he's covered in pimples, he is not taking the duck. I don't think I have any choice in the matter. If Dan likes me then I will automatically like him, if he hates me, the same. I let others set the emotional temperature and then I react according to it.

It doesn't help that Dan and Paul's brother are constantly pulling me aside and telling me to scram, to leave Nina and Paul alone, to stop being the fifth wheel, or the third wheel or whatever numbered wheel I am. At the same time, Nina is pulling me over and hissing through her sparkling white clenched teeth, "Do. Not. Leave. Me. Alone. With. Paul." Which is hard to misunderstand. My loyalty is to Nina, of course, so I stay.

So I follow them everywhere, their unpaid and mostly unwanted chaperone. I'm there to protect Nina's virginity and, in so doing, I realize I'm probably keeping Paul's intact too.

I follow them to Cocopah school dances and to school baseball games at which I never glance, or the after-games, the players still strutting around in their tiny seventh and eighth grade-sized uniforms, showing off. I follow them out past the school and over our tiny stretch of desert, before the bulldozers, to the convenience market, to lurk there outside the door asking strangers to buy us Boones Farm wine for a dollar a bottle. Getting drunk seems like it might be a worthwhile pastime.

I follow them to the shopping plaza that circles the convenience market, with its collection of struggling stores. We make our rounds into each of the newly-opened tiny shops – a candle store, an arcade, a health food store, a clock repair company – and then we watch as the owners proceed through the life cycle of each business. They are opened in a fit of optimism, later they're beset by worries, and, finally, they close one by one. The candle store guy is sure he's sitting on a gold mine. He tells us confidently that the center of Scottsdale is projected to move north and envelope him within twenty years, and then he'll be sitting on a gold mine of candles, but right now we can only see what he's envisioning by squinting at it, all the way down the full length of Scottsdale Road to the other end. That's where the center of Scottsdale is.

There's a liquor store, which we never step inside, sure we will be shooed right back out again. There's a cowboy bar owned by one of our classmate's families, and there's a vacant two-story building that I decide would make a perfect location for a commune. Just me and Paul and Nina in a commune together forever.

I follow Nina and Paul into the desert to watch Paul and Dan ride their dirt bikes, the brown dusty air enveloping me as I watch, coughing and choking. I follow Nina onto the back of a dirt bike, careening through the desert like a lunatic, soon, I'm sure, to be sadly dead, as Dan seems determined to shake me off the thing.

I follow them to the arcade in the shopping center where I spend my evening doing several activities. I can watch Nina and Paul fight and make up all night, maybe referee for a while with the wisdom of a tween King Solomon. I can mess with a pinball machine and watch impotently as the steel ball zooms past my flippers every time. I can chain smoke outside, or at least pretend to, since I don't inhale. Or I can play air hockey, my true God-given talent. I can't run, I'm an all-around, run of the mill klutz, I can't climb a rope or run a mile. But my Olympic sport, if I had one, if they had this one, would be air hockey.

I follow Paul and Nina to a tent revival set up at a

hotel on Scottsdale Road where a fiery preacher exhorts the audience to accept Jesus as their Lord and Savior, to come on down to the stage when they are ready to do so. The preacher's staff fans out among the audience asking people, "How about you?" and "How about you?" and "How about you?" and I sit there cringing, skulking, hoping not to be asked, the secret Jew.

I watch as audience members stand and walk to the stage as if in a trance, joining the preacher, collapsing on the stage in the fervor of this moment, and I wonder, am I supposed to have a fervent moment too? Am I supposed to give myself to Jesus? I don't know much about my own religion, but I do know that we don't believe in Jesus. Still, there's something about the new converts' shining, converted, eyes afterwards that's very compelling. Suddenly I realize that Nina is walking up there too. Fourteen-years-old, stick thin, wearing low, low-cut pants and a high cut top, dirty blond hair, narrow green eyes, picked out eyelashes, and a smile and teeth so beautiful, so straight, and so white that they could have come from heaven, she walks up there.

I stay glued to my seat. I remain Jewish.

There are two people who think I'm beautiful when I'm fourteen and, unfortunately, neither of their opinions count to the eighth grader arbiters. They both count to me.

One is Mr. Rizzo, the owner of a pizza place near my high school. He calls me "Lovely Linda" each time I walk in. My companions gasp in astonishment, actually do double takes, look around to see if there's another Linda in there who is actually lovely, or if he's mistakenly called Nina by my name.

As a matter of fact, I think he's joking too, maybe making fun of me, but he's not.

Paul and Dan try to straighten him out, saying, "Nina's the pretty one, Mr. Rizzo." And he looks around and sees Nina, the underdeveloped stick, who lacks my Rubenesque curves, and says, "That one? Ha! Lovely Linda is the most beautiful!"

Nina seems amused and bemused by Mr. Rizzo. She has a studied reaction – one raised quizzical eyebrow which means that his choice is clearly beyond sanity – that maybe he's senile and requires no reply. His lack of mental acuity is fully expressed by that eyebrow.

And then there's the other person in the world who thinks I'm beautiful at fourteen – Paul's dad.

As we pour into Paul's house, Mr. Harris, some kind of confirmed elderly bachelor, house-husband-type, wearing house shoes and a worn Mr. Rogers-type cardigan, only has eyes for me. There is apparently no Mrs. Harris, just him and his household of raggedy-haired, motocross-bike-riding boys. He has somehow single-handedly spawned these sons, I'm never sure how many of them are loping about.

He sees me and it's the pizza guy all over again.

He says to Paul as he walks in, "Is the beautiful Linda with you?"

I flush, I blush, I even cringe a little, because I know what will come next – the utter amazement of my companions.

Of course, it's hard to imagine how these two see any potential in me. I'm having an unfortunate, ultimately four-year-long, awkward phase, with my dark hair cut into wings, pimples dotting my face, and makeup that consists equally of Clearasil and beige cover stick. I have a Dudley Do Right chin, of course, and a black unibrow staking out the edge of my forehead. I smile and a full set of silver braces show, maybe some rubber bands attached to hooks on the upper and on the lower, snapping my jaws together as I spoke.

So, no. Not attractive.

But they see something in me. Some glimmer, something I assume is inside, because it's definitely not outside. Maybe something I'll grow into. I'm stunned that men exist of this ilk. I wish both of them could be rolled whole into my father.

It's January 4th, 1974, and I am in a pitch-black room with about a dozen other teenagers. We are having a make out party. For some reason, I'm not sure why or how it happened, I'm making out with Phil Wilson, a pimply-faced, long-haired hippie who is known by his floppy suede hillbilly hat with roach clips attached to the brim. This is his signature look. It's so much his look that one day at school he takes it off for a second, revealing the crushed, lifeless hair beneath it – hat-shaped of course – and he is unrecognizable.

His hair is long and greasy. His skin is a study in pre-Accutane acne, pock-marked where there aren't active pimples, pimples moving in and pimples moving out, all leaving new pock marks. He has a studied sloppiness – shirts out over jeans that are too long, hems ripped up, and button-fly Levi's. I can't imagine why he'd have buttons in the way when all he seems to want in the world is to take those pants off, stat.

I'm not attracted to Phil, but I've already learned that I don't get to choose. How this was conveyed to me through my limited lifetime so far is uncertain, but I do know that the gage of my attractiveness is set on boys' barometers. If they like me, I'm attractive, and if they don't, I'm a "dog." When Phil and I somehow flop down on the bed together, I think, well, I didn't think I liked Phil but now I guess I do.

Phil's main attraction is that he is a sex maniac, which is an attractive quality at the time. No one knows if he's actually had sex – we are only in 8th grade after all – but my God, the impression is that he will die trying. Each girl is his Mount Everest, and he seems ready to climb to get to that goal.

He chooses me the night of this party, and this is a bad choice as far as these goals go. I have never made out before and back in Skokie I'd spent a considerable amount of time and effort protecting my breasts from ever being touched during various rough and tumble games at a synagogue youth group. I don't know what I am saving them for, maybe for my own private Paul Harris, my own going-steady boyfriend, not just someone who gropes me on a bed in a pitch-black room. I need a commitment if I am going to wheel out my breasts.

The party was at my friend Mona's mountainside house. To be specific, it was in her bedroom in her mountainside house. We don't seem to know yet that at real parties you stand and talk and drink and then retreat somewhere in privacy to have make out sessions. So we cut out the talking and the standing and the drinking and cut to the chase, collapsing in make out session piles on Mona's bed, on her bean bag chair, behind her vanity, on the floor.

Mona's mother is a gentle, somewhat befuddled, southern Christian woman who had married an older Jewish man. She seems a little bit in over her head, frazzled maybe by the difference between her teenage years and her daughter's, maybe ready for us to have a sock hop. Mona, instead, stuffs us all in her bedroom and slams the door in her mother's face saying, "We're going to listen to music."

This is my first make out session ever and Phil and I have somehow scored the bed. I end up having a sexy, Hollywood-ish, rolling-around-the-bed-type of make out session that day with him. I'm French kissing for my first time and, good news, I really like it. Beforehand it hadn't sounded so great. As a matter of fact, I find it a great improvement on what passed for my first experience kissing, back in Skokie, which was a bunch of synagogue youth group girls lined up next to a group of synagogue youth group boys and hiding from our activity counselor and, working our way down the line, kissing each boy with a closed mouth. Something seemed to be missing. In fact, I could stay like this for a year, maybe more, kissing and kissing and kissing, being hugged, and complimented. I'm wondering why I hadn't discovered this before. I am so happy just laying here on my side like Brigitte Bardot.

Then, suddenly, there is an intruder. One of Phil's hands decides to go wandering, just a flicker above my waist, so that I'm not quite sure it's a problem. Maybe it's part of making out? But his hands continue encroaching, making their way north and south on my body. I don't understand. Why couldn't the hand just stay where it was, passionately wrapped around me? Everything was perfect up until this point. But now there's a soft touch at my side, then an inch lower and an inch farther. There's an over-the-shirt, under-the-shirt, over-the-bra, under-the-bra, controversy among my classmates that I haven't known much about till now, but Phil does. He has an inexhaustible army of hands all lined up at his side ready to head out into battle. I lose my concentration for kissing, intercepting all these hands. When he inches his octopus arms around me, I have to remind myself that it's okay to do this, or at least part of this. Though my instincts say run, defend, I'm not in Skokie anymore where I know who I am. I'm in Scottsdale and I need to be like everyone else. Phil and I just roll and roll and roll. My breasts – both of them – stay safe, tucked safely in my bra.

I come away much hugged, much kissed, and happily anticipating having a boyfriend of my own. He said many romantic-sounding things, like that this wasn't just a one-night thing, that he really likes me. I believe him, even though, at the same time, I am worried that maybe I don't really want a raggedy boyfriend who wears a floppy hat with roach clips attached to its brim. Is that my type? Also, won't sustained face to face contact give me his acne? I'm barely holding back the tide of my own pimples.

We burst out of Mona's room hours later, hair disheveled, clothes in disarray, devouring the innocent snacks her mother has laid out, all of us plotting belatedly how to get into the liquor cabinet to spike the punch. I'm floating when I get home, wondering how this will change eighth grade for me.

I'm sitting in the kitchen staring at the wall phone that

weekend, willing it to ring, but the phone doesn't ring, despite Phil's assurances. Not Saturday, not Sunday. Immediately, the world spins on its head and all my concerns about the floppy hat/pimple situation disappear from my brain. Now I desperately want him to call, need him to call. I'm sure he'll be the perfect boyfriend; I'll just have to tie his hands down.

With my friends, I parse out all the possible reasons he hasn't called. Maybe he went camping. Or four-wheeling. Or motorbiking. Or he's in a stoned stupor in the desert behind his house. All of these are both possible and impossible explanations, all intended to string me along to Monday when I'll see him.

Nina assures me he likes me and my mind gloms onto that happily. "Linda, he thinks you're SOOOO cool! Not like you used to be at all!"

On Monday we're back at school but he avoids my eyes. I can immediately tell that I'm not going to have to worry about acne transference or the whole floppy-hat-with-roach-clips issue. I clearly don't have a boyfriend.

Our make out party is the talk of the school – who was with whom, how far each couple went, which in 1974 means how far did the girl go? The truth is that boys are expected to grab all they can and rise in status because of it and girls are the gatekeepers, the ones who tell the boys yes or no. They are always blameless, and we are tramps. I intercept a rumor, something about how far I went. He does nothing to refute this gossip. He grows in stature and legend, and I became a little smaller and diminished.

Nina helpfully tells me what everyone's saying about me. It's my word against everyone else's. She tells me the only solution to solve this problem is to go kick somebody's ass, but I'm not sure whose. Maybe the entire eighth grade?

Ultimately, there are problems in our little group of newcomers. There's a battle over the top position, a problem with someone maybe being crazy. There's a fistfight, a broken nose, trips to the principal's office, suspensions. One of my friends disappears, yanked out of school by her parents, another moves back home because Arizona didn't work out.

Arizona isn't working out for me either, as a matter of fact. But apparently, I am staying put.

Ten

Ingathering of the Asthmatics

I am running in slow motion around the track at my school, a great racetrack of a space that I'm sure is only meant for horses and jockeys. There are girls so far ahead of me that they're coming up behind me on their second lap, and other ones so far ahead of me that they're already done running and resting on the bleachers. I know, to my chagrin, that I'm expected not just to run on this track, but to run around it several times, to achieve something called a "four-minute mile." I don't know it right then, but I'm about to be the winner of the "five-year mile," because, over the course of eighth grade and all of high school, I will never finish those laps.

My Physical Education teacher, whose skin is tanned to a leathery bark, exhorts me to run faster. This she does by leaving her laconic pose over by the bleachers. She charges over, closer and closer and even closer until she stands, shorter than me, yelling up into my face.

"You need to run that track, now!"

I've come to a dead halt. I say, "I've got asthma. I

can't run."

She scoffs and points at the lead sprinter, a thoroughbred dot in the distance.

She says, "Tina's got asthma too and she can run a mile in four minutes. Why can't you?"

She sneers at me. "You're just making excuses, Burt."

Could anything have prepared me for Physical Education class in Arizona?

First, and this was an affront, there are girls who are athletic. Back home among my Jewish classmates, this problem just didn't seem to exist. I figure it's because I've been plunked down in the middle of a gigantic non-Jewish population. Maybe it was the lack of inbreeding?

Then there is the fact that since so many asthmatics flock to Arizona, my PE teacher doesn't quite believe in it, or she thinks it can be fought against, resisted, or that I can rise above it with determination and willpower. Again, just look at Tina Bird! She was asthmatic and look at her running! Even her name sounded like she'd fly around the track. From this one example, my PE teacher seems to make her decision about asthma.

The final thing that is awful about PE in Arizona is the weather, since the thermostat doesn't seem to know it's fall and time to cool off. The teacher is aware of this, but she's tough about physical fitness, like it's okay to die if you're not strong enough to survive this – a one-woman Darwin's theory. There is a mile that must be run outside, around and around the track. PE never gets called off, it never gets moved inside, there are never any days of fun and games. And there is never any water.

Back in Skokie, my Jewish classmates and I, raised on whatever exercise Twister and our banana seat bicycle-riding provided us, fell apart on gym days. Told that the boys were better than us at everything, we were expected to stay girlish and pretty and noncompetitive, unless we were cheering for the boys.

There was my elementary school gym teacher who dreaded seeing another Burt girl show up in her class. My five klutzy older sisters had already ruined our athletic reputation, all of us in turn standing next to the gym's fifty-foot oiled rope dangling from the gym ceiling while she barked, "Climb it!" Burt girls didn't climb. We only swung uselessly on the bottom knot.

The junior high gym teachers, on their sliding scale of expectation, expected only one thing from the girls, to dress out each day in the uniform – a one-piece cotton shorty jumpsuit that pulled at the crotch – and then we'd get an A. It was a stress test of tough love and belittling, a pressure cooker of dressing out in tiny gym uniforms and being told that there was never a reason not to dress out. We were yelled at on the first day of class like it was an army bootcamp. There will be no excuses. Don't even try to miss gym class because of your period, everyone's got a period, even them. We look at them with horror.

Apparently, the only excuse for missing class is death. If we are a corpse just sitting there in the locker room, yes, then we can miss class. And if you're sick, wheezing and crackling along with sudden-onset adolescent asthma? Well, dress out slowly, creakingly, taking the full hour of class, and then, when you're done, just turn around, go back in the locker room, and, slowly, creakingly, change back into your regular clothes.

That was my experience with gym teachers, tough love all around, not this strange new thing called PE, or this leathery tanned teacher with flinty blue eyes who seems to know before she even makes her demand, that I cannot make it around that track. Not even once. Those eyes are equipped with some type of PE superpower and have already checked my BMI, assessed my muscles, tested my cardiopulmonary capacity, and discovered my poorly kept secret – that I'm hopeless, just one of the Seven Burt Family Klutzes, similar to the Seven Dwarfs. I am Wheezy. She is disgusted.

There seems to be a consensus among Arizonans that the state is getting too full around 1973. That the real Arizona, the real Scottsdale, a cowtown, ranching community, is getting destroyed by all these new arrivals and maybe it's time that the proverbial door to Arizona should be slammed shut, definitely before any more asthmatics get there. There is some wonderment at who, exactly, was responsible for this Manifest Destiny movement of asthmatics, shifting a whole population from east to west, just stopping short of California. I was one asthmatic too many, and maybe should have been left in New Mexico somewhere, knocking on the door of Arizona.

Everyone is moving there with health problems. Asthmatics clog the streets like it's one big hospital. People too ill to live out regular life spans in other locales live out life spans of heroic proportions in Arizona. My parents move me there to do the same.

My Chicago doctors enjoyed warning us ahead of time, saying that moving to Arizona might not help, that I'd most likely develop allergies to trees and plants there and that Arizona doesn't cure everyone. I remember hearing this, I remember my parents hearing this. I remember the indecision and warning flying in one ear and out the other. Then the certainty – my dad's decisive, "Chasia, pack up the house. We're moving to Arizona."

And now that we've moved to Arizona, I'm supposed to be healthy. I'd better be healthy.

At first it seems like I really am cured. I mean, I haven't gone off my asthma medication or anything, but I am moving around – this is a big improvement – and going to school – also a big deal. There was some idea that the 115-degree August and September days were going to dry my lungs up into some type of overall desiccation, that Arizona will cure my asthma and make me run wild and free, gulping deep breaths of the clean air. When there are signs that contradict this – inaudible wheezing, then audible wheezing, a gradual bending over of my back – there is complete denial. I try not to mention it. No one else mentions it. If I admit to being sick won't our whole move look futile? The script has been written and it is important that I play my part correctly – sick in Chicago, cured in Arizona. The act rapidly frays.

My mother and I are in the car on an endless and frequent drive to the doctor.

When we move my mom has a hot lead on a doctor, a Jewish doctor, but the referral comes from a friend of the family who lives in Tempe, so the doctor is down there. It's not like the old trip my mom used to make with me to Gurnee, Illinois the year before, to save my life with the only doctor who had a nebulizer in Illinois, but suddenly she's schlepping me back and forth, twenty miles there and twenty miles back, to the doctor we somehow inherit.

We drive and drive to our doctor appointments. Phoenix has only one freeway at the time, one that's of absolutely no use to us for this drive. We drive down Shea and hang a right at Scottsdale Road, then we take that for about a gazillion miles till we arrive in Tempe, waving at our store near the intersection of Scottsdale Road and McDowell as we pass by. When we cross over the river bottom separating Scottsdale from Tempe, the air changes imperceptibly. We are suddenly in a college town. I look around and gawk. In five years will I be one of these bewildering college students with purpose, with somewhere to go, with a skateboard maybe and a Primatene Mist inhaler tucked in my backpack?

My mother and I are really good at this doctor thing, we have a lot of experience. My value as a co-pilot depends on the state of my lungs. Sometimes I'm a regular passenger, talking and yakking all the way down. Other times, lacking air, I'm silent, the only sound in the car my audible wheezing. My asthma is the instant, complete, destroyer of my personality.

This doctor we inherit is of considerably lesser quality than the doctor we left behind in Chicago. This one's rude, brusque, pompous, and has a mean streak. For some reason, my mother is inordinately attached to him, probably because he's Jewish, like he's the only island of Jewishness we'll find in this God forsaken place, so we'd better hang onto him.

115

It's not like he ever encourages her. He never chit chats with her, he cuts off her soliloquies in mid-sentence, never lets down his I'm-the-Doctor demeanor for one second. This is no deterrent for my mother, who continues to treat him as if he's her best friend, to chat amiably, to play Jewish geography with him, even as he's slamming the examination room door on her, mid-sentence. I cannot for the life of me understand why this is our doctor. Why have we picked this insufferable, overstuffed egotist to take care of our health? Is he our only choice?

My mom, who trusts no doctor completely and is sure they're all trying to kill me, feels as comfortable as she can with Dr. Levin. He possesses everything she looks for in a doctor. He's Jewish, which is good. The Holocaust Survivor inside her always appreciates that, in this country, Jews are allowed to be doctors. He's got a superior, supercilious manner, and this is fine – she expects a bad personality to go hand in hand with being a good doctor. However, she doesn't want a doctor who treats her poorly because of her accent or origins, but she realizes that this is not the case. He treats everyone with the same scorn.

This doctor is young in 1973 and just starting out, so he puts up with some of my mother's foibles, like her complete inability to understand two basic rules, making an appointment ahead of time, and letting the doctor be the doctor.

Because my mother cannot possibly make an appointment ahead of time, we get to the doctor's office and plant ourselves in his tiny waiting room preparing for a long wait until the nurses can squeeze us in. She gets very friendly with the front office staff, believing that the staff is running the show. Unfortunately, at this office, this isn't true and, after they squeeze us in for years with no appointments, the doctor orders them not to do this, that if we show up again unannounced, they should let us sit there and learn a lesson. He leaves us out in the waiting room for hours until my mother sniffs and leaves.

Besides the drawback of the twenty miles in each direction to see Dr. Levin, when my lungs finally creak to near halt and I have to be admitted to the hospital, I get admitted to one near his office, not our house. I end up booked into a tiny hospital there, so small there's only one floor and each room looks out on its courtyard, like a tuberculosis sanitarium. It seems I've been sent there to wheeze and gaze fondly out the window at life.

Arizona doctors seem to have a different point of view about hospitalization. In Chicago I had laid quite happily half-dead on my fold out couch in the basement of our house, or in my mother's bed, for months on end. No one ever mentioned the hospital. Maybe in Chicago, the hospital is where you go to die. Dr. Levin does not hesitate for one minute. Into the hospital I go. Is there a reprimand in that to my mother for failing to keep me healthy? A reprimand to the entire family for being stupid enough to believe Arizona would cure me? A pat on his back for showing us how futile the move was? Maybe. Either way, he will begrudgingly save my life.

But before I can get booked into the hospital, before I can get into one of those rooms with a view of the courtyard, my mother and I must get through the emergency room.

Turns out I'm not so much going to the hospital as my

mother and I are going to the hospital, it's not just me being poked and prodded as much as we both are being poked and prodded. We are the asthmatic Bobbsey twins.

There's this one difference – she's the only one of us with enough air in her lungs to yell about it. She is the terror of the ER. She has a few core beliefs, such as that doctors know nothing, that she knows more than them with their fancy shmancy degrees, and that, left in their clutches, they will kill me. She has no patience for the random doctor working the emergency room, and heaven help them if any fumbling intern tries to treat me, troubling my mother by pulling out the gigantic Physician Desk Reference book to look up my symptoms, or the definition of Asthma. They all get to feel the Wrath of Mom. She's on them like a cat. She argues, she demands, she gets another doctor. And another doctor. Finally, she gets Dr. Levin hauled out of bed in the middle of the night. If asthma is our disease, Dr. Levin is our crutch.

I can tell the staff believes my mother to be the problem here, falling somewhere on the line between overprotective and insane. I can see the looks they give each other behind her back and to the nurses when they think she's not looking. They don't realize that, like all proper Jewish mothers, she has eyes in the back of her head. Her paranoia over being a greenhorn in this country becomes compounded with her paranoia over losing one of her children, her war years, and her sister's death in 1969 – admitted to the hospital alive, discharged dead. Her hackles are permanently up.

But my mom can only stay and guard me at the hospital so long. Once I'm admitted, even she has to go home, leaving me to the eager-to-commit malpractice apparatchiks at

118

the facility. Because, while they might find my mother annoying, interfering, the stage mom of all asthmatic children, I am comforted by her presence. I know that it's only her standing between me and death.

She saves my life over and over again.

Other than the whole bent over, nearly dying, can't breathe, wheezing and general suffering of it, I find the hospital to be a pretty cool place.

When left alone, a troop of hospital employees come marching to my bedside. There are the bossy nurses. There are cafeteria workers delivering the food, whom I really like because, even though the food is awful, I do get to fill out an order form every night for the next day. I live for that one moment of surprise, of absolute magic, when the food is delivered and I get to whisk of its cover.

I like chatting up all the nurses who take me under their wings as an alternate daughter. I love the way I never know who's going to pop in, this doctor or that, the nurse, the chaplain, the candy striper, my room the center of the universe, all paths leading there.

Of course, I don't mind all this attention. First, I am overcome with the happiness that when I get out – if I get out – I'll get to tell everyone at school that I'd been in the hospital. That's worth a lot right there. Also, I've got all the eyes of the family trained upon me, even the sisters who hate me are stuck coming to visit. And if anyone anywhere needs to find Mom – guess what? She's with me. Where else is she going to be? She's at her thirteen-year-old daughter's bedside saving her from the doctors who want to kill her.

There's one downside. Somehow, I get a bad roommate – Jo Beth, or maybe Mary Beth, something Beth, with two names like the Petticoat Junction girls – her hair black and choppy, like someone just hacked it off at home while they just happened to be chopping the heads off of chickens.

We try to get to know each other but we are from different planets. I have never been to an agricultural fair, I've never raised a calf and brought it to show, nor have I ridden on a tractor or gone to church. She, on the other hand, has done all these things and nothing else. She's never heard of Chicago and barely knows where Scottsdale is. We lapse into the moat between us. She perks up a little when she realizes that I'm "one of those Hebrews, like from the Bible," but I lose her when I tell her we don't believe in Jesus.

She says, "You don't believe in God?" flabbergasted.

I say, "Of course we believe in God!"

She says, "If you don't believe in Jesus, you don't believe in God. Jesus *IS* God!" She nods her head definitively and I wonder for one horrible moment if she is right. I know so little about it I'm struck dumb. I'm actually not as sure about what I'm saying as she is about what she's saying. We lapse back into silence.

Day after day we sit in our respective beds, glaring at each other balefully. When my mother comes to visit and my roommate hears her accent, her mouth hangs open in surprise from her side of the room. A foreigner!

It's okay that we've run out of things to talk about because after a while I realize that all conversation is diverting from my new primary purpose in life, which is to watch my IV bottle sway precariously overhead, emptying, drip by drip by drip, the nurses oblivious down the hall. I worry over each and every air bubble, waiting for them to travel from the bottle, into the tubing, into my arm, and kill me.

This is my full-time job.

Despite my asthma, despite the hospitalization, there's more smoking in my future.

Since I have bought a group of friends at school with the cigarettes I get from our store, suddenly I'm part of the crowd smoking in the bathroom at school – coughing, smoking, blowing, ashing, and cigarette-borrowing friends. It becomes epidemic, me buying friends with cigarettes, they, in turn, using me for cigarettes, and then watching me closely while I smoke my own. I carefully pretend to inhale the smoke and then puff it out quickly. I don't inhale.

One day a teacher rushes in and busts everyone smoking. A few of us get away, though the teacher glimpses me as I run in an asthmatic slow motion. Hauled to the principal's office, he calls my mother while I'm sitting there stewing, telling her I was caught smoking at school. My mother calls him a liar, tells him that this is impossible because I have asthma. She hangs up on him, which I really appreciate because the paddle he uses for corporal punishment is hanging on the wall behind him. I get to watch as he breaks out in a sweat as he's hung up on by a crazy woman with an accent. I'm in his office again a few weeks later, this time he calls to tell her that I was part of a group of kids caught drinking beer at school. She hangs up on him again, saying, "My Linda would never do that!" I can hear her outrage through the phone.

And she's right that time. I was actually sitting with a group of kids when they cracked out a six pack of beer. The principal began marching across the entire field to bust us. Spotting him, the silver beer cans, glinting in the sunshine, are thrown over the fence behind us into a neighbor's yard.

Still, right there in the principal's office, I get to smirk, and Mr. Beal gets to sweat. The paddle stays on its hook.

Right or wrong, my mother is my greatest cheerleader.

On my fourteenth birthday, my sisters lure me out to our station wagon with the promise of a birthday present. Ah, finally. The love I have sought from the twins is coming my way.

I get in the backseat of the car, slide in on the cold blue vinyl, instantly smell smoke, and start coughing. My cough is not an auspicious start. I think perhaps my sisters are going to teach me how to inhale cigarettes, but, instead of a cigarette, my sister Sherry pulls out a baggie, a little pipe and a lighter and the next thing I know I am smoking pot. Apparently, they'd had enough with my geekiness, my penchant for colored pens, my non-stop journaling. In one fell swoop, they turn me cool with some pot in a pipe. I stumble out of the car eventually, sleep well that night, and realize the next morning that I will finally fit in at school.

Pot saves me. Things change. I can suddenly show up at parties not only knowing how to smoke it, but carrying some to share, courtesy of my sisters. I'm ahead of other kids in this regard, being able to earn the druggie respect of my peers, their awe. I can't fistfight with them, I'm not prettier than them, and God knows I can't ride a horse better than them, but I have mentors right inside my house who teach me how to smoke pot and that, it turns out, moves me right to the head of the line.

It's quite an accomplishment, graduating eighth grade. I've been through the trial by fire of my classmates, I've been befriended, dumped, and befriended again. I've had the thrill of crushes on tall blonde boys, I've misinterpreted gestures such as the throwing of gum into my locker as a reciprocated crush, yet not misinterpreting other actions, like the day that boy calls me a dirty Jew.

My mother, who doesn't always know what's going on, seems to know I need a gift, something to acknowledge the end of this tough year. She buys me a Sounddesign stereo, which consists of a turntable, an eight-track player, and two speakers. A fifty-dollar present from a woman who has never spent a cent on anything but food, shelter, or fabric.

"From me and dad," she says. I am so amazed. My heart is so full and so warm, and I am thinking such kindly thoughts towards my dad all that day.

Of course, there's a problem when my mom makes this choice – to include my father in the gift giving when he had no clue. There's a problem because the minute she includes him, she can't do the most prudent thing, which is to tell me not to tell him he's included. Most certainly she can't tell me not to thank dad.

I wait and wait, and he comes home as he usually does, like a tornado whirling through the hallway. I burst out of my room. I run to him, hug his stiff, unyielding body. "Thank you,

123

dad! I love it! Thank you!"

He peers at me suspiciously. Says, "What's this?" He wants to know what he's being thanked for. I hear warning bells going off in my brain. He doesn't know? I show him the stereo which, to his immigrant eyes, looks like it cost a thousand dollars. For this he works and slaves all day? For this he moved to this country?

He turns black with rage, then storms back to the kitchen to yell at mom. He mentally tabulates, calculates the repacking of the components, the returning of the stereo to LaBelle's Department Store, the price of an angry wife.

The gift, it turns out, was from my mother.

For our eighth-grade graduation the girls are to wear pastel-colored dresses, the boys, suits. Mom searches through the collection of couture clothes she used to make and sell to department stores in Chicago and gives me the only one that is even halfway appropriate, a navy, pin dot, balloon-skirted and balloon-sleeved dress from her one and only collection. I stand out like a navy shmear among all the proper pastels of my classmates. On one day in early May we gather on the bleachers, flooding well beyond it, for a final picture of our class. The principal seems somewhat relieved to see the last of us, what with the broken nose issue, the smoking in the bathroom issues, the question of how long, exactly, he was going to be able to put off using the paddle on his wall.

Years later my tormenters turn out to be just a bunch of skinny little kids squinting into the sun.

***

It's the summer before high school and I think I have a boyfriend. Nina tells me I definitely do.

First there is a wild rocketing make out session. There are the usual hands everywhere – part boy/part octopus. And then something new, there's a declaration of love and an insistence that we are now boyfriend and girlfriend. I barely know him, but if someone wants to be my boyfriend, I know that he automatically gets the job.

He then loops a gigantic hairy arm around my shoulders. We walk that way awkwardly – I'm too tall, he's too wide, the brim of his cowboy hat keeps trying to take out my eye – but we lope through an evening of anxious attempts at booze buying, anxious attempts to get comfortable making out in the brambly desert.

For that one night I'm the girlfriend, maybe even the wife-type person. I need to be solicitous, I think, I need to take a fond interest in him, though I just met him that night, don't know him, and don't particularly like him. I've seen other girls do this and I need to emulate them, I'm sure.

And, anyway, then he's gone. Nina and I continue roaming aimlessly through our territory – pizza joint, candle shop, arcade, Shop-n-Go. At first, we can't decide my on my status. Am I taken or not? He clearly told me we were boyfriend and girlfriend. Then he's gone forever and I'm not sure. Sometimes I take solace in the fact that I have a boyfriend, wherever he is, especially when Nina's long blonde hair attracts boys and I'm the consolation prize, for runners up only.

I string him out, longer and longer, to mythic proportions, until this boyfriend and I have been going steady the entire summer of 1974. I don't exactly tell Nina about this, after all, she actually has a living, breathing boyfriend who hangs around, is corporeal. I tell myself that Tim and I packed a lot of relationship just a couple of hours — too much making out, a proffered "I love you," a declaration that we were a couple, the arm like a tree trunk slung across my shoulders. If I spread that quality time out, comparing it to Nina's relationship with Paul, where nothing is ever said or declared, where Nina is always high tailing it out of any romantic clutches, then I'm sure we actually dated the entire summer, even if it was only that one night.

I figure right about the time I'm about to start freshman year in high school might be a good time to "break up." And I do that, telling no one.

Eleven
Teenage Wasteland

We're speeding along on our way to a desert party, rattling in the cargo area of our friend Luke's 1960s Bondo-colored Dodge van, no paint left on it, gears that grind, and a shifter that comes out of the floor like a drum majorette's baton. He turns suddenly. Not at a street, but at a bush. Sure enough, before him lies a rutted path, rutted by the wheels of the thousands of other teenage cars zooming this way before him, the jeeps and the embarrassing family sedans, and station wagons or the infinitely cooler VW vans. Because, of course, there are delineations of cool cars among us hippies in the 1970s, with a VW van at the pinnacle. Any hippie van is second. A VW bug is third. Everything else is fourth, just happy to have wheels.

Luke knows the way to the party – every party – and it's purely by instinct. He's one of our new friends, a junior at our high school. The junior guys are extremely interested in the freshman girls, so we're automatically interested in them knowing seniors are out of our reach. He befriends my little gang, Nina and me and three others, and we become his little freshman followers, especially because we can't drive. He will pile all of us in the back of his van and take us to boondockers.

He makes a right at the initial bush, a left at a certain cactus where the road forks off in different directions – God forbid we should end up at a neighboring high school's boondocker – he makes other turns, his dim headlights weakly lighting up the eerie nighttime desert landscape. We are alternatingly jolted and bouncing, our heads nearly grazing the ceiling. His wheels hit ruts high on one side and low on the other, gone on one side and a rock on the other, or just straight jitters for miles at a time. He makes a left at a tumbleweed, a smooth arcing turn around a ravine, and we are there.

Luke is blind in one eye so it's conceivable that this might affect his driving. He doesn't wear a patch or anything, he just has one unseeing blue eye, dull and blank next to his seeing one, framed by his long orange hair, his lumberjack shirts, torn, baggy jeans. No one ever mentions the eye because that would be uncool, and above all else, we don't want to be uncool. Anyway, he's an upperclassman hippie so everything he is or does is considered perfect the way it is, unquestionable. He's our ride and it's not like we have any choices here. We are freshman.

Luke has adopted us in his way. We're fledgling hippies, barely able to roll a joint properly, more apt to blow into a bong and make a real mess rather than inhale its contents, prone to smoking confusing-looking pipes upside down. There was also that one time I was handed an apple

128

pipe and I took a bite out of it.

Since he's adopted us, he's in charge of delivering us to the quintessential Arizona desert party, a boondocker. A drive into the desert, a keg appearing from somewhere, some music source involving a woofer and a tweeter, and a bonfire. Who really needs chairs or such luxuries as bathrooms?

We come upon the party like it's a hallucination, an illusion. First there is nothing, just dark sky and glittering stars and cactus coming at us like sentries, and then there are people and a fire, and a party lit up in the headlights. We get out and find our legs. Luke says, "Are you ready to party?" because "party" is a verb around this place and this time. We are.

Luke's a junior but he uses the term loosely. He's planning to finish out his "bullshit, mother fuckin' four years" of high school just like he's supposed to. And if by some chance those four years of art classes, shop classes, auto mechanic classes, and smoking pot out in the field add up to a diploma, then great, he'll have a diploma. If it doesn't, then he won't. It doesn't matter to him like it doesn't compute. Four years is four years. It's kind of a jail sentence, and when it's done, it's done.

He is part of an old-fashioned commune-ish hippie family that lives in some ramshackle wreck of a house out in the wilds on the northern edge of town. He, mysteriously, has no mother, there is just a father there and a bunch of brothers, all with long red hair, all with two eyes each. Nina describes their home as "really bitchen," which I envision as meaning beds and blankets everywhere, the other orange-haired siblings running throughout the house, and that, when it's nighttime and they're done with that day and ready to move onto the next, they simply fall wherever they're standing. That's where they sleep, bedless, showerless, eyeless, diploma-less.

Certainly one of the good things about being a teen in the Arizona desert in the 1970s is that there's a lot of isolated space to have these parties and to have make out sessions with boys, if you don't mind rolling into a pile of brambles. The best location is one we refer to as Pima and Bell – an intersection of dirt and cacti and scrub bushes and tumbleweeds and power lines that will one day turn into a gazillion houses.

We party till the fire burns down, till the beer runs out, or until helicopters suddenly start circling overhead busting us, searchlights beaming down like we're runaway convicts.

I might be in high school, but there are things I don't understand about it.

I don't understand the difference between Pom and Cheer, to me they're all just a gaggle of skinny blondes who race around the school in a pack wearing identical flouncy micro miniskirts. I have no time or patience for parsing out the differences between this flouncy skirt and that, these bobby socks and those. All I know is that they stare though me like I don't exist when we pass each other in the halls at my high school and that they appear to be waiting for me to drop out or get expelled.

I don't understand what "Varsity," or "Junior Varsity" mean, though I do remember reading those terms in Archie comics. I don't understand the rules of any sport anywhere. I am completely bewildered by the fact that the boys I hate the most, the ones most likely to call me "Chin," come to school about once a week dressed identically in football uniforms in what I am told are our school colors – I wasn't even aware that we had school colors. Other days some of them wear white sweaters with letters on them and I'm informed with some amount of gravitas that these are "Letterman" sweaters. Literally, they've "lettered" in a sport. The lettered athletes are considered fine, upstanding, the best my school has to offer, yet when I end up at the same party with some of them a year later, I find that they're incapable of drinking politely, but are instead boisterous, belligerent drunks. They destroy property. They must be thrown out of parties. All while my hippie friends sit, quiet as mice, passing joints, the owners of rich interior lives.

I don't understand it being a matter of life and death and heartbreak and defeat and drooped heads and crushing disappointment when our team – whatever team – doesn't win a game. Again, I barely know there's a team or a game or that these are scheduled week by week by week throughout the fall, that boys are tumbling over each other, crashing into each other, suffering brain injuries, all for the love of this game. I don't understand the sheer noise of games – what is the constant din? Are people talking, yelling, shouting, encouraging, fighting, coaching, flirting, competing? Yes. Do they ever shut up? No.

I do understand that being the freshman sister of hippie twins who are cool and in their junior year puts me in a great place, an alternate universe to the jocks. I'm immediately a cool hippie freshman, with what seems to be an inexhaustible supply of pot thanks to the cash register at our family store and my sisters.

I understand that, in the UFO design of my high school, with ramps leading out of the main building to the ground, that hippies hang out under the north ramp. It's here in between classes, or instead of classes, that I find my people.

I've finally arrived.

There are rules associated with being a hippie. Even though I want to believe I'm now a wild child, in some ways, I feel as rule-bound as the jocks. I can't show up at school wearing high-waisted polyester pants and those girls can't show up in a pair of dirty, patched jeans, like I do. I can't do a cheer and they can't do a modern dance while stoned. And, mostly, I can't seem to recreate myself the way they do, disappearing over a summer and coming back tan, with bleached blonde hair cut into Farrah Fawcett-Majors hairstyles, sudden goddesses. Have they had makeovers and gone to finishing schools?

I sneer at the jocks with their rigid dress codes, the girls with their high-waisted polyester pants, their strappy shoes, the boys with their letterman sweaters. I revel in my belief that we have no dress code at all.

There is a gradation of cool among the hippies, all judged by how worn out your Levi jeans are. Basically, the day you buy the nearly black Levi 501s, made of some industrial cement-type fabric, that's the day the fledgling coolness begins. I show up at school in them and everyone knows I just got new Levi's, it's an open topic of discussion. People gesture at their own jeans-clad legs, a comfortable shade of faded blue, reminiscing about bringing them home from the store way back when they were little green freshmen too. My new jeans label me a brand-new hippie, just starting out. They are the most uncomfortable pants ever conceived, yet I am willing to take on this multi-year project, to know that I'll only be comfortable in these pants in the third or fourth year of use, to put up with the huge investment of discomfort, laundry detergent, and humiliation. I will do all of this to be cool.

There are so many problems with these pants. They're men's pants built for no hips where I have hips, and a gigantic square waist where I have a narrow one. They are alternatively busting and loose, gaping at the waist like I'm wearing a wheelbarrow, showing my underwear when I sit down, either pulling or hanging loose. No one thinks to make these cut for women in 1974, or, for that matter, Jewish girls with Old Country bodies. They are considered perfect just the way they are. If they don't fit a particular person, then the person must change, never the pants. And, what's more, there's a leather label with the size clearly indicated sewn outside the pants. No female on the planet actually wants that. It's like wearing a scale.

Is it possible to understand how my very soul longs to fit in the right pants, to look right in the right pants, to have the right pants be the right size and fit me in just the right way? I watch my friends as they effortlessly don their button fly 501s. There is, apparently, no problem at all in the world with them getting these pants on their body. But my body is shaped like a fertility goddess, some Jewish thing. Small feet, big hips, small top.

Besides the jeans, there are other clothing requirements. Gauzy shirts, bras or not, our hair au naturel, maybe hairy legs. Our clothes should be evocative of the slightly earlier hippie era including Woodstock and Haight Ashbury and anywhere in the world but 1974 Phoenix. Everyone else looks great like this – young and naturally beautiful. I look insane.

Besides clothes, I have to know my way around pot paraphernalia like rolling papers, bongs, pipes, and roach clips. I need to be aware that hippies use sandwich bags to hold one ounce of pot exactly, which is called a dime bag, and we roll it into a cylinder and lick the edge, like that seals it shut. We need to know what a bamboo roller is or how to make a perfect joint ourselves, with nothing protruding. There are flower tops in there which are the Cadillac of what we're looking for, and exploding seeds, the bane of our existence, and little sticks. And this must be broken down, mashed and smashed, into a pipe bowl or somehow rolled into a joint without things sticking out all over. It should be smooth, not bumpy.

I need to know how to hold the carburetor on the bong while taking a hit and that hash doesn't stay lit. I have to know that anything can be a pipe, even an apple. It's important not to eat the pipe. We have to be inventive about this pipe thing, even treating the mall tobacco shop like a head shop, cruising in there, reeking, and endlessly mulling over the pipe choices while the bearded owner stands behind the counter, humorlessly watching us.

I must share to be cool, even if I'm the only one who ever has any pot, even if the other ones are all mooches or bogarts. And I need to know those terms, mooches and bogarts.

There's never a question that pot leads to speed and speed leads to cocaine and Quaaludes and hashish, and that all roads lead to acid. I sit in the family room and watch the news about whether marijuana is an entry drug, but in my new world it's all mixed up together. If you're "cool" you spend parties doing something, whether it's smoking a joint that's making its way around the entire room, taking an unidentified pill, or being handed a dime of coke, it's assumed that if you're a hippie you do it all. Drug dealers are not what I see on the news. A drug dealer may be a friend of mine who decides to buy a pound of pot and sell off some of it to make his money back, or it might be one of my sisters' boyfriends who buy a pound and has me sell a few ounces at school. It might be me.

Also there's this saying: we're never going "straight," just forward.

We listen to obscure rock-n-roll. Low-voiced DJs who for sure have better taste than me and more arcane musical knowledge than any human being alive, DJs on radio stations that have no commercials. There are guitar riffs that never end and are wholly enjoyed by people cooler than me since I only enjoy the vocals and nothing else. Musically, it's my great secret that I never matured beyond my junior high favorites of Carly Simon, the Carpenters, Bread, and Carole King.

There are other music-related issues. I need to go to concerts even if I hate them and hate crowds. I need to know that Jethro Tull is not a person, but Leon Russell is. That The Who is not a question and Chicago is a city but also a band. And that Yes is not only an affirmative answer but a musical group. I need to be able to differentiate between ELO – Electric Light Orchestra, and ELP – Emerson, Lake and Palmer.

Despite the hippie mandate to love everyone, it's my

secret that I don't. I see meanness, pettiness, and conceit, all around me. There are a lot of people who hang out with us who I'm supposed to adore, like the Junior class males who prey like hawks over the Freshman class, plucking the girls' virginities one by one by one.

Then I take my marijuana interest a step farther, becoming a farmer of a type. I begin to think about all those seeds I'm picking out of the way as I roll my joints, all those seeds I pull out of the pipe before I light it, so they won't explode in my face. And I think, aren't seeds, well, seeds? Couldn't I grow plants from seeds, like pot plants? So I get some Columbian seeds from a friend and plant them in a clay pot on my bedroom windowsill. I guess I think maybe I'll become a marijuana farmer and till the unused portion of our desert acre. I'll start small, with this little pot plant on the windowsill, incognito among my other houseplants.

My mother dusts around the plant, waters it a little and frankly admires my green thumb. And so there it grows in the window by the front door until it's about three feet tall and skinny, since I can't bear to pinch it to make it bushy. One day my brother-in-law is walking up to the house, sees it in the window, and recognizes it. He tells my mother. She tells me I have to give it away. Even then, I can tell she makes up her own story in her mind about how it got there, something like maybe I thought it was just another houseplant, a strange-looking Coleus or Creeping Charlie. Because, according to her, I don't smoke pot. I am a good daughter.

After my mom tells me the plant must go, I mull over what to do with it. I can't just kill it. This was my Colombian cash crop – the future of my drug cartel, an empire to start on the back of this one skinny little plant. I give it to a friend, and he solemnly swears to plant it somewhere amid the brambly desert behind his house and split the crop with me. A few weeks later, alas, he declares that the plant has suddenly died. I'm over at his house soon after that and there's a suspiciously familiar pot plant thriving. I cannot call the police about this theft.

Of course, I have horrible asthma and inhaling pot smoke into my lungs is probably not good for this. My friends around school, suddenly amateur pulmonologists, declare that marijuana is good for asthma. This doesn't seem to be true. The further I go into my freshman year and the better I become at being a hippie, the worse my asthma gets. I'd heard from these same expert friends that hair could be analyzed and reveal drug use, so whenever I go to see Dr. Levin, I wear my hair pulled back and watch his hands closely, ready for a sudden yank.

My mother hauls me back to his office. She has continued her love/hate relationship with him, as in he hates her, and she loves him. She makes no appointment, just appears with me in the office in a series of emergencies. He wrinkles his brow, looks at me quizzically, and wonders aloud about what new allergen has entered my world, infiltrated my lungs, and destroyed my health. I look at him and shake my head. What could it be?

"Must be Arizona," I say. Everyone in Chicago had predicted that all the asthmatics who were swarming to Arizona for a cure would actually get sick here too. I am willing to jump on this excuse.

He nods. "Yes. It looks like you've developed allergies to plants and trees here."

I'm relieved. I am not the little sickly asthmatic thirteen-year-old I'd been the year before when we moved here. Now I am a conniving fourteen-year-old liar, committed to my new place in society as a hippie. Treat me for allergies, not smoke inhalation.

He makes no quick moves towards my hair. It remains intact along with my secret.

Twelve

Money Doesn't Grow on Trees

Here's my dad on February 28th, 1975. He's ebullient, enthusiastic, optimistic, energetic. He's sitting at our dinner table with that unsigned contract before him just waiting for his signature to buy a store just like the one we already have, but on the west side of phoenix. Two stores to which he can be enslaved.

"Ah, Linda, here, read this contract. You tell me it all sounds good, for a second store." My dad shoves some papers across the dinner table towards me.

I look at the incomprehensible contract. I say, "You're buying another store? That sounds great!" I say this because I have some idea that we'll be rich if this happens. I say it because I believe that my father can do anything. And I say it because I'm trying to leave the house for the night. I've taken forty dollars out of the bag of store money that he stashes in his closet every night to pay for my next day's plans, both shopping and shoplifting.

I am fourteen. A high school-ditching, class-flunking

pot head. These are my secrets, and my dad knows nothing of this. He thinks I'm still the smart, college-bound child who moved to Arizona a year and a half earlier.

I have a big weekend planned, first spending the night at my friend Rina's house to do acid, and then shopping with Nina the next day. Or her shopping, me shoplifting. Rina and I had searched high and low for a place where it'd be okay for us to be incapacitated, where we'd be safe even if we were lying around in a stupor. We found it, planning to sleep in a camper parked next to her house that night.

Mom is at the table. Since she's unhappy with this whole idea, since he can't get a "yes" out of her, Dad has bypassed her opinion and has moved onto me. She's unhappy about it for real reasons, like because our present store is like a foal standing on very wobbly, knobby-kneed legs, partially collapsing under its own weight, almost toppling, but rising and shaking uncontrollably. Dad sees the few times it's stood and decides it's time to start building his empire – a string of produce markets as far as the eye can see, strung across Phoenix, from east to west, who knows, maybe we'll be nationwide? For now, though, he'll start with one other store, also in a converted convenience store building, on a street which slices diagonally through the heart of Phoenix. This will be his second Farmers Produce Market.

I've been raised with a feeling of economic security my whole life so, unlike all my father's admonishments to the contrary, I do believe money grows on trees, that there will always be a steak on the table, a dad in his recliner, ignoring us, a newspaper rustling in his hands. The particulars of how he manages this prosperity, our trajectory straight up, I'm sure,

140

whether we own a laundry in Chicago or a produce market or two in Arizona, I don't consider to be of any interest to me. I do know I don't want to sit in the kitchen all night reading an incomprehensible purchase contract.

Not being conversant in Contract Law, I barely know what I'm reading though I read the contract. I agree with Dad because disagreeing is not an option. Mom sits at the table fuming. I know this is wrong but if dad's paying attention to me, I'll run over anyone to get it. He eats, he talks, he discusses, and he smiles, and this is so rare an occurrence that it's like watching a mountain crack.

When I dash out of the house that night, I don't kiss anyone goodbye, including my father. I am fourteen, after all. I had stopped kissing my parents like a little child long ago. I thought they'd always be there like rocks, like monoliths, especially Dad. I lose that opportunity, then, to take one last look at his face before I would never see it again, to kiss his living cheek, to look in his eyes.

The older me, the director of the rest of my life, is jumping up and down out of my director's chair because she knows that I will replay this scene in my head over and over again for the rest of my life. She knows that the fourteen-year-old me will regret this moment, this omission, that she'll think about it for years. I shout down to the fourteen-year-old me, "Get over there, you idiot, and kiss him goodbye!" But I never move an inch toward him. I always leave the house, dashing out with the money in my purse.

The next day I wake up at Rina's house, after spending the night in the tiny, cold travel trailer her stepfather Cam has parked in the driveway. It's my fourth and final time using acid. We'd emerged from the trailer sometime in the night, staring at the world around us.

"Look, Rina," I point at the asphalt, "each little chunk of the street forms the petal of a daisy!" How had I failed to ever notice before that the entire street was a field of black daisies as far as I could see?

That's the happy part of the acid trip. In the bad part I realize that I'm done. Even if I like doing this, if I like seeing a field of daisies where there is none, the beauty of this pretend world can do nothing but distract me from my real life, the land of tar and blacktop streets. I don't know it, but right when we wake up, my dad has three hours to live.

I walk over to Nina's house, and Nina and I get a ride to the mall from my sister Sherry, who's just zooming by on her way to our store, a three-block detour.

"Why doesn't Nina's family ever drive you anywhere?" she asks when we get in the car. I'm embarrassed being interrogated in front of Nina. I thought it was obvious – I carry 90% of the burden of this relationship, and so my driver sisters must too. And anyway, Nina's family never drives us anywhere. They're stuck in their house by some type of centrifugal force.

We zoom down Scottsdale Road, Sherry barely stopping the car at the corner of Scottsdale and Camelback to eject Nina and I at the 1975 version of Fashion Square Mall, with department stores at either end and a few luggage and shoe stores scattered between them. There's an outdoor escalator to the second level which emerges from a grassy lawn at the far end.

We are shopping for the day. Or maybe I should say that I'm shoplifting, and Nina is window shopping, because she leaves home every day with a completely empty purse, not one cent in it, the purse just for show. We both want everything in the world but only I can get it, either with store money or nimble fingers. I pride myself on this skill, on my ability to walk in a store without a sweater and walk out with one, a talent so honed that I have stolen record albums. No one can steal a record album.

But Nina has no money and will not steal. She is a Christian, she tells me. When she really wants something, like the tiny yellow gold crucifix with a miniscule white gold Jesus writhing and dying on the front of it, she looks at me like I imagine my future children will look at me in toy stores. There is a wistful sighing and pouting, and then she puts a bright brave face on, pretending she is okay without the cross that now she'll want forever and ever but which she can't afford, ever.

I'm not aware of this ahead of time, but it turns out there are a lot of choices when it comes to crosses. My only entanglements with religious necklaces before this were when I lived in Skokie and every Jewish girl got a Star of David for Chanukah one year, or when, right after we moved, I brought home a half cross/half Jewish star and excitedly showed it to my father. What a perfect blending of our Jewish selves with our new home in non-Jewish Arizona! He grabbed it from me, breaking it in half and tossing it in the trash.

There are white gold crosses and yellow gold crosses, and there are combination pieces with both colors, like the one she falls in love with. There are eighteen karat and fourteen karat ones, big ones, small ones. I agree to put little crucifix on layaway, knowing there will be a painstakingly slow payoff. Week after week we will need to go visit the cross at the mall.

Nina is happy enough at this outcome to give me some kind of a compliment.

"Linda, you are the best friend ever! I am SOOO glad I stayed friends with you even when everyone used to ask me, 'Why are you friends with Linda?' and I'd say, 'Yeah, I know it's weird, but you don't know her. She's SO SO SOOOO great!'"

She doesn't really have to say anything. I don't put the cross on layaway because I'm "so great" or "so nice" or any of those reasons. I put it on layaway because I'm stuck with her – we both know it – and I'm still buying my friends.

At the end of the day, the stores close, we leave, the managers clicking the locks behind us.

I've been so busy shopping and shoplifting all day, that I don't know anything has happened to make this day different from all the other days of my life, until no one shows up to drive us home. It turns out there were ambulance rides that day, firemen and paramedics that day, that my sisters and mother waited in a hospital chapel for word from a doctor that day.

All of this because earlier in the day, my father was standing in the back room of our store haranguing my sister Denise for some produce-related transgression – did she put out the yellow bananas, forgetting to save the green ones for later?

Then he clutched his chest and fell to the ground.

Much later, after all the stores are shuttered and dark, a friend of one of my sisters shows up. She is silent the entire drive home. I ask questions that go unanswered, they just float in the air above our heads till they fade away. No sound. I have no inkling of disaster, no forewarning, no foreshadowing. I'm convinced that this day will be like all the other days of my life, coming home into our evening house, the cool spring air, my father in his recliner blasting the TV volume, me sneaking off to my bedroom with my stuff.

I walk in the house loaded down with stolen goods, shopping bags and record albums and the sweater I was wearing and the money in my wallet and the wallet itself and the memories of all the money I'd stolen and the profits from the store Dad would never see. I walk in the house with the stuff in my arms and the stuff in my imaginary arms that I carry around with me for the rest of my life, and the minute I walk in, the minute that door shuts behind me, my little sister walks up to me and says, "Linda, Dad died."

And I drop all those things I'm carrying out of all those arms. I drop all the things I've ever stolen. I drop them, and I don't know where they go because I never see them again. I think Dad takes them as reparations from on high, as payment for all the sets of forty dollars that I stole from him, now playing *Lynyrd Skynyrd* albums up in heaven.

Suddenly I see me from outside of me, Linda below in the foyer, as I imagine my dad seeing me. There's no hiding from this father, now everywhere. Can he see how truly despicable I am? Does he instantly know I stole from him and from the store? Does he know about the drug use, that the Linda that he thought was so good was really so bad?

When my father dies, it's like a spaceship has picked him up, it's so complete. Where could he have gone? His presence, just the day before, was there, and now it is incomprehensibly missing, like someone carved a hole into the painting of our family. I am still squinting at the fine print on the contract he wanted me to read the night before he died for the store he never bought, the second in his imaginary nationwide chain of failing, small, miserable produce stores strung across the country. His shoes still stand in his closet, pointing all in one direction, perhaps a clue telling us which way he went, to maybe follow him. His rings, his wallet, his watch, all sit on his dresser, like maybe he's walked into another room, just momentarily left the picture we're in, just out of sight.

His death changes that moment, and it changes the part of the day that had already happened, and it changes the night before. In some way it colors all the life that had gone before.

That day and the days leading up to it become slow motion in my memory, strobe light images, flashing and darkness, image after image piling up. Me, stealing money out of the store cash bag, my father, raging through the house. Me, smoking pot, doing drugs, ditching classes, shoplifting, smoking cigarettes. He, assuming that I am still the innocent thirteen-year-old Linda who moved with them to Arizona. Me, reading the contract he hands me at the kitchen table. He, dying at our store. Me, walking in the house, leaving everything, the entire world I had known, behind me, that last second before I knew.

Thirteen

Where He's Gone

The first thing that happens when my father dies is that all the relatives fly in from Chicago, collapsing as they get off their airplanes, wracked with inconsolable grief, insisting Dad cannot have died. The idea that this has happened is completely inconceivable, beyond belief, out of the realm of reality. They are stumbling, prostrate, distraught, wrecked, bleary-eyed with tears. They have come here not so much to bury their brother as they've come to find him, to prove this thing cannot have happened. They knew nothing good could happen from this move to Arizona. Didn't they try to talk our dad out of it? Hadn't they wanted to keep him in Chicago where they could watch over him? Because, obviously, our mother had failed to do that, had failed to keep him alive.

Someone, somehow, covers all our mirrors, puts a wash basin and cup by our front door, places low stools around our family room. Little black button pins with a ribbon attached appear on each one of us, the easier to rend our clothing, as required of Jewish mourners. I have no idea what any of this means. Dad lived secularly, agnostically, with himself at the center of the universe in the place usually reserved for God. Despite this, he will be buried Orthodox.

Suddenly we are searching our closets for funeral clothes, not the halter tops we normally wear, or the patched-up Levi's and Earth Shoes, but grown-up clothes. Since none of us own anything black we end up dressed in a mismatched assortment of the most somber-colored clothes we can find, navy and green, brown, and gray, our L'eggs hose-clad beigy legs sticking out below.

Two days later, a limousine pulls up to our house and we make our way to the Jewish funeral home where we are all seated behind a *mechitzah*, the lace curtains which separate women from men in Orthodoxy, like a mantilla around us, muffling the room, muffling the people. There is a coffin in the front of the room that is supposed to contain my father but this, of course, is impossible. No box on this earth is large enough to contain my father.

After the service, we get back in the limousine, now with the hearse in front of us, with that box in the hearse, with the impossible knowledge that our dad is in the box, and travel miles and miles across town, across Phoenix, with about a thousand cars behind us, headlights on. We make our way to the cemetery at the south end of a highway, the Jewish section at one end of a Christian cemetery, snaking our way past angels and flowers and weeping Jesus statues to find the gates to the Jewish section. We know we've arrived by the stones on the graves.

Dad's not quite buried yet. His gleaming brown coffin is on a cart, wheeled over from the hearse, next to a perfectly square-cut grave, one with meticulously trimmed up sides and a perfectly squared off bottom. There are no unwashed, scruffy, Dickensian gravediggers here standing around with bent shovels, week-old beards and threadbare clothes. This grave has been dug by a machine.

My dad's older sisters are crying, distraught, and falling forward over and over again onto his coffin. I look at them angrily. Do they have to land on my father, their heavy bodies thudding against the wood, their grief hijacking our grief?

My sister Sherry walks up to me and rolls her eyes. Without moving her lips, she says, "Oh my God, when are they going to stop?"

I answer her, but I'm not as good at ventriloquism.

"I don't know. Can they make this any worse? They're upsetting Mom."

This should have been my mom's show, but how much more complicated is it being the dead man's wife in a bad marriage than it is to be his sisters? My mother stays in her seat, mainly because she keeps fainting with shock. She's not the throw-herself-on-a-coffin-type. My mother's Litvak family tends towards stoicism and anyway, she'd already taken a tranquilizer before we left the house.

Finally, the aunts faint dead away and are hauled off by the uncles, who hold their listless bodies, fan them, and wave smelling salts under their noses.

For this is the way you do a funeral in the Old Country – your wounds bleed and you die with your dead, crawling into the casket. There's no restraint, there are no niceties, just raw grief.

I'm standing there in the grass with my six sisters, my heels sinking into God-knows-what below me, with God Himself somewhere above, the sun beating down on us, when the rabbi pulls up in a big Cadillac, jumps out, looks at his watch and starts the service, though people are still parking their cars, still walking up, still adjusting their ties. He starts talking about nothing, although it's supposed to be about Dad.

Except for the yarmulke placed flutteringly upon his head like a bird suddenly landed there, he is indistinguishable in his slickness from a TV evangelist. His Hebrew is awkward, like he's been to divinity school and not seminary, like he's never gotten the accent quite right. He moves the service along at a fast clip, doesn't customize it, except for glancing down at the appropriate intervals to slot in Dad's English and Hebrew names when needed.

"Harry Burt," he intones pompously, and then, with his strangely accented Hebrew, "*Tzvie ben Gershon.*"

He doesn't know it, but he's a litmus test for our family that horrible day in March in the blinding Arizona sun, Dad in a coffin and Mom collapsing at our feet. We haven't had any real use for our religion all the days of our lives up until then. But now that we've been laid low, we're looking for God. We need the rabbi to scoop us up and pour religion on us like a balm. We need him to tell us what we need to hear, something that will go in our ears and travel all the way through to our eternal souls. What does he know about death, and what can it teach us about life?

It may look like we're standing in Beth El Cemetery that dreadful, sunny day, the tombstones boxing us in, the green grass carpeting the ground, but really, we're at a fork in the road. My family is about to catapult out of Judaism, but if he says just one right thing, we might stay. It's a lot of pressure to put on a mediocre rabbi, stuck in the backwaters of Phoenix in the 1970's, a rabbi who excels in good enough but not great.

We can almost put up with God appearing in the person of a puffed-up popinjay arriving in a gleaming Cadillac, wearing a three-piece suit, bluffing his way through the service. We can almost handle that. We don't care what he looks like as long as he opens his mouth and we get pearls. Pearls.

But we don't. We get the prayers for the nonmembers. We get the next rabbi up on the rabbi rotation list for the unaffiliated Jews who died in Phoenix that week. And just our luck, we get him.

He delivers his lifeless sermon for the lifeless. He fumbles with the card that tells him my father's English and Hebrew names. When he's done, after he's waved us all seven of us over to Dad's new subterranean home and we've thrown our handfuls of brown dirt on Dad's brown coffin, the Rabbi hops neatly into his waiting Cadillac and zooms away.

Back at our house, I can't help but wonder where all this Jewishness came from anyway? We're barely Jewish, living in 1970's Christian Phoenix, eating bacon, not a Bat Mitzvah among us. Suddenly, with our father's death, Judaism shows up, like we moved and left it behind in Chicago and it finally finds us, panting after a year and a half on the road. But someone directs the rituals surrounding my dad's death because it strains belief that anyone in my immediate family could have uttered the words, "We'd like an Orthodox funeral," or "We'd like the women separated from the men." I didn't know there were different types of burials, different types of Jewish funerals, I didn't know that besides being muffled in grief, I could end up muffled behind a curtain, the funeral before me hazy, shimmery, dream-like.

But someone who knew more about this than we did showed up and arranged everything, leaving me stumbling with it, mystified by it, holding prayer books backwards, like English books. I don't know that there's such a thing as the Mourner's Kaddish, I don't understand the funeral or the shiva, and by the end of the shiva I have lost my mourning pin. Each night I know something's going on because the men are restless, gathered around, fidgety, prayer books in hand, awaiting a tenth man for the minyan. I know nothing about why everyone's here, how it honors my father and should help us begin to creak into our future. I peek beneath the covered mirrors to see how thin I am, knowing my dad would really have appreciated my weight loss, and thinking maybe starving myself will serve as a fitting penance to bring back my father.

I can't quite decide which is the absolutely worst part of sitting shiva.

There are all the people, mostly strangers. I wonder, how did my parents manage to meet all these people in the mere year and a half we've lived in Arizona? We'd been mostly hiding from the Jewish community, yet here they are. They are eager to come to the shiva, to connect to the tragedy, to find out more about the tragedy, to shake their heads sadly at the tragedy and the disaster of a grieving widow and her seven daughters.

There are the conversations I overhear. He was just alive on Friday! Oh, you saw him Saturday morning, getting in his truck leaving for the store? Yes, he was alive then too. Yes, then he died a few hours later, alive in the morning and dead in the afternoon! Somehow this idea that he was alive when last seen is supposed to refute his death, like maybe with a report of a definitive sighting, it will all turn out to be a terrible mistake and my dad himself will just walk through the door.

There are my aunts and uncles, distraught, surrounded by strangers who can't possibly comfort them because no one can comfort them, no one's loss can compare to theirs – just repeating again and again, how could this have happened? My Uncle Sid catches me in the dining room and says, "What are you upset about? You only lost a father. I lost a brother!"

And then the food begins to arrive. The tables are groaning, bending, swaying, breaking under the heft of the kosher-style platters that have arrived from near and far. The food is supposed to keep the mourners from starving, but we can't eat, unable to concentrate on this most mundane of tasks.

The people who come to sit shiva have no such problems. They eat like they've never seen food before. They eat because the platters of food begin arriving and no one can possibly resist that much corned beef, pastrami and brisket, rye bread, challah, bagels and rolls, pickles and side dishes and desserts, like a pop-up deli has materialized before their eyes in 1975 Phoenix.

Everyone eats and talks and exclaims over the food and talks about whichever side of my dad they'd known which, interestingly, has nothing to do with the side of him I'd known. There's an impression that Dad himself is hosting this shiva, he wants them to eat, is cajoling them to eat, to eat for him, that by the very act of eating they're honoring a man who would never want someone to go hungry in his house.

Chewing loudly, they exclaim over the death of Harry, shake their heads mournfully over the death of Harry, tsk tsk over the death of Harry. There's a general postmortem over the death of Harry – how did it happen, how did Harry stumble into this, what were the warning signs that he ignored and that can now be blamed on him so that his death was not only predictable but his own fault? And how can they, being now clearly armed with this knowledge, avoid the same fate? I stand nearby listening, weary and incensed with this conversation. Sometimes people laugh and I look over quickly to see who it was, who dares to laugh in our shiva house? How dare they talk about anything but death?

There are the cars pulled up in the new circular gravel drive Dad just put in two weeks before, like he knew he'd be providing massive, overflow parking after his death. There are cars lining our access road, cars lining both sides of our street.

The scene plays out night after night – the people, the food, my mother at the kitchen table surrounded by platters piled high, her face distraught, tears flowing, tranquilized by her doctor. She listens politely and absently to anyone who's talking to her, listening to Cantor Kushner, whom, we find out, is not just a Cantor, he's also a life insurance salesman. I sit cringing at the direction of the conversation.

"Chasia," he says, using her Yiddish name, "you tell me – what will happen to the girls if, *God forbid*, something happens to you?"

He doesn't wait for an answer because he knows the answer.

"Such a tragedy for the girls, no father! You want to leave them like Harry left you, no warning? Poof! And gone! Destitute!" He motions in the air just how she'll disappear. Then he opens his briefcase with a flourish and presents life insurance forms on the table, made out ahead of time.

My grandfather, having nearly disappeared into something we call senility in the 1970s, suddenly slips back, but too far back, like his brain is time traveling. He reverts from the kitchen table in Scottsdale, Arizona, 1975, to a rough-hewn house in Krivich, Lithuania, 1942. He loses his old man's shuffle, loses his English, regains his Yiddish, his pack-a-day cigarette smoking habit, and his coherence. The urgency of my father's death brings him back to other deaths during the war. He is planning a run from their village into the forest, past the Nazis guarding their house, an event that actually took place thirty-four years before. An event that resulted in him sitting at this table, my mother sitting at this table, me sitting at this table.

"Chasia," he says to me in Yiddish, calling me by my mother's Yiddish name. "Chasia, we'll escape in the middle of the night when the soldiers won't expect it."

My grandmother looks at him sharply, "*Yankef!* We're not running anywhere! We're in Arizona!"

I look to my mother for help, but she is sitting there stunned, glazed-eyed, sitting on the other side of our round, brown laminate kitchen table from me, signing life insurance documents.

I nod at my grandfather. We will escape.

***

I slip out of the cacophonous house, onto the gravel driveway, in my hose, no shoes, still in the green outfit I wore to the funeral, the noise disappearing with the shut door behind me.

There's the desert, empty and brown. There's the silence, then the noise pouring out the front door of the house every time it opens. The sun setting in the distance, my dad dead another day.

Our lives had a cadence that is suddenly broken. It wasn't exactly a good cadence, a heart-warming cadence, but it was our cadence. The familiarity of my father coming home, yelling and blustering – we're all *schervas*, we're bums, we're *goniffs*. He and Mom taking up their new pastime of fighting unto divorce – teetering, slipping, and sliding towards divorce. He, cranking the TV volume higher, higher, and even higher – his eardrums destroyed as a child – as he walked through the family room on his way down the hallway. As he went, he'd take time to stick an arm into every bedroom along the way, flicking off every single light, even if we're in there, or studying, suddenly plunging us into darkness.

When his arm snaked into my room, I'd send up a plaintive wail, "Da-ad!"

His response was always the same, for years the same, almost reassuringly the same, "What do you think? I'm made out of money?"

He'd make it to his room and change – outside clothes to inside clothes, then taking up his post in the family room, in front of the blaring TV, on his recliner, a newspaper fully opened in front of him.

156

***

When he dies it's like someone has dug up our family room and left a hole in the middle of the house. The TV is no longer blasting, we are suddenly allowed to sit in the recliner, there's no rustling of the newspaper, turning off of our lights. We jump over this hole each day, clinging to each other, eventually building a bridge over it, as families do. The bridge is constructed piece by piece as we re-mold into a different family.

Some of it is formed by identifying with our mother and our absolute relief that we have one parent left and it is her. In honor of our living mother and in sympathy with the way she was treated during this twenty-four-year marriage, we form a type of unspoken agreement never to honor our father's memory. We don't swear solemn oaths, our hands crossed over our hearts, rather it comes out in little verbal slings about Dad and how different life was without him around, life was better without him around. He was a troublesome father for so many reasons, after all. Philandering, yelling, distant, stingy. Why should we mourn?

We were all married to dad, all scorned. We are all our mother.

There are the pat reasonings we decide upon – our answers to Dad's inexplicable gone-ness. At least he didn't die young, I say to the nodding heads of my fifteen-year-old friends, all of us so young, and to us, forty-seven so unimaginably old. There's not one part of me that doesn't think that my dad lived a long, full life.

We're sure he would rather have died than slowed

down. He couldn't stand being sick for one day, couldn't stand being any less than a "man" – how would he have handled this? We shudder. We decide for him, can almost hear him saying that he'd rather be dead.

Also, the reasoning continues, if he'd loved us even one iota, he would have told the doctor about the chest pain, told the doctor about the rapidly disappearing stockpile of Nitroglycerine tablets, told the doctor that, rather than slowing down, he was speeding up. If he'd loved us one iota, maybe he would have acted like a regular, mortal patient, not Superman. If he'd loved us, he would have had life insurance and not rejected it superstitiously. There's some kind of nebulous feeling that in not taking care of himself, he proved he didn't love us enough to stay alive.

Over the next months, our family rehashes our lives and Dad's life. We become accustomed to his absence. Now we can walk around partially undressed, a family of women. Up until Dad's death, Mom had an unequivocal relationship with death. All death was miserable, incomprehensible, tragic, beyond belief, the dead all sainted. Dad's death causes her to reexamine all that. Our father, a saint? Ha! She laughs to herself, remembering things that we don't even know. What freedom she now has to criticize him when he can't talk back! What freedom for us all – living so long in absolute terror of Dad and his moods, his moodiness, to start with a whisper and move to a roar.

Half defiant and half still fearful, we turn away.

And there's the fact that, even though I know he's dead, even though I put rocks on his grave, shoveled the dirt, symbolically tore my clothing, rode in the limo following the hearse, after all the mourning rituals are done, the mourners have finished the last crumbs from the last deli platter, I realize I am not alone.

My dad is gone yet my dad is distinctly not gone. I feel my father all around me, a continuation of his presence. In my mind, he has the same judgments, the same prejudices, is still quick to anger. It's this father who hovers over me in the foyer, who flips through the strobe light images of my life so poorly lived, of the lies told. This dad forms the judge and jury and sentences me.

Though the world inside our family appears to have stopped on the day my father died, the outside world just keeps on moving.

We tick forward through the Jewish rituals, though the devastating funeral, though the week of shiva. We live in our bleak envelope of mourning.

Then, suddenly, it's a week later. How can this be? A week? I don't understand. Is time just going to continue marching on, the calendar pages just keep on flipping, leaving my dad far behind? It doesn't matter that I am still frozen in the foyer, my arms loaded with shoplifted goods, still standing there listening to my sister walking up and saying, "Dad died!" It doesn't matter at all if I'm frozen.

There's the reality that I'm just going to have to live like this, traumatized both by my father's life and by his death, my guts churning, mentally peering into his grave and waiting for him to pop back up. I understand that I just have to get used to the idea, that I have to get used to being frozen in one primary scene in my life.

He dies on a Saturday. The Friday afterward is my fifteenth birthday. Does one celebrate a birthday right after a father has died? I have no idea. Is it called off, suspended, postponed? I'm fifteen and ignorant of all Judaism. I have no rabbi to call and find out what the shiva protocol is on a child's birthday occurring during the week – is something supposed to come in the way of my birthday? Is something supposed to come in the way of the shiva?

Then eight days after he dies is a Rod Stewart concert, one I'd saved up for, one for which I'd bought my ticket months ago. Does one go to a concert right after a father has died? Right after shiva? What's the shiva for concerts? Who would I ask? To go or not to go? When do I resume my regular life? How do I resume a regular life? I make little forays, test runs, to see if, indeed, I exist in a world that no longer contains Dad, if I can go on living.

I go to the concert. I go because I'm ready for life to get back to normal. I go because my ignorance of Judaism is legion, I have no idea if I shouldn't go. I go because I have no idea how to mourn, how to grieve, and the best tool I have in my arsenal is denial and the best exhibition of denial is to go to a concert. I go and I stand with the crowd and sit with the crowd, I sing with the crowd, and I grow silent with the crowd, I scream with the crowd and light matches with the crowd for encores at the end, though my mind plays my frightening new normal back to me every second – Dad is dead, Dad is dead, Dad is dead.

I'm half an orphan. The only thing stopping me from being a full orphan is my mother, tranquilized by her doctor and in full grieving. I'm not ready to be parentless and there isn't exactly anyone else stepping in to take over the task of raising me with three more years of high school left to hoist me into college. The years yawn ahead of me. How can I guard my mother's existence to ensure her survival? How do I make sure she doesn't disappear the way Dad did?

And because time keeps ticking on relentlessly, refusing to stop so that I can stare at the death of my father like a massive collision in a roadway, the way I'm psychically looking at it in horror for years, the following Monday dawns just like Mondays always do and I go back to school, and we reopen our store.

I walk back into school terrified – will someone see my heart? I'm a complete wreck but I decide right away that as far as my public persona goes there will be no change. I might be cracking into little pieces on the inside, but I can't talk about it on the outside, I can't accept condolences, care, love, or even commiseration from anyone else who also has lost a parent – no condolences from anyone. I'm sure if I have to talk about it for even one second, I'll shatter into a thousand tiny pieces.

The only tool I've got in my toolbox is to pretend it never happened, and my sisters and I had already decided it was for the best, right? The litany of thoughts dance in my brain, that he didn't love us, he didn't care or would've taken better care of himself, he didn't love our mother, he would've hated surviving that heart attack. Over and over. I stuff this away, soldier through it, I let it sit inside.

My first day back I walk into my social studies class from the field where the hippies hang out, the backside of my jeans brown with dirt. A popular girl who's never spoken one word to me during all of eighth grade, and during all of ninth so far, a girl who lost her father in seventh grade, suddenly says something to me as I walk into class.

She says, "Linda, I'm so sorry about your father."

I look at her dumbly, numbly. I'm not ready to deal with things at school that make me cry, or things at home that make me cry, or things that make me cry ever, anywhere. I can't afford to let that river of tears start flowing again, they might never stop. How can I talk to this sweet person, so different from me, so obviously well-raised, with manners and condolences and who knew what else? This girl who probably had no secret life she'd hidden from her own father? She doesn't seem to have a gaping hole inside of her like I do, and which hides the unbearable question, did I kill my father through my stealing?

I am dumbfounded. I don't know what to say. I walk silently past her.

Fourteen
Widow Maker

I know rationally that my father died of a heart attack, but that doesn't mean that I don't think I killed him. I certainly do. I am sure that with my stealing of store money and his apoplectic response to the accounts that just wouldn't balance, I killed him. It's my own awful secret.

But it turns out that others in my family think the same thing.

One sister tells me she knows she killed him for a fact. Earlier the day he died, she and Mom drove down to the store to get fifty dollars from him to buy new clothes and he refused to give it. Mom yelled. My sister yelled too and then, afraid of him, locked herself away in the store bathroom.

She tells me that she stood in the store's miserable, squalid bathroom, with its cement floor, filthy sink, chipped porcelain toilet, a tiny window set up high stuck open with a view of the dumpster, and she waited for Dad to calm down. Like maybe she'd have to stay in there forever.

Finally, she heard the ding of the register as Mom

opened it, saying, "I'm taking the money, Herschel. Try and stop me!" Then the tap tap tap of her heels as she marched over to the bathroom and said, "Come out, we're leaving!"

They drove away. One last image – Dad standing in front of the store, his face red with anger, watching them.

But another sister is sure that she was responsible, at least in that she couldn't revive him. She was a nursing assistant in training at Bryman Nursing School, learning mouth to mouth resuscitation and CPR and how to give shots, and how to write up chart notes in doctors' offices, among other duties. When Dad fell to the ground in the back room of our store, she and an actual nurse shopping at the time came running. The real nurse kneeled to one side, taking Dad's pulse, but knew immediately that he'd had a heart attack so severe it's called a Widow Maker – there would be no reviving him. My sister thumped on Dad's chest, trying to restart his heart, but this was considerably worse in real life than in the classroom. Should she do CPR? Was she supposed to touch that mouth, the mouth that had yelled and screamed and sneered at her for her entire life, put her mouth on that mouth?

And another sister, who saw him fall, also thinks she killed him. If she had been quicker to call the police, the hospital, the fire department, in those days before 911. Had she killed him because, in a panic, she'd dropped the phone and run out of the store trying to flag down someone in the road to help?

Or was it that Dad was hell-bent on killing himself? We all knew he'd had a previous heart attack while we still lived in Chicago. Mom knew, the extended family knew, his doctor knew, but somehow Dad himself didn't seem to know this. Sure, he'd known that in 1972 he'd had some kind of problem that landed him in the hospital for several days. He knew the doctors called it a heart attack, but he was only willing to call it a mild heart attack. He went to the cardiologist grudgingly because what do the doctors know with their fancy educations? Heart attack!

At our store he would leap in one bound into the bed of farmers' pickup trucks to inspect boxes of fruit, and then unload those boxes of fruit. At restaurants he'd order Fred Flintstone-sized steaks marbled with fat, and then enjoy a nice cigar afterwards. After our store closed each evening, he careened around town with Gene and Lou, drinking and getting mixed up with women. Many times he'd call my brother-in-law and tell him to meet him out at some bar – the party was just getting started.

At the store and at home, he is mercurial, his anger flashing easily. He storms through our house. We all hide in our rooms, relieved when we realize we're finally too old to hit with a belt. He could calm down when necessary. He did this whenever he was on display, in the middle of our store, charming customers. He did it when he was pretending to be just one of the guys with the other walking timebomb men.

But there are two truths going on in my family at the same time. There's the truth that my father is not supposed to be doing these things post-heart attack and there's the truth that he seems invincible, too strong to die. There are so many reasons why it's inconceivable. He's the King of our house, the boss of us all, and the King doesn't just die. He can't die because he laughs at death, he thinks doctors are stupid, and that he is much smarter than his doctors, with a street intelligence honed in Siberia during the war and the Black Market of Germany after. He's not going to pay attention to doctors when they haven't done an honest day's work in their lives. He can't die because he fills up the house the minute he walks in and takes all the air with him the minute he walks out. That kind of energy doesn't just die and disappear.

He can't die because dying is for normal men, *schlemiels* who let themselves die. He'd tricked death before and would do so again.

It's the perfect storm. The store kills him and his decision to buy it kills him. Lou and Gene, his carousing male friends, kill him. We kill him – each fight, each disagreement, each explosion of his temper, kills him. Our mother kills him, and steaks kill him. Cigars kill him and his heart surgeon kills him, and the woman he was having an affair with kills him. The Nitroglycerin pills he swallowed like candy kills him. All of us killed him and none of us killed him. Or maybe he killed himself through a string of bad decisions, one after the other like dominoes falling, ending up at a grave.

And the relatives back in Chicago? They believe that Arizona killed him.

A month after my dad dies, on one of my days off from work, Nina and I are walking to a Los Arcos Mall on the unavoidable route past Ray Korte Chevrolet, in front of the leering eyes of the used car salesmen, whom we're convinced want us bad.

"Don't even look at them, Linda," Nina says.

I look because I only know what I look like through the eyes of men. I dare a glance. Sure enough, they're looking over, but probably only at Nina. There's an intensity of their gaze that makes me look away, like they have the right to look but I don't have the right to look back. I get the sudden, sure feeling that this gaze is no compliment.

We're off to the mall to shop. I am carrying forty dollars as usual along with some pot hidden in the torn lining of my purse, which I think is a cunning hiding place. It's a productive day. I had recently made the final installment payment on the crucifix I'd put on layaway for Nina and now she's inseparable from it, the little white gold Jesus hanging dead on the yellow gold cross. There are no Jewish stars in the cases at the jewelry store.

Finally we're upstairs in Broadway Department Store and I'm carrying four shirts I like, but I'm thinking why should I waste good money on them if I can get them for free? And so I make my way in a zig zag diagonal line across the entire store, visible to cameras, to detectives, to store clerks, to shoppers. I make my way to the bathroom, ostensibly to try them on, and then I stuff these shirts in my bag. I walk out and Nina and I head in a meandering, serpentine path to the exit which I'm hoping mimics how paying customers shop. I stop and exclaim over merchandise here and there to prove I'm not in any rush to get out of there.

As I'm stepping one foot, or just the toes of the one foot, over the threshold separating the department store from the rest of the mall, a man in a suit walks up very close behind me, puts his hands on my shoulders, and says, "I'd like you to come with me, young lady." And I am turned around, blushing bright red, marched back in the store, up the escalator, and into a back office. He hands me off to a female store detective.

She finds the shirts immediately. She seems to relish the task of searching my things. She has all the time in the world and appears to enjoy this task. Then she searches my purse, finding both an asthma spray and cigarettes, which seems to dumbfound her. She opens my wallet and is agog at the sight of over forty dollars, more than enough to have paid for the stuff I was stealing, which she says.

"Why you have more than enough money here to pay for those shirts!"

The she notices the rip in the purse's lining. I'm a purse girl. I only wear leather but, because I really have no money at all, I carry them and carry them until they fall to pieces, hence the torn lining.

What a sinking feeling, that moment when I know I have pot hidden in the lining of my purse and that purse is in the hands of a store detective. I have a fleeting thought – maybe she won't find it? And then she says, "What's this?" and the pot is in her hands.

"What's that?" I say, playing dumb while looking at it like it's a dead mouse, which is probably in there too.

She looks at me like she just hit the jackpot. She is elated. What a great day to be a store detective at Broadway Department store at Los Arcos Mall in South Scottsdale in 1975!

"We'll just see what the police have to say about this, young lady."

Nina is charged with the misdemeanor of shoplifting, but marijuana possession is a felony. I have to go to the Scottsdale jail. First, though, she tells me never to enter

Broadway Department Store again. She takes a picture of me to put up on her wall, like a wanted poster, but in this case an unwanted poster. I know I'll never step a foot in there again.

The police arrive and I am marched in reverse down the escalator, through the store, this time with my hands handcuffed behind my back, a police officer by my side. Faces turned upward toward me, watching the spectacle. A public shaming.

It turns out this police officer works this stretch of Scottsdale Road and he knows everything that happens on it. He somehow knows it was my dad who died inside the produce store a month before. He knew my dad.

Since the officer only has me for the time it takes to drive me from Los Arcos Mall down to the white-celled Scottsdale jail, he seems to try pretty hard to make an impression on me. Scared straight in a police car.

He loads me in the car and says, "That was your dad who died in that store last month? Oh boy. I knew him pretty well. Used to stop by on my beat. He'd be pretty ashamed of you if he saw you now."

It's 1975, when even police officers have to pretend they're hip about pot, so he says, "Look, pot is pot and who knows, maybe one day it'll be legalized, but right now it's not. Then he throws in the clincher, the things he just has to say, the things that traps me in that car for the next twenty-seven years, riding up and down and down and up Scottsdale Road forever, hands cuffed behind me, trapped listening to a police officer trying to make an impression on some spoiled rotten shoplifting fifteen-year-old.

He says, "But a thief is always a thief."

And I hear him say that I'll always be a thief, that it's no use trying to escape my fate, that it's in my DNA now. Years later I realize he was saying that our views about pot might change over time, but views will never change about shoplifting, that a thief is always a thief. Don't be one.

I remember the ride in the police car, I remember my sister Francine coming to fetch me a few hours later, since my mother has a standing policy that she will not pick any of us up at jails. In a lifetime of remembering almost every minute, I don't remember my time in the Scottsdale jail. Nothing from the officer's words in the police car until my sister arrives. Only the image of a jail cell with white bars, like something out of Andy Griffith's Mayberry drunk tank, but nothing else.

Soon it's Monday and everyone at school knows about Nina and I getting arrested. This is not considered to be a big deal among my crowd – though I certainly have fallen far in the last month, from bereaved orphan to felon. Someone points out that you probably can't become a psychologist when you have been arrested because you can't have a criminal record. Everyone knows I plan to be a psychologist and we are experts on the ins and outs of juvenile crime. We have a deep belief in our records being expunged at eighteen.

I don't know what to do with this information. I have a gigantic list at home of all the things I want to be and all the things I want to accomplish in my lifetime. Psychologist, writer, doctor, lawyer.

One of my friends pipes up, "Wow, Linda. I wish I could give you my record. I'm not planning on doing anything with my life anyway."

Months later, I'm sitting in a small office downtown, the probation officer looking across his desk at me.

Nina had already had her appointment with him, and she'd warned me that he was a pervert, that he'd asked her what she was going to do for him if he let her go.

She said, "Linda, this guy is a perv! I was pissed! I didn't know what to say so I just smiled like I'd do something for him. But hell no!"

With the appointment looming, my mother and I had concocted a wacky story to tell him. At least, I understood that we had fabricate a story but, by the time we're driving to the appointment in August, she believes it's true.

She's muttering darkly as she drives outraged that her innocent, misunderstood daughter could be arrested and go through this humiliation.

"With your asthma they think you'd smoke *something*? A friend gave you the *thing*."

She literally cannot say the word 'pot.'

She continues, "And you threw the *thing* in your purse. You forgot it was there! Of course you were surprised when that detective lady pulled it out! You never thought about it again!"

I'm reminded again that my mother is always on my side, even when I'm wrong. I can't break her heart again.

The conversation with the probation officer goes unexpectedly – I never even get to tell my elaborate alibi.

He says, "You're a smart girl. The girl you were with," he shakes his head, "she's no friend at all."

I think to myself that this is most likely true.

He continues. "You'll be lucky if you have two or three true friends in your lifetime."

We have a long discussion. It's just about the only hour of father/daughter time I've had in my life and he's not even my father.

Then he asks me the question I knew was coming.

"What will you do for me if I let you go?" he asks.

I hear the words, but it's nothing like what Nina said. There is nothing tawdry about this. It's a sincere question, an appropriate question, and it is deep.

I look him in the eyes and, in maybe my first mature action ever, I say, "I would thank you."

He nods, satisfied.

He says, "You're free to go."

Fifteen
In Cars We Trust

My sister Denise and I are rolling down the road in the family Pinto Station Wagon listening to the radio, an endless cycle of top forty hits – Captain & Tennille's *Muskrat Love*, the Eagles' *Hotel California*, *Sister Golden Hair* by America, with a little BJ Thomas and John Denver thrown in. I'm aware that in music too, I've come of age in a worse world than my oldest sisters. They got the Beatles and Motown. I get Tony Orlando and Dawn.

Once we reopen the store after shiva, my days of carefree childhood end. Dad's death has left a hole which must be filled by me, the fifteen-year-old shoplifting, wage-stealing, profit-eating, daughter. Mom makes the executive decision that I'll start working seriously now, not just moseying around the store when I can't get out of it. I'll have a real work schedule.

No more walking in a meandering path with Nina from school to her house, then from her house to Rina's house and then from Rina's house cutting through the golf course to my house without a care in the world. Suddenly, instead of finishing up my busy days at Chaparral High School ditching my classes, flunking my classes – I'm beginning to get a dawning realization that these may be related – smoking pot in the field all day, all that ends. Now my sisters, both enrolled in Distributive Education, time for which they spend at home sleeping, pick me up after school, one or the other twin. I climb into our Ford Pinto with the exploding gas tank and head down to Farmer's Produce Market.

It soon becomes routine, that Denise and I are a work team, and we drive to the store together. On the way to the store, our conversation has its pattern. First, I get yelled at for whatever I've done wrong – tried to get out of work, I'm late, I overslept if it's a weekend, whatever. There's always yelling because in our family we're yellers, that's just what we do – the yelling of the older sisters to the younger ones, the younger to the older. Once we're alone on the endless desert run, the stretch of no lights, no stop signs, no nothing, we quiet down.

We're driving on our endless loop from north Scottsdale to south Scottsdale, a meandering car ride to our store, since my sister must use sneaky backroads and avoid Scottsdale Road whenever possible. Sundays are the worst because normally I'm out partying late the night before, when unwitting bar owners have allowed teenagers to enter. After the snooze alarm, after the rolling over of our bodies, the rolling of the eyes, the disbelief that somehow once again it is morning, after the evaluation of the clothes in the closet, any matching pair of shoes on the feet, the hastily grabbed food in a kitchen which contains no food, there is also, every day, the problem of the car.

Of course, just getting to the store is a problem. First there's the firing up of the Pinto. This car takes its time starting. There's the attendant half fear/half excitement – will the car start at all? Will I get out of work? The looming disaster of the store just not opening today hovers above me.

It's a process, getting the Pinto to actually run. First it doesn't turn over at all and, through Denise's pounding on the pedal, invariably the engine floods. We must retreat into the house to wait for this problem to resolve itself. Sometime later, we come back out and there's some action. The car engine turns over a few times, though it immediately dies out. It wheezes. It gasps. It rattles, and around here a rattle is a good thing. We can actually get to the store on a rattle. On cold winter mornings, one of my sisters runs out to our driveway and starts the car so it warms up. Sometimes we forget it's running out there and it runs out of gas.

Finally it starts and holds. We jump in. Denise revs the engine, gasoline fumes shimmering all around us, and we take off.

On Sundays we get to the store and the customers are waiting outside for us to open. The first time we open right after our dad dies, the customers stumble in, to buy, to console.

A lady says, "That man died? The owner? The handsome, friendly man?"

I look at her in confusion. Friendly? Handsome? I cover my surprise. Of course they're talking about my dad, he's the only one who's died. I nod a numb yes.

We pull open the huge glass sliding doors and then, as the customers swarm in, we turn on the lights inside the produce cases, fill up the milk in the cooler, spray down the vegetables, turn on the tinny radio up high in a corner, and power up the register. Denise immediately plants herself on the second register counter to smoke and ash her cigarette in a soda can. I make a mental note not to drink from that can. Of course, I forget it in about an hour. How many times have I drank coke-flavored ash?

On days off, the car routine works a little differently. We wake up late and a quick glance around the house reveals that one sister or another is missing something essential – cigarettes, diet pop, sunflower seeds, corn nuts. Upon these we live. We must go to the store. Denise is the automatic driver on these outings, born to live behind the wheel. She wears her nightgown, a low-cut, ankle skimming, evening gown of a nightgown, Dr. Scholl's, and carries a purse that doubles as a garbage can, ashtray, and sink. She can't get out of the car wearing a nightgown, of course, so one of us has to come with. We get in the Pinto, and it is warmed up and ready to go since it's so late in the day, sitting in the gravel driveway all night and all morning poised to load some of us up, slam the doors, and screech out of there, barreling out of the driveway.

My sister drives one way only – fast. Her only speed is fifty miles per hour. She doesn't start out slow and speed up, she somehow starts out at fifty. I jump in fast while the car is erupting from the driveway, a pin ball about to be flung out into the galaxies from our u-shaped driveway. This car is most similar to Fred Flintstone's, with the car just a shell around us and our feet running on the ground below providing propulsion. We're at one with our surroundings mostly because, with everything broken, non-existent or is disrepair, we *are* in our surroundings, literally in the open air. In the summer, the steering wheel is burning hot, our legs stick to the vinyl seat, panting in the Arizona heat, in the winter we're freezing cold, with wind blowing in a stuck-open window, trying to speed to get to our destination but knowing that if we accelerate above fifty mph the car will simply grind to a shaking, shuddering halt.

My feet are invisible on the floor below, covered with garbage, the evidence of a thousand late night runs to Jack in the Box, the paper bags left in the car for time immemorial. Fast food logos have changed while our car remains uncleaned. It's a rolling museum of American fast food in there.

"Shoot, the lane's ending, hang on!" Denise says, the road narrowing in front of us. She's a highly skilled driver, especially considering the challenges of driving in Arizona. Since all of Arizona is under construction, every road dug up, new ones being paved, ones that were never paved now gleaming with black top, and thickets of road hazard signs blinking, like driving an obstacle course. The workers close lanes, they dump one lane into another, until our lane merges over and over again and has nowhere left to merge, just a tiny dot at infinity. Arizona is a work in progress.

There's one section of the automobile laws that we have memorized backwards and forwards – the decrepit car laws. In other words, how bad can our cars get before we'll actually get pulled over for something? There's a sliding scale, from things that are bothersome to us to things that are bothersome to police officers, and we will do anything to keep the car from falling from one category into the next. A tilted rear-view mirror that flops over again and again once adjusted? We're unlikely to get pulled over for this. Bald tires? It will never rain so we'll never skid and come to the attention of an officer. There are the broken seatbelts, doors that won't open, windows that won't shut, and air conditioning that never works. We have windshield wipers that are reduced to fibers and windshields which have cracks so long and complex that we peer through them like puzzle pieces, trying to get a unified vision of the roadway. Our windshields only crack right in front of the driver's seat, never the passenger's.

Our cars don't have working turning signals, but it's hot out and the windows have to be rolled down and then up again, so it requires some evaluation. When is it worth it to roll down my window to signal a turn? If I'm in a right turn lane, no. The right turn lane *is* my turn signal. If I'm in a left turn lane, same thing. If I'm alone on the road, not one driver coming near me from behind or in front, no. After all, if I'm going to turn myself into an absolute jackass by sticking my arm out the window to make obsolete hand signals indicating the direction of my turn, there'd better be a good reason.

We expect a lot of mind-reading from the drivers in the road along with us. Sometimes, when we're sure we're at one with the road and the other drivers, and we only have one working turn signal, we just use the one turn signal to indicate both right and left. We are not going to be opening and closing these crank windows every time the car moves.

On the other hand, there's never a reason to get in the car after someone else has been driving and make any complicated adjustments. These cars require no adjustments at all. The rear-view mirror doesn't have to be adjusted because it's hanging by a thread at a 45-degree angle and my sister has her head craned sideways just to use it. The driver's side mirror doesn't have to be adjusted because there isn't one. There are no complicated buttons, no lumbar adjustments. There's just a lever under the seat that takes the whole front bench on a dizzying ride forward and backwards, sometimes it catches in a good spot, sometimes we have to try again, forward and backward, hoping our passenger will pull their side so we don't get stuck at a crazy angle.

We are aware that, at the officer's discretion, any one of these things could be the cause of a citation. We are also aware that only one thing will absolutely get us one – a broken taillight. We live in fear of broken taillights.

If worse comes to worse and we break down, our mother gets us towed off any roadway with her handy AAA membership card. It's transferable to any member of her family, a situation she abuses, almost running AAA into bankruptcy with all of us breaking down all over Arizona in our various household cars, in our boyfriend's cars, in Mom's boyfriends' cars, in everyone's cars, at least one a week all over town, the tow trucks' flashing lights beating a path to wherever we are stuck.

Once towed, there isn't exactly a plan. The car can't be towed to a repair shop, that's out of the question because there's no money for repairs. So the car is just towed back home to our acre out in the boonies. It gets deposited there, steaming, overheated, clunking, delivered by the tattooed tow truck drivers, all of us piling out of the cab of their trucks and thanking them for the ride. The car simmers there, lies fallow, stirs in its own juices, maybe heals itself.

We go back out there in a month or two, put the key in the ignition and listen to it roar to life.

Sixteen
Matchmaker

The biggest problem with having a widowed mother in the 1970s is that she has no plan to stay that way - single, widowed. She is determined to pair herself off again. There's an appropriate mourning period, a tranquilized period; a fuzzy, blacked-out period where the question of whether I've lost two parents and not just one looms heavily. I realize my vulnerability as a now-fifteen-year-old near-orphan. I need to raise myself, and fast.

During her tranquilized phase, my mother sleeps fitfully on a cot in our living room. At first, this is understandable because when the relatives descended on us for the funeral and shiva they were given all the bedrooms and we were all shoved in the living room. As they leave, trudging off wearily to return to Chicago, to return to Florida, to an unthinkable future without their brother, we return to our rooms, our mother the only one still in there.

I say, "Mom, why don't you go sleep in your bedroom?"

She cries out, "I can't sleep in our bed without your father!"

So she sleeps on in the living room, her fancy bedroom with its king-sized bed standing empty, assumed to be holding his ghost.

When she finally wakes up out of this state, she immediately decides it's time for her to rejoin life, to snap out of it, maybe even to start dating. Then she packs up Dad's clothes – I wonder, is she making room in the closet? – packing up even his Polish cowboy ensembles. The bola ties, cowboy boots, the stuff he wore right before he died.

After all, as she is reminded by all her friends, she isn't getting any younger, and it's not like she and my dad were a great love match. Optimistically, there is a chance for romance.

She bounds up out of this mourning cot and resumes her place in the half-empty marital bed. This, in turn, triggers some international Jewish matchmaking network, like maybe there were sensors planted there and, realizing there is an empty side of the bed, this mobilizes a worldwide network of *shadchans*, cranking them into action to get my mother remarried. The whole world seems to be looking for my mom's next husband. People all over the globe are trying to match her up, on the hunt for her next husband. They find *schlemiels*, they find *schlimazels*, they find *schmendricks*. They are looking under rocks, in crevices, under bridges. They are putting notes in the Wailing Wall in Jerusalem.

The matchmakers evaluate my mother like she's a horse, and the general consensus is that she's got baggage. She has an accent which belies her immigrant past in a time period in which no one talks about the Holocaust. She has seven daughters, five still at home. Also, she lives in Arizona. What self-respecting Jew lives in Arizona, they want to know? No one lives in Arizona, that's who, and certainly no eligible widowers.

On the positive side, some likely widower might be ready to retire to Arizona and there she is, desperate for male attention and owns a nice house on an acre. And, yes, a pool. And won't the girls be out of the house in a few years? Or, as it turns out, boomeranging in and out of the house over the course of a decade? There's some presumed wealth, a belief that my mother is also a rich widow, but that's only because the matchmakers don't know one important fact – that my father died with no life insurance, and we are broke.

Did we mention the pool?

They all readily acknowledge the futility of their task. It's almost impossible. A widow with seven children – could that sound appealing to any man ever? But children do not stay young forever and my mother is not yet forty-five. There might be some man on the planet somewhere looking for someone to support him and let him live in her nice home in Scottsdale, to cook his meals and iron his shirts and support him while he swims in the pool all day.

The men come from all around. One comes from Pennsylvania, another from Chicago, leads here and there. There are the short, the fat, the bald, the poor, the hairy, the loud, the opinionated. Nothing works out. My mother is, in some ways, married to her daughters. She is both available and completely unavailable at the same time.

Since all the neighbors up and down our block had socialized together as couples, Mom gravitates to them when she first wakes up out of her tranquilized state, but she soon discovers that there is no longer a place for her now that she is unmarried, whatever the cause. A man is always an asset and automatically assumed to be an eligible widower, but their doors are shut tight against Mom. After all, she just might make off with their husbands.

These women guard their men. They guard them no

matter what they got in the great marriage lottery of life – fat, balding, rude, smelly, overbearing. They cater to them, jump to do their bidding, laugh at their unfunny jokes, and keep themselves attractive for them, their hair backcombed in gigantic helmets around their head, their bodies trim by playing tennis or sweating in saunas, and wearing fashionable polyester pants suits or dresses, whatever the husband prefers. They are going to stay married forever.

It's unfortunate – messy – but sometimes someone dies, like my dad, like Ethel Shapiro. And when Ethel dies, she leaves her husband Mickey behind, one of those men who have been catered to, pandered to, doted upon like miniature kings in their fiefdoms. This is the type of man available to my newly widowed mother.

But before my mom settles her gaze on Mickey, there is Jewish Singles.

"Linda, *mamaleh*, remember I need the family room tonight for the Jewish Singles party."

I sigh heavily. I will be dodging the Singles all night trying to beat my usual path between my bedroom and the kitchen, wanting to avoid detection.

Our home is suddenly filled with an endless queue of unemployed men with bad hairpieces and shirts open to their navels, each revealing a three-inch-long 14k gold chai tangled up in their chest hair, ogling our home in Scottsdale, sitting on its prime acre. Their Long Island accents grate on my nerves.

She is popular, that is apparent. She hosts these parties, and the men show up in their golf attire, like they spent the day golfing instead of living in their soon-to-be repossessed cars. Of course, we're frauds too. We have nothing but that house sitting on that acre and that has twenty-eight and a half years to go on its mortgage. The men don't know that.

My mother is charmed by all this male attention, but I am annoyed. It's like having a new, stupid, younger sister who has no idea how to date, no idea how to say "no," no idea how to use modern forms of birth control, no idea which guys are just too good to be true and so, indeed, *are* too good to be true. She is easily impressed, easily excited, entering into relationships quickly, taking on the men's interests, their family problems, their medical problems. This is familiar territory to her. Not only has she been catering to Dad all these years – catering to a tyrant – but she has a Lithuanian brain forged in the 1930s, and a Holocaust Survivor brain that is savvy and knows how to survive. Surviving means marriage.

My mother and I hit dating age at the exact same moment, a fact I find scary and disconcerting. She hasn't dated since 1951. She leaves the house on all these adventures ill-equipped, a time traveler from 1951 landing in 1975, Fiddler on the Roof and Helen Reddy vying for space in her head. We send her out there, a cyclone of hairspray engulfing her heavily coiffed head, some type of Mod outfit on her body, the door slamming behind her.

Mindy and I, as the two youngest daughters, become the potential stepchildren to a series of men, the scary teenagers whom they need to charm in order to marry our mother. I glare suspiciously at the intruders.

During my mom's forays into the dating world, she never forgets that Mickey conveniently lives right across the street, a widower across the street, so close it is almost *bashert* –

these things can't just happen by accident, can they?

Mickey Shapiro is not going to be left alone, sitting in the gloom of his home day after day, glaring out at the world. Not with my mother widowed nearby. Soon after Ethel dies, my mom begins bringing Mickey food every couple of nights. First a brisket, then a chicken, then some matzo ball soup she just happens to have lying around the house. She is seducing him the only way she knows how. There is some belief that the path to a man's heart lies through his stomach.

For some reason, long before Ethel died, Mickey had taken a virulent dislike to all seven of us. His natural attitude was one of dislike, he had to be convinced of a reason to move up from "dislike" to "tolerate." We were vulnerable to criticism, our parents preoccupied with both their failing store and failing marriage. There was a level of discipline that just didn't exist on our side of the street – my parents had lost the battle with their American daughters. Then my dad dies and by the summer of 1975 it's apparent that my mother is running a lax operation. With the drinking age set at nineteen in Arizona and no one checking IDs, some of us take to sneaking into bars, ending up in clutches with men in parking lots, pressed up against their cars or in ramshackle pick-up trucks parked on dirt roads. We are up to no good and Mickey knows it. We come zooming home at two or three or four in the morning, our car careening around our mutual corner, music blasting.

Unfortunately, Mickey either doesn't sleep at all or he is an alarmingly early riser. By the time we get home after barhopping while the bars are open, and then party hopping after the bars close, he is up for the day, stomping out around his front yard in the pre-dawn in his pajamas, yanking a garden hose behind him, and watering the bushes. He never waves hello, just stares. Glares. I feel caught, even though he's nothing to me. I refuse to believe he's anything to me. It's impossible to believe that life could be that cruel, that having lost our previous tyrant – our father – we're just supposed to take on a whole new tyrant voluntarily.

Once he and my mother start dating and because he cannot shut up about how our she is raising us, he seldom comes over to our house, their relationship takes place almost exclusively across the street. But at Passover he climbs down out of his recliner, he stands up, he yells at his boys to hurry up, and then he makes his own personal Exodus to our house – we're stuck with him for the Seder.

He and the boys arrive, Mickey's aftershave overpowering, my mom and I, both asthmatics, wheezing. His boys wear the neat pale blue suits mandated by their father and shiny black shoes, their hair slicked down, smashing their natural waves. They call my mother "Mrs. Burt," no matter how many times she tells them to call her Helen, or Helene, the "e" added after our dad's death, her new identity. After all, they don't obey her, they obey their father, and their father demands formality. Mrs. Burt it is.

We have a lock-down Seder, enforced reading till the bitter end, and then, starving, we'll eat anything when it's over, even the hard-boiled eggs and parsley. Though we read our mother's haphazardly and crookedly-copied *Haggadot*, with the names of long-ago seder participants written in beside each paragraph, then scratched out as they die, there's no understanding, for me at least. Hebrew looks like hieroglyphics to me, there are too many rabbis, too many sons, too many unpronounceable names. The English I read, but do I believe a word of it? Does anyone at this table? Mom, of course, is an atheist because of the Holocaust and Mickey is most likely an atheist because as far as I can tell, similar to my father, he thinks he is actually God. His boys are Bar Mitzvah Jews — they can read Hebrew but don't know what they're reading.

So we sit there, mindlessly intoning words about slavery and Egypt and surreptitiously thumbing our Haggadah copies to see how many more pages we have to sit through, when suddenly Mickey stands up and his hand comes smashing down on the table, bringing the Seder to a halt. He starts yelling at one of his sons in an apoplectic, profanity-filled, shouting fit. His face turns purple.

"Goddamn it, Jake. I saw you turn the pages of that Haggadah, you little bastard. Did I tell you you'd be respectful to Mrs. Burt who nearly killed herself making this Seder?"

Apparently, we aren't supposed to page ahead to see how many pages stood between us and freedom.

Jake is looking straight down at the table.

He says, "Yes, sir."

"You little *pisher*, wait till I get you home! And your tie is uneven! Are you supposed to have an uneven tie?"

"No, sir."

"And you will not open your stupid, little, goddamned, pissant mouth during this Seder one more time, you got that? You will be respectful to Mrs. Burt who spent all this time cooking such a lovely meal!"

"Yes, sir."

Then, just as suddenly as he started, Mickey stops

yelling. We look away, down, at our soup, at the matzo, out the window. Anywhere but at him or Jake. When it's possible, I glare at my mother for bringing him into our house.

The Seder resumes awkwardly, but never recovers. There's no way to recover, the rest of us are aghast. At least when Dad was alive, he could be depended on to get drunk and oblivious at a Seder, but there's no way out of the hell of Mickey Shapiro.

But Mickey recovers just fine. He chomps on his Cuban cigar, slurps his soup, then ashes the cigar into the empty bowl while he waits to have his dishes cleared away and be served the next course. He never notices any tension. His suit-clad legs remain spread, his big gut resting between them as he continues arguing politics with his mouth full, shouting down anyone who dares to disagree with him.

No matter what my complaints had been about my dad, the certainty that he'd been the most miserably unsuited partner my mother could possibly find post-war, it turns out I was wrong. My father was actually a fine, nice, pleasant, charming fellow compared to Mickey.

My mother searches the world over, she searches Israel, Mexico, Canada, and the U.S. She searches under rocks, across oceans, and beneath bridges. Finally, she finds exactly what she is looking for, right across the street. When she pairs off with Mickey Shapiro, she proves to me that no matter how difficult and troublesome and angry and fickle our father had been, there was still an even more difficult, troublesome, angry, and fickle man in the world – her new boyfriend.

To match my mother's broken boyfriend picker, I've got a

broken picker of my own. Mine settles on a boy I meet at school as a freshman, Greg Scott.

I'm already aware of where I fall on the high school supply chain. I'm not quite cool enough. I'm too pimply, I have awkward hair, and a body weight that starts careening up and down the scale. This doesn't go over well in 1974 when the beauty ideal is Cheryl Tiegs. It's necessary for me to ratchet my taste down, way down, to the freshmen boys, guys with grown out shags, haircuts that had successfully escaped the barber for a few months. The guys who are always scrounging for pot, scrounging for a ride. The immature freshmen are my league.

From the moment I meet Greg, both of us part of the incoming freshman hippie crowd, I'm a little interested, mostly because in a sea of blondes he has black hair. At first, I don't think much of him because he's too short, in a way where I knew that no growth spurt was expected. And skinny. If I ignore the skinny and short thing, he is handsome with the craggy head of a model, the light eyes. His walk is distinctive, the walk of all the partying guys. Loping in a side-to-side pitch, cowboy boot-clad, his shoulders rolling along, dipping one way and then the other, his pants slung way low, held up by a thick leather belt, the square imprint in a back pocket attesting to his Marlboros.

But when I catch him staring at me a few times, I decide he likes me, and this automatically triggers my liking him back. I proceed to have a maddening, nonverbal, crush on him based on this only. He's my big crush, the one that lasts for all of high school, the one I boing back to automatically and in between any other guy I meet. This crush lasts through all my friends' scoffing and incredulity, insisting that even *I* am too good for Greg Scott. It lasts through his dropping out of school, dropping back into school, then dropping out and in one more time before finally disappearing.

When I walk out of a classroom in one of the four random semesters that his high school career coincides with mine, he is easy for me to spot. I look for short and skinny, I look for black hair, I look for the telltale crouching over a joint, passing joints with gingerly-held roach clips, cupping a joint carefully while eyeing up the general area for our resident narcotics officer. I learn right off the bat that he's troubled — like James Dean-troubled, with a dead mother and a remarried father. Instead of making me shy away from him, this information draws me near because I dream of saving Greg from himself. It feels very romantic to me and, though I'd planned to be many things — a psychologist, a writer, a professor, a doctor — I'm willing to chuck all of that for whatever Craig wants me to be, if I can get him to talk to me.

There are a lot of reasons I believe we're meant to be together. First of all, he's older than me, one whole month older. This doesn't often happen to me with a March birthday and since I'm still wandering the planet believing my future husband needs to be older than me, this seems important. Then I find out that his deceased mother was half-Jewish. No, I can't envision him in a yarmulke but, at this point, I can't envision myself in a synagogue, so that's okay. But beyond all that, the biggest reason I know that I'm meant to be with Greg is sheer romanticism because I believe he has a matching, acute, miserable crush-from-afar on me. This is ultimately all I need for fuel.

There are the staring years – freshman year, some of sophomore year – where we stare holes through each other's heads but if our eyes meet, he looks away, not like he was caught, but disinterested, like he wasn't looking at me anyway, and isn't that wall behind my head fascinating? There are the talking years containing brief conversational bites, where I try to get information out of him before he flies on past me, always on his way to a party somewhere, anywhere. I have to do all the conversational heavy lifting after plotting it out with my best friends for weeks. He's either uninterested in everything or he's only interested in where the party is, where the pot is, who's got it and how to get it.

I'm certainly willing to have an unrequited crush for the rest of my life. A requited crush just seems like it would be overwhelming, yet, even I need more information to have one that's unrequited. Like which half of his mother was Jewish? This is critically important to me because even though I come from a bacon-eating, Sabbath-breaking family, even though all our traditions have been scattered to the wind, there's still this little spark of a spark in my Jewish soul. Am I headed towards a chuppah?

I look frantically for clues. His father's name is Sid. That sounds Jewish to me. I learn that his father started his own car leasing company, so I check off a few more clues – entrepreneurial equals Jewish, car business equals Jewish. This makes me frantic, could it be? I catch him as he flies by me into a car revving up in the parking lot, stereo blasting, ready to screech out.

"Is your dad Jewish?" I ask, running alongside him.

He says, "No, my dad's not Jewish. My mom was

half."

He doesn't seem to know what I'm talking when I yell, my voice barely audible over the screeching car, my eyes wild, "Which half?"

Greg disappears as high school continues – he's there for freshman year, in and out for sophomore year, back for part of junior year, and gone forever by the time we should be seniors together. He pops up before me or disappears behind me after rumors of him sweep all over the school – he's coming back, he's not coming back, he's working, he's not working, his dad will give him a car if he finishes high school, then that he totaled out that car and then another. Craig cannot drive to a store without totaling out a car. I never hear this information firsthand, rather rumors float along in the air and finally find me. I'm always amazed at how long it takes for people to tell me news about him. Don't they know I'd like nothing better than a daily newspaper blaring out a headline containing only the title, "Greg!"

He flits in and out of my life, in and out of high school, crashing through his father's car inventory. After a while there are no more rumors of him returning because there's no chance he could ever catch up. He'd be a senior by age with a freshman's credits. I move towards the midpoint of high school, I move beyond it, leaving Greg behind. But I'm still sure I can fix him.

I'm raising myself while my mother's preoccupied with Mickey Shapiro, preoccupied with her newly-single life in between their breakups. It turns out I'm not much of a mother.

Seventeen

Jewish Girls Gone Wild

My sister Sherry is sitting on the edge of the bathtub in the hall bathroom. Denise, her twin, is standing at the sink, brushing her teeth.

"What if the world ends tomorrow? I really want to know. Listen to me. You have to answer. This is really important. If you knew the world was going to end tomorrow, you'd just die a virgin?"

It is 7:00 am, early for the harangue to begin, for existential discussions about whether the loss of virginity, in and of itself, constitutes a meaningful life. This reflects the seriousness of the discussion.

"I don't know. I guess so." Denise says.

"What do you mean, you don't know? You can't die a virgin! You have to have sex! Everyone is having sex except you! There's not one sophomore who's a virgin — well, maybe a couple of cheerleaders, but no one who's cool."

"I know already!"

"Well, what are you going to do about it?" Sherry

glares at her twin.

I overhear them talking, arguing, day after day. At least, I overhear Sherry talking and arguing day after day and Denise agreeing that she needed to get rid of her virginity as soon as possible, that it is an emergency, that maybe she should call in some assistance, give it away to a passerby, anyone really, not so much because she didn't want to potentially die a virgin, but, more likely, to shut Sherry up.

I hear the message clearly, that virginity isn't an asset. It isn't something to be treasured or "saved" for one's husband, it is to be tossed away as soon as we can, a barrier between us and a full life. Virginity impedes us from what we should be doing, like having serial lovers, to pretend it's normal to have sex, to wake up with guys, to roll over with guys, to be casual about whether guys call or not.

My mother is too busy to guard us, first she's too busy mourning to realize what we're doing, then too busy with Jewish Singles, then busy with Mickey Shapiro, on an endless trip back and forth from one side of the street to the other, and our father isn't there to act as the all-purpose policeman. Like prisoners whose wardens have gone on strike, we look around, we sniff the air, we realize no one is watching us or will notice anything we do, and, finding ourselves free, we slip out until it's pretty much Jewish girls gone wild around here. No one can stuff this genie back in the bottle.

First, I go wandering off, having fun with other teenagers, hanging out at open parties at our high school, dressing up in some kind of version of "sexy hippie," and lurking around keggers and boondockers looking for guys to be my boyfriend.

I *get together* with guys, which means that I roll around in the desert, roll around on top of scrub bushes, or roll and roll and roll, until I roll right on top of cacti, having wild make out sessions. It feels like I am beautiful if I am desirable, even if it's just for a few hours.

Things change when our friend Wendy moves from Chicago to Phoenix. She is raring to go, just like me, but insatiable for guys, guys, guys. We soon decide we don't like guys our own age, they aren't mature enough. We've already ruled out Jewish guys because we just assumed there weren't any here, the law of large numbers and all that. We like older guys, guys out of high school, or guys from other schools, or college guys, even community college guys, guys who can appreciate our qualities, which are largely overlooked by younger guys.

Sometimes we wander over to the west side of town where things are a little wilder than in Scottsdale. As we drive west, change is in the air. The smell of exhaust from countless taped together broken tail pipes is palpable, the sound of broken mufflers roaring through the air, some intentionally broken, some not, jacked up muscle cars, their rear ends hoisted in the air. We are definitely far from home.

To continue our slide, to go from bad to worse and then to impossible, we begin to cruise the main drag, Central Avenue.

It's a summer night in 1975. I'm in our family station wagon with Wendy and my sister Denise. We are cruising Central Avenue, the go-to place of hot rods and kit cars, where every car is driven in slow motion to let everyone admire their gleaming wheels, then they get to the turnaround point – the Jack in the Box – and do it all over again. We don't exactly have a cruising-worthy car, I'm aware of that. We join the stream of cars, cruising unironically in this station wagon. I'm also aware that, as teenage girls, we might potentially make up in appeal what our car lacks.

We pull up at a stop light, the engine rumbling, which sounds cool but isn't – our transmission is about to hit the pavement. A car pulls up beside us full of sweaty west side guys, I'm sure, and they rev their engine at us where we sit in the car, our legs stuck to the vinyl of the front seat, sweating, not touching any of the chrome because while the car was parked it heated up to over 200 degrees. They start revving their car, ready to race our family station wagon. When the light changes, we smile wanly at them because we know there is not really going to be a race – this car can't race - and also because our theory of attracting males is that we will smile at anyone, even them. The light turns green, and they blast off.

I say, "Go get them! They were cute!" I say this mainly because I am fifteen. My sister is seventeen, perhaps she should know better, or perhaps she should know our car better. Who knows? Maybe this one glorious time the car won't let us down. We fly from the stoplight and streak down the road, our car a lightning bolt of wood-paneled sides, towards the next stop light half a block away. My sister presses on the gas just a little too hard. We hear a wheezy, airy sound, and the car comes to a dead stop.

It's sad but true that I know we can't attract the best of guys, that there's a downward slope of men on this hill of cruising and, lacking a hot rod, driving a station wagon, we

196

aren't very high in status. It's a war of competing interests after all. The guys are looking to show off their cars and have sex. I am looking for a boyfriend, even if it starts off looking an awful lot like a one-nighter at first.

It's not that I think this is all we can get or all we deserve, but rather that there's some inner convoluted need to be the most desirable girls ever to some group of males somewhere, no matter how low I have to go. This backfires of course. It will take many revolutions up and down Central Avenue to find out that the more I devalue myself, the more I am devalued.

I'm aware that we're most likely the only Jewish girls cruising Central, also probably the only girls from out in the boonies of North Scottsdale. I know I'm slumming. I'm still in high school, so I have no real idea of where I'll eventually fall on the scale of life. Maybe I really am destined to end up cleaning my boyfriend's car's chrome wheels with a toothpick each weekend while pretending that I find that rewarding work. Or maybe I'll end up President. Who knows? Right now, I'm fifteen and an underperforming high school student. We're the same.

Bored cruising, we park at the Jack in the Box at the end of the line, and place our order, the usual – six regular tacos, three orders of onion rings, and three diet cokes, because we are never, ever, allowed to drink fattening pop. At age fifteen, I've already learned that I'm allowed to eat calories only, never drink them. Even later, when we go to bars, I drink a diet coke and rum. There is no justification for a wasted calorie.

Then we open our tailgate to more easily welcome

guys. We're open for business.

We take all comers. Whatever, whomever, talks to us, we talk back. Anything goes. Push, tug, or pull, everything's okay. Spanish-speaking guys come by and, sure, we'll give it a shot, communicating by hand signals and charades, even though I know enough Spanish to tell that they're calling us *putas* to each other. Skinny guys with shifty eyes, that's okay. Cowboys with mouths full of chewing tobacco, round Skoal containers outlined in the back pockets of their Wrangler jeans, spitting tobacco juice out every now and then, in between offering us a ride on their "horse" and laughing their heads off if we say yes. That's okay. We even end up at parties where I find out with some consternation that *we're* the party.

What could be a greater guy magnet than a stupid fifteen-year-old wearing a tube top to hold up the buoyant breasts that exist only for an unappreciated decade, before life takes them away, before aging? Nothing is holding them up except for the sheer miracle of youth.

I know I'm kind of cute here in mid-teenhood, yet early in the summer I'm always standing by mystified as my sister and Wendy meet guys and I'm left alone. I wonder, am I emitting some type of male repellent, or are Wendy and Denise emitting a special pheromone? Do guys have some kind of built-in radar which tells them that I'm a virgin? I try to pretend I'm carefree and kind of wild, but it comes off false. Thy point their testosterone-fueled brains our way, and I'm left waiting on couches for make out sessions to end. I'm constantly being given advice by the guys we meet, mostly that I think too much. I don't know how to think less.

Our summer of cruising Central finally ends when the

police bust it up. They begin giving out tickets to anyone who circles around the street more than one time in two hours or so, while they stand out there with clipboards and pens and write down license plate numbers, and then pull us over the second time around. Everyone decides en masse to move the whole operation over to Metro Parkway in Northwest Phoenix, circling Metrocenter mall. We show up once but it's too crowded and the police are already there waiting for everyone, handing out citations before people even begin to drive. It's over.

There is nothing to do now but to get fake IDs. Of course, that's possible for Denise and Wendy but I don't even have a driver's license. I'm at the mercy of whatever fake driver's license someone at school loans me. Sometimes I'm a blonde nineteen-year-old and sometimes I'm a very tall twenty-five-year-old. Sometimes I make it past the bouncers and sometimes I don't, which makes me high risk for Denise and Wendy, schlepping me along at all, knowing they could end up driving all the way down to a bar just to find out I wasn't making it past the door, and then schlepping me back home again.

It's simply not an option to stay home.

One night, primping, I take a last look in the mirror. I'm satisfied with what I see – with my curled wings of hair, with my eyebrows tweezed away until there is only one hair connecting with the next hair and the next, forming a skinny arched line over each eye. I'm satisfied with everything, our plans for the night, my male-magnet outfit, my makeup. I'm happy with everything, except that my mother is getting ready for her own night out right next to me. She asks me to pass the mascara. I sigh heavily.

I wonder at the crazy twist of fate that's cast me into the dating world at the exact same time that my mother has been re-hoisted into it. Instead of being watched over by a zealous, overprotective parent, I find myself instead zealously guarding her from loser after loser in an ever-descending spiral. Our matching spirals zoom downwards in unison.

My mother is beautiful, with a pointy nose, a tan, and a great big poof of ash blonde hair floating in a fluffy cloud around her head. She's thin, except for a permanent belly from the six pregnancies that resulted in seven daughters, so this is our fault, of course. She keeps herself in tip top shape playing tennis in a tiny white dress with Mickey Shapiro when they happen to be dating, spending the whole game chasing tennis balls. When they're not dating, she gives up tennis, since it reminds her of Mickey, and takes belly dancing. She is self-conscious about her war-ravaged teeth, malnutrition-damaged, gold teeth originally replacing the ones she lost. She has gum surgery after gum surgery.

Lipstick is the name of the game for my mother, her favorite makeup. There's nothing she can't do with a lipstick. Lipstick for her cheeks as blush, lipstick for her lips, of course. Sometimes, when she needs to write an emergency note and can't find a pen, she uses a handy nearby lipstick to write it down. Then there's the dried-up mascara, smudgy, uneven, used by all of us.

She smiles at me, or maybe at herself, nods her head, preoccupied as she fluffs up her billowing fuzzy blonde hair and powders her shiny face. She envelopes her head briefly in a cloud of, first, hairspray and then Youth Dew cologne. Finally, she pats herself down and is ready to go.

All my friends think I'm lucky to have such a lenient mother, and one who's dating too! What fun to live in an all-female household with no rules, where we can run through the hallways in our bras and underwear! We never walk around naked.

"Where are you girls going tonight?" my mother asks me.

"To the library," I say this with aplomb, knowing it's the truth. We're going to a bar conveniently named The Library. I'm aware that there's no real lie in my answer.

"Why the library so much suddenly?"

My mother is clueless. She's preoccupied, either dating Mickey Shapiro or dating a string of men at Jewish Singles. I'm trying to grow up as fast as I can, to quickly zoom through my teen years and leave for college before Mom makes the mistake of marrying one of these men, especially Mickey. Every now and then, normally because of Mickey commenting on the hooligans she's raising, she gets alert, starts asking questions. My nightmare is that she'll end up with him and they'll decide to shack up in one house or the other and then I'll be the one Mickey yells at during Passover, his new child.

"We ran out of books! It's so boring in Arizona in the summer!" I answer. Is she suspicious at how studious we've become in the middle of summer?

"Won't you be cold in the library dressed like that?" a flick of the hand at my outfit.

"Oh, this is just what's in style."

I'm wearing elephant baggie jeans, my hair fluffed and

ruffed. My perfume is heavier than my makeup, though I haven't discovered eyeliner yet.

Denise and I are wearing tube tops – it's hot out! – along with jute wedge shoes and carrying fringed leather shoulder bags, so heavy they almost drag on the floor. Wendy can't wear tube tops due to her double-D chest, so she wears a strapped halter top which kind of operates as a rope and pulley system for her chest. Not being a Burt girl like Denise and I, who would never wear shorts because of a mutual hatred of our white, pasty thighs, she wears shorts. There are a few unspoken rules for Burt girls – no shorts, absolutely no bathing suits, and no fattening soda pop after age fifteen.

My mom gives her face one final pat.

"I look good." It's half question and half statement. Yes, mom, you look good.

She goes on her way, and we go on our way, heading out into the hot summer night.

The combination of these tube tops, the Library, the Front Line, a teen bar we sometimes go to, hormonal males and teenage girls looking for love, is a success. I'm wearing these clothes because I want to meet a lot of guys and, even though I'm not good at math, I'm aware of the unerring equation that teenage girl + tube top = guys. I look around as we walk in, automatically sensing whether I'll have a good time or a bad one, mostly depending on the number of girls prettier than us. The three of us have an intuitive type of communication, knowing whether we should abandon one place and drive miles across town to another place where our youth will compensate for whatever we're lacking and guarantee attention.

The Library is where my sister meets her future husband, ending up on the dance floor with him all night. Mike is cute and young and rough-mannered. He satisfies all our family requirements to meet a fixer upper. That neatly checks off the dad box, since for the first decade or two after our dad's death various sisters date versions him – bad-tempered, self-made, drinkers.

As the summer winds on, each time we go out, I end up somewhere unplanned, in clutches with older guys in parking lots, making out while pressed up against their cars, or in ramshackle pick-up trucks parked somewhere, the desert night quiet around us. I stay out all night, sleep in late the next day. I'm having the time of my life, thinking this is what being grown up is all about, what being female is all about. I'm sure it's a compliment to be groped and grabbed.

I'm not exactly trying to be easy or sleazy, I'm trying to fall in love. Or, like my mother, end up with a guy who's good enough anyway.

I'm raising her and she's raising me.

Eighteen

The Silent Phone

I wake up well enough the next day, floating on the romance of the night before. This happens dozens of times. I'm full of my stories of the evening and eager to tell my sisters about the great guy I met. I'm optimistic he's my new boyfriend, or maybe I'll marry him, and of course I gave him my phone number – it would be unthinkable to make out with someone and not give him my number. And he has the greatest occupation ever, or I'm not sure of his occupation, it never came up, or he has the best job ever, even if he has no job and is living in his parents' basement smoking pot all day. I officially love a fixer upper, thinking every guy I meet is a hardworking blue-collar guy who's going to work his way up to the American Dream, just like my dad. At home, I open my diary to a fresh page each time, writing detailed accounts of the night, of the make out session, of each thing each guy said as if it all were a promise.

Then the inevitable question from my sister Sherry comes zooming at me, puncturing my fantasy.

"Did he call?"

I soon learn what the next day brings, the inevitable downside to all that rolling around and making out with strangers – waiting for phone calls. While I'm still floating, exuberant, I think the phone call is just a formality. I'm so certain that he's going to call that he could almost not call, and I'd still be able to live on the fumes of the night before. Isn't that true?

The day winds on and on with a silent phone and I start thinking that maybe I need to hold back a little, be a little more reticent in my story telling, holding something in reserve for after the phone call comes. Because, after all, how am I going to switch from "he is the greatest" to "I didn't like him that much" or "who?" when he doesn't call, having committed myself so heavily before?

I think, am I insane? How could my impressions be so far off? Was nothing last night as romantic as I imagined it to be? Eventually I realize that I'm not crazy, it's all true and it all absolutely doesn't matter. Anything that happens on the first night is never going to lead to a second night.

Despite my burning gaze willing the phone to ring, my imagination conducting the awkward but satisfying first phone call, most of the time the phone doesn't ring.

"How many days should I wait to see if he calls?" I ask Sherry, the expert. Because one of the rules that govern us is that girls are the waiters, the waitees. We hand out our phone numbers but would balk at taking one. We must be chosen, and we never choose. I am trapped in a female-centered inertia, the only question is how long should I wait before I give up waiting? The fine difference between actively waiting and chalking a guy off is very slim.

She shrugs. She does not have this problem ever. All the guys she meets call her.

Anyway, I get it. If he doesn't call, I can wait my whole lifetime. If he does, it better be by Wednesday.

We're at the Front Line, the teen bar in a seedy area of town. They serve soft drinks only, forcing us to spike our cups in the bathroom. There's the drunken wild laughter, the dancing, first fast and then dangerously slow. There's the eventual awareness that someone somewhere in this room has narrowed his gaze upon me. We meet and in the microcosm of an evening we zoom through all the stages of a relationship - talking, dancing, kissing, and, finally, driving off in the desert night in his VW bug to a dead-end street by a canal. The wild embrace, the roaming hands. Suddenly, it's time for my choice - is this guy as good as any other guy in the whole wide world on which to throw away my virginity?

Getting rid of my virginity is an emergency at this point, I think. Maybe even a family emergency. I know I can't live through one more day listening to my sister Sherry haranguing me about it, I need to enter the world of my sisters with all its attendant concerns – boyfriends, birth control and orgasms. I even need to enter the world of my mother, her door firmly locked at the end of the hallway.

The drive home after a make out session is distinctly different than the drive there. I had some kind of power at the beginning of the night, but it's gone now, firmly in his grasp. The power to call or not call, the power to say yes or no, after trying his best to change my no to a yes earlier. Would he call?

Would we date? Will he be my first boyfriend? Would we finish that story from earlier in the night and fall in love?

But no. Somewhere on the drive home, somewhere between the canal and my house, he makes a decision. I am not consulted. I can see him shaking himself alert as he realizes my age, frowning when he looks down at my number, like he's been in a fog and now some crucial fact is swimming to the surface of his brain.

"How old are you again?" he asks me.

"Fifteen," I chirp, now jumping through hoops. "You're nineteen, right?"

I make some ill-timed joke about statutory rape and how my mom is really cool about all this stuff. He doesn't seem to take this very well. The moment he remembers I'm underage is palpable. I can almost see the mental imagery floating in the air above his head – a judge's gavel slamming down, a clanking jail cell door. He drops me off and zooms away. Does the little piece of paper with my number on it flutter out of the window as he drives?

I walk in the house vaguely worried, but also exultant. Finally I can take my place among the sisters, a sexually active member of our family. I can't wait to tell my sister Sherry that she no longer has to ask me if I'm worried about dying a virgin.

I wake up the next morning, look in the mirror and I'm surprised. I look exactly like I looked the day before. Why would something like this not show on the outside? I peer in the mirror looking for a difference on the outside that shows the change on the inside. I see nothing, just the same old me, no scarlet letter appears magically on my forehead. I have cast off the purity required of an earlier generation for marriage – like ten years ago – and find I'm a little frightened. What have I done? Will anyone ever marry me now?

I wait for my sister to ask me what I'm going to do about my virginity if I knew the world was ending tomorrow. I am ready for her question.

My sister doesn't ask. This one day of the whole year she doesn't ask. I can't resist, so I tell her anyway. She is uninterested, disinterested even, in that particular way that conveys she doesn't remember ever being interested at all.

At work I'm still suspended somewhere between the glee of the night before and the faint worry about whether he'll call. My sisters know to give him the store number if he calls at home. Only the phone doesn't ring. I try to keep the store phone unused and unoccupied; I try to answer it every time it rings, but there's no call. My brother-in-law, who's heard about this escapade from my sister, who heard about it from Sherry, who heard it from me, consoles me in his own inimitable way.

He says, "He's not going to call! Do you seriously expect him to call?" He scoffs at me. "Why would he buy the cow when he got the milk for free? He already got what he wanted!"

I, apparently, am the cow.

It turns out I don't have a boyfriend. The phone doesn't ring. Just like that, with no sound at all, the relationship has run its course, a mad dash of a one-nighter. I am used, I am sullied, I am devirginized and, yes, I am milked. Worse, I have to face my brother-in-law's smirking face at work. At the edge of my brain comes a faint thought – maybe relationships aren't meant to be operated backwards, from intimacy on the first date to getting to know each other after that. I ignore that niggling thought.

"What are you dressing up as?" Wendy asks me that Halloween. This holiday now has nothing to do with candy and everything to do with meeting guys.

It's an unspoken rule that we don't dress up for Halloween as, say, a rabbit, or something that requires makeup that obscures, makeup that doesn't show us off, or makeup that would deflect us from this primary purpose. The main criteria for Halloween outfits are that they are sexy, I'm aware of this. I can be a hooker or a nightclub singer. I can be a madam of a bordello. I can be a Playboy Bunny, a sexy waitress or a French maid.

I answer Wendy. "I'm going as a prostitute."

Since I have no budget for a real costume, I choose my own conception of a prostitute, dressing in my usual clothes but taping some Monopoly money at my cleavage.

I end up meeting a guy named Kim – yes, a guy named Kim, like *A Boy Named Sue* – and he becomes my boyfriend for a lingering, anemic, unenthusiastic three months.

Kim has an apartment in some crummy area of Phoenix with a couple of other nineteen-year-olds living there, smoking bongs day and night while tough girls flit in and out, looking at me like I'm just some spoiled Scottsdale Princess that Kim's brought home for amusement. They don't know this, but I absolutely can't be that since we have no money. Yet, I'm aware in a classist type of way that I'm slumming. I try to act like all this is normal, just life – bongs and filth and mean, competitive girls who are ready to kick my spoiled/unspoiled ass if I look at them wrong, but really, I can't.

I have decided that since I officially Have A Boyfriend, I am going to consummate the relationship. I think this is just what we do in the Burt family, have serial boyfriends and serial sex.

Kim's bedroom contains one piece of furniture, a waterbed on which we end up after making out standing up. There are hands groping and clothes unfastening and me, worrying about my body – is it too fat? Does my control top hose leave an imprinted line running unevenly down my abdomen? Do my hips pop out of their restrain after being set free?

And then we slosh onto the bed. I am immediately criticized for not being lively enough. I make a mental note to become lively, which, as discussed with my friends at school, means that I'm not to lay like a corpse but do pelvic thrusts during the act. But if I move, the waterbed develops a wave and some type of mini tsunami rolls through it almost catapulting us over the edge. I'm not sure how to climb out of this thing.

I guess I don't get any better with time, or the second time, at least. I don't age like a fine wine, or maybe he's dating one of those nineteen-year-old tough girls hanging around his place, the ones who probably know how to do this better than me.

Kim is some kind of drug addict, I'm not sure what kind and, at first, I'm not even aware of this. It only occurs to me when we are on our very last phone call. He calls me intermittently, drunkenly, with noisy parties going on in the background. The phone calls get disjointed, we get disconnected midway, midsentence, mid-syllable sometimes. He slurs his words, admits to all the dope he's popped or smoked, admits in a heedless way that he's doing all this to retaliate against another woman, I guess the woman he's really involved with. I'm just the girl he calls to talk about her when he's messed up.

The relationship ends. I'm not sure who breaks up, I think it might have been Kim, but I've started to realize that in these grown-up relationships many times there is no clear winner or loser, people just fade away, stop calling, or both lose interest at the same time.

I'm not unhappy. I mean, I didn't like dating a guy with a girl's name anyway, I didn't enjoy explaining this to everyone over and over again, acting like it was normal, just part of my lexicon, correcting people innumerable times, "No, not *Ken*, *Kim*!"

There's one more quasi boyfriend. I meet a guy named Hal who is a salesman for Truly Nolan. This is a step up for me, a guy with a job. I'm not as thrilled later that week when he picks me up for a date driving his Truly Nolan Bug, a car that has black rodent ears on the roof, a long tail on the end, and whiskers on the front. At the end of our date he gets pulled over for speeding since he's pretty noticeable in a yellow bug with ears and a tail. Hal avoids the ticket by selling the police officer pest control services. I wait in the car, the apparent girlfriend of the guy who drives a rodent.

I look around at the wreckage of my nascent love life and assess how it's going. I am fifteen years and nine months old. I have had sex three times with two different guys, and I have really, really hated it. I have hated it somehow even more because I've been reassured that I would love it. I have been betrayed by promises of fireworks. I give up.

This is awkward because just as my sisters had raised me to be a hippie, I'm sure I've also been raised to be sexually active. The basic message I've gotten is that I am a Burt girl and Burt girls have sex. After I toss away my virginity, I am to have sex with my serial boyfriends. Boyfriend, sex, breakup. Boyfriend, sex, breakup. Sometimes, certainly, there's just boyfriend, breakup. And sometimes just sex, sex, sex, sex – no boyfriends, no breakups.

There's only one problem with this entire scenario – I'm not built for it. I'm a train wreck, stumbling, emerging emotionally bruised and battered, waiting tearfully and desperately for phone calls that never come, imagining myself in love and married to guys I never see again.

There are other expectations I absorb, not just from my family, but from my friends. Not only am I supposed to be having a lot of cool hippie boyfriends and sleep with them, but I'm also supposed to have overwhelming sexual urges, use terms like "I'm SOOOOO horny" or "I need to get laid." This is our patois, though I'm imagining something more like a torrid make out session rather than a terrifying naked guy. My sisters know something is fishy. They interrogate me and discover I am a great frozen iceberg. They provide helpful hints for my next boyfriend, having no idea that I've already decided there will be no more boyfriends. I'm in danger of becoming the family prude. As far as I can tell, some kind of wall has appeared between me and this life, maybe the Berlin

Wall or the Great Wall of Vagina.

I give up on everything. I'm not good at any of it. I figure I started too early, or I'm broken. A physical deformity or frigidity is not out of the question. Maybe I'm just the old obsolete Eastern European Jewish model, a psychological chastity belt conveniently built-in for fidelity and monogamy. If I were Catholic, I'd most likely be intended for the convent. Either way, I'm not built for this.

I decide not to do it anymore until I'm ready and to hell with being hassled. I'm going to wait till I grow up for grown up things. I become revirginized, regain my innocence. As the next three and one-half years pass chastely and quietly, as I have make out sessions that go no farther than over the shirt, maybe under the shirt over the bra, as I slow myself down to a near halt, as my virginity grows back inside my head at least if it can't grow back in my body, as my sisters tease me mercilessly about having sex once every light year, I think that somehow, someday, I'll know when it's time to say yes.

Nineteen

Death of a Store

One day I'm at the check stand with a customer weighing her produce when I realize that there's not only a cockroach inside her bag of oranges on the scale, but there's one on top of her back-combed hair and another one inside the scale, obscuring the number I'm trying to look at. I slam my hand against the side of the scale, trying to dislodge the roach, surprising the customer, but managing to get an accurate weight and price on the oranges.

I wonder – should I take something off for the weight of the roach?

After Dad dies, my brother-in-law gets roped into working at the store. He might have had other plans for his life rather than putting on a green produce apron and being our manager, but once he hitched his wagon to the Burt train in 1971, that was it, he keeps getting tethered to the ground. Just like George Bailey getting stuck in Bedford Falls in *It's a Wonderful Life*, Larry gets stuck in the produce store.

He is there to oversee Farmer's Produce Market's last few dying, writhing spasms before rigor mortis sets in, just to watch the last few customers run out the door of the building never to be seen again, with, yes, cockroaches in their hair and in their produce bags. Just to watch my sisters grab a few more packs of cigarettes from the cigarette display wall and sit on the second checkout stand smoking all day. Just to watch me steal my salary from the cash register and sell beer to my high school friends who drive all the way down there from the north end of town.

The thing about having a family business is that the arguing and complaining and talking about the store never ends – it's there when we're at the store and it's there at home, since now that Larry's the manager, he gets to argue with Mom all the time about plans he wants to implement and which she wants to resist. Finally, after arguing for weeks, when even she can't deny that the cockroaches have taken over and that we're probably selling more cockroaches than produce, he prevails in his decision to bomb the store. Not with dynamite, though that might have been a good idea, but with insecticide. We close for a day while the insecticide bomb goes off and then everyone but me – I have an asthma exemption – shovels out their hard little corpses until the place is habitable again.

My idea to save the store is less dramatic and less violent.

I'm a hippie so, of course, I think this place should look hipper, more like the burgeoning health food stores popping up here and there, instead of like a sad, old, abandoned and repurposed convenience store with a polyglot assortment of coolers and tables inside holding the produce and broken-down cash registers. What we need, I think, is a diagonal wood exterior.

I argue my point, "It's so in style, so modern, and we should have a cutesy sign to play up the natural food angle!"

Unfortunately, no one is enthused with my idea and for some reason they're the bosses, not me, the teenage cashier. My idea has some merit, however, so it gets downgraded and downgraded to basically "cutesy sign" which, of course, we're not going to pay someone to create, so I am handed some cans of paint and a paintbrush and am told to implement this cutesy sign on the front window, in my self-taught graphic letters. I spend a Saturday happily out there painting "Fresh Delicious Fruits and Vegetables" on the window. Customers come by all day and say, "Wow! You're an artist! If you can do that, why do you work here?" I look at them. I'm sixteen by then – what else should I be doing with my life? It hasn't even begun yet. It's either sit behind that register and ring up bags of cockroaches or sit out here and paint.

I paint.

Finally, three things happen: the cockroach army advances, the new, more resilient ones who have survived the insecticide bomb, a fruit fly swarm descends, appearing out of nowhere, and our income dries up. The paid employees who are not indentured family servants notice the shift and quit one by one by one, to get real jobs at the real grocery store across the street. To do anything, really in the world, except work there.

Nothing can save the store. Not the insecticide bomb, not Larry's college business classes, not my hand-painted sign in the window.

We lose our business with the help of everyone

involved. Dad's ghost haunts the place, causing a fluffy white cloud to appear in an otherwise clear sky only above our store. Mom orders the cheapest, most cockroach-ridden produce she can find. I eat all the profits in the first of my teenage weight swings. And my sister sits on the second checkout stand smoking cigarettes and ashing on everything in sight. The customers abandon us in one fell swoop.

By 1977, our store is for sale, or at least something is for sale. It turns out we own just about nothing. We don't own the display cases with the lights we flip on at the start of our workday and off at the end. We don't own the sprayers we use to hose down the vegetables so they'll look shiny and wet. We don't own the building. We don't own the two cash registers with their broken side doors, the spools of register tape that keep popping out, the change drawers that won't stay shut. We don't own the coolers where we go to fill up the milk, the eggs, the cheese, first throwing on the giant men's coat that hangs on a peg by the door.

We don't own the coat.

We own the name, Farmer's Produce Market. For that, in July 1977, my mother gets four thousand dollars. And we own the debt. Twelve thousand dollars to Associated Grocers for produce bought but not paid for, a debt that my mother painstakingly pays down dollar by dollar over the next five years.

Instead of fulfilling Dad's dreams of making us rich, the store makes us poor, eating up all of our money, until there's nothing left. It's gone and so is Dad. One day we close the store for good, sliding those plate glass doors shut for the last time.

My mom's paperwork tells the story. There are liens from the IRS, then satisfactions. There are lawsuits against her for debts incurred on behalf of our store, finally satisfaction and suit dismissals. Short of a judgment, a lawsuit, or the IRS, my mother is not going to pay a bill willingly, even after she starts making money. She doesn't want to pay anything associated with any of this, even the lawyer who handles all these lawsuits, waiting until he, too, files suit. And then, attorney-less, she pays.

After Dad dies and we lose the store, we have just the shell of prosperity. There's the house, saddled with its burdensome mortgage for twenty-eight more years. There's the acre lot filled with broken and semi-broken cars, and the aging Lincoln Continental that my mother has somehow agreed to buy from Mickey Shapiro. He doesn't drive old cars.

With all that debt, all those collectors, I learn when to hang up a phone. I have a sixth sense about whether a person calling our house is from a collection agency. A collection agent is never heard out, I know my job – I immediately hang up. If someone dares to ask for my father by name I answer with a resounding rejoinder of, "He's dead!" which normally will end a call abruptly. The front door is answered cautiously and suspiciously and is never opened for process servers. My mother is officially never home.

No one really talks about money, just about outsmarting the collection agencies. I know that my mother is scraping by, keeping this house and pool afloat through some magical combination of determination, sweat, perseverance, and optimism.

The family in Chicago doesn't seem to know about any of this. Our mother is proud and will not ask for help. It didn't help that our father had painted such a picture of his Arizona prosperity – of the pool, the house, the acre, the store – that there was probably never a question in their minds that our mother was left a very rich widow, indeed.

"Why are we doing this, Mom?"

I am mortified at our errand one hot July day after losing the store.

We are driving, driving, driving, from north Scottsdale to South Scottsdale, to apply for welfare.

We'd accepted food stamps at our store, my parents continually amazed that customers could tear these out of a little coupon book to pay for food. We'd then send the food stamps into the state and receive real money back in exchange. To my mother, if money is being given out for free, she is getting in line. This is how we end up driving in our aging Lincoln Town Car on our way to a welfare office on a hot July day in Arizona.

I don't approve of her overall scheme. I'm sure that we aren't the people that food stamps are meant for, that this is one more example of my mother trying to get something for nothing, and it mortifies me. Real poor people are the ones food stamps are intended for, not us. Like people who are really starving. Yes, it is true that we have no food to speak of and that I've opened the panty door more than once to find only Saltines in there. Yes, we have no money except for the Aid to Dependent Children government checks that show up because of my father's death, a set amount for each of us still in school. As we finish school, or as school finishes with us, the money dries up. Yes, we share clothes, depending on who's the same size. Yes, haircuts are out of the question because they cost money. One sister takes the vintage Liberty Head silver dollars my dad gave me for safekeeping and spends them on cigarettes.

But the glow from Skokie that I was born with cannot subside. It is a glow of denial, the glow of a now dead but hard-working father who I thought was immortal and who got up and worked every day without fail, bringing money in without fail. It was the glow of shying away from anything bad, from my parents' Holocaust stories to financial concerns. The glow of proving to them through sheer optimism that nothing bad could ever happen to us. My brain shut down at the thought of it, my ears shut, my eyes. I'm a product of 20th century America – everything is just fine as long as I don't think too deeply about it.

Really, we're just broke. Mom lurks around the house pondering how exactly she's going to pay the mortgage, pay the outstanding bills from the store, put food on the table, and I watch her when I'm not rattling around the empty pantry, or with my sisters, buying one dollar of gas at a time.

I get in the car with my mom anyway because I'm her little pal for zooming around town, and we head off. I note that she hasn't dressed down, even though she's going to a welfare office. A smart pumpkin-colored polyester suit, square-heeled pumps, a jumbled, aging leather bag, and her hair – never touched by a hairbrush, only by someone putting rollers in it, done in a perfect ash blonde bouffant. My mother would never dream of visiting a government office without looking snazzy. She wasn't some greenhorn! She knew how to look sharp, like an American.

I, on the other hand, am dressed perfectly in my role as a welfare teen, wearing ill-fitting jeans and an over-washed top, both of which could easily have come from a garbage pile somewhere. Since I haven't yet figured out the broad categories of hair or makeup, my hair lays in lank brown shanks next to my oily skin. It certainly isn't my happiest thought, but it is true – my mother looks better at forty-seven than I do at seventeen.

We pull in the parking lot, and I note that we appear to be the only ones pulling up at the welfare office in a Lincoln Continental. I try to calculate the mathematical improbability of being Jewish, driving a Lincoln, albeit an old one, and pulling up at the DES office, but the statistics are out of this world. Knowing we're an anomaly, however, doesn't help my humiliation.

Whether we truly qualify for food stamps or not isn't the issue with my mom. Yes, we lost our store. Yes, she is having a hard time getting a job that pays any money maybe because all of her formal education took place in Lithuania and was interrupted at age eleven, on the day the Nazis marched into town. Somehow, in the space on the job applications for "Education" there's no room for her to write in that her education was interrupted by Nazis, by the fact that in the forest there was nothing but survival, that she wasn't able to resume her education until she arrived in a Displaced Persons Camp after the war. That she tried to be just a regular American college student when she got to the U.S. in 1949 at age nineteen, but she wasn't like the other girls, bobby-soxed,

221

poodle-skirted, girls who hadn't starved. There's no way to fit that on the application.

My mother is determined to get these food stamps and in that she has no shame. After all those years of accepting food stamps at our store, now it's her turn. Maybe she thinks it's War Reparations of a type, and she's a Holocaust Survivor, so she qualifies. God knows Germany hadn't paid her anything. Maybe it started further back, when my mother was living in the forest that stretched out through Eastern Europe and running from the Nazis, begging food from house to house in Polish villages. What were food stamps, really, but paper food?

"You're coming in?" She asks me, half statement, half question.

I roll my eyes. This means no.

"Maybe the clerk will ask me something I don't know."

"Please, Ma. I just can't." I still have no conception of how broke we are.

"Fine. You wait in the car."

I nod.

She goes in the office. I hide. She comes out with the food stamps and pulls the car back out onto the road. I emerge. She might not be embarrassed by applying for welfare, but she's savvy enough to insist that we grocery shop here, twenty miles away from our house, where there's no chance of running into anyone she knows. That kind of shame she understands.

Then we drive and drive and drive, all the way back up to north Scottsdale from south Scottsdale. Till the next week when we do it again.

There are many difficulties for my mother after my father dies. Like this difficulty of being destitute. The difficulty of being single and trying to sort through all the losers and bums to find a gem, which is not her forte. Now she sits pondering her next move while shuffling the unpaid bills like a poker player as collection agents pound on our door and ring the phone off the hook.

She begins entertaining new occupations. What kind of job should she get? What kind of job *could* she get? She'd been taught how to sew in the Displaced Person camp and, for the next twenty-five years of her life, while ostensibly a Skokie housewife, she was also a seamstress, once even creating her own label with a friend and selling their dresses in department stores in downtown Chicago.

Naturally, then, she thinks she should work in some field related to clothing. She takes a job at I. Magnin, a high-end department store known for its fleet of foreign-accented saleswomen who know how to fit clothes. My mother lasts one day. No matter the alleged prestige of working there, my mother somehow knows that she can do better than this, than the insulting $4.25 an hour, that she can not only hustle more but that she can be the master of the hustle.

She decides to go into sales.

The Amway folks come by to give her a sales pitch, but she's put off by their Christian air. Then the Fuller Brush people come by, but she's uncomfortable with the idea of lugging brushes from door to door. She toys with the idea of selling for these companies but decides against them. She finds her heart just isn't in cleaning. Then she hears about something new – a diet in a can – Slender Now – the 1970s precursor to Slim Fast. Like Fuller Brush and Amway, Slender Now is sold only out of people's homes in some kind of primitive pyramid scheme.

She throws herself into the dieting world with fervor, rising in the ranks, becoming an area manager, and eventually using our entire house as her warehouse, stacking cases and cases of products everywhere, lining the closets, the tabletops, even encroaching on my bedroom when new shipments arrived.

"Ladies, do you want to get your life back? Your figure back?" My mother is like a fiery preacher, exhorting the women gathered in our family room. I sneak through the living room on my way to the kitchen to avoid detection. It's a tent revival in there, with women sobbing and hopeful and buying. It helps that my mother is completely genuine.

Selling Slender Now is the perfect product for my mother to sell. She's spent years battling a maddening five to ten-pound weight problem and so she understands the dream of losing weight, the belief that the weight loss would change her life, and she understands the excess weight as an eternal adversary and permanent foe.

My mother, the dieting optimist, can convince anyone that this diet will work, and it *will* work for them with her cheering them on. She is permanently on the diet since she considers herself a walking advertisement for her products and she's no huckster, she has to believe in what's she's selling. She might never have been more than ten pounds overweight, but it was a very unhappy ten pounds overweight, as she would remind us. That ten pounds was enough, ultimately, to destroy her happiness and her health, ruin her marriage, since Dad had made fun of her for being fat while apparently all of his girlfriends had no problem keeping their bodies trim and sleek. If only she'd had this diet back then!

She is on the phone constantly, more than ever before and that's saying a lot. I listen to the dreams she's selling, and these become my dreams – the dream of the once-thin body, how if I had it again then everything would be fine, my whole life would be better. She tells them about the diet plan, about how they'll be transformed, how their lives will change, how their husbands will love them better, or their boyfriends, or their boyfriends and their husbands, both at the same time. She sells a lot of product.

I go on the diet several times, of course. How could I resist? It was free, all I had to do was crack open one of the cans stacked around the house, replace two meals a day with delicious milkshakes, and eat up to a pound of meat for the third meal – my interpretation of the directions.

Ever since I'd emerged from our shiva cocoon after my dad's death, food had called to me. One day, sitting on the second island at the store, waiting for customers, the aroma from some just-delivered, fresh-baked tortillas wafted through the air to me, and that was that. So I understand my mother's presentation – I want to magically transform too.

I am amazed that on this diet I lose weight with the metabolism of a teenager. Of course, I *am* a teenager. I can lose the majority of the weight in three hard weeks on the diet. Three weeks from despised to revered, three weeks from ignored to sought after, three weeks back into my thin jeans.

I love the weight loss time periods, all the attention I get from everyone at school, all the compliments and the admiration for my newly svelte body appearing from out of nowhere. I also enjoy eating my way back up because I longed for the food I had been avoiding. This also stops the stream of compliments immediately. Somehow, I am more comfortable when my outside serves as a test of true friendship, of loyal boyfriends, of no boyfriends. I gain it all back.

My mother knows her customers well. Sure, here and there was an actual overweight woman looking for a diet to turn her life around, but most of the women buying from her are just like Mom, women who believe that a ten-pound weight loss will transform their existence. They sit there, a sea of normal-sized women on our couch, listening to Mom's *shpiel*, nodding their heads and getting positively teary-eyed over her weight story, over the intractable ten pounds. They also had lost their husbands' love due to their weight problems! They also had suffered from debilitating diseases and humiliation at the doctors' offices! They also had not had one day of peace or happiness, all due to the eight to ten pounds that were destroying their lives!

It helps that the diet works.

Just when the refrigerator is full, the pantry stocked, and there is gas in all our tanks, there's a sudden rumbling about trouble in the company, something about regulations and broken laws and pyramid schemes. Overnight, almost the entire Board of Directors ends up in jail or on trial, under some type of investigation. The entire structure falls down.

We end up with cases and cases of stale Slender Now powder in our closets and desperate customers calling my mother day and night for some product, like junkies for a fix. She doesn't know exactly what to do but she does know she's not allowed to sell it any longer, instantly losing all of her income.

Again the upscale department store beckons, this time offering her $4.75 an hour. Again Mom says no. This time she is buoyed up by her success with Slender Now and has a legitimate sales resume along with the awareness that she's a natural saleswoman. She is going into real estate.

Twenty
One-Woman Habitat for Humanity

My mother covers the phone receiver with her hand, shushing me when I walk in a room talking.

"I'm on the phone with a client!"

She does this like this is an unusual situation, like it's her first real estate client ever. I recognize that that's exactly what makes her amazing at her new occupation, she treats every client like they're her first, and she treats every client like a VIP even though most of her clients are poor. To her, every home buyer and home seller exists in a beautiful, perfect balloon, the only balloon in the sky. She will concentrate her considerable effort on each, regardless of the outcome for her bank account. She is a one-woman Habitat for Humanity.

When my mother gets licensed as a real estate agent, she doesn't get hired at a regular office. No John Hall for her, none of the regularity of Coldwell Banker or Century 21. There are long complicated reasons why she doesn't go to these places – her sewing background will just not allow for the little gold jackets as required attire, maybe there's too much floor time answering phones, or brutal percentages for agents. She has some inner barometer about the type of place she can thrive and instinctively knows it has to be less corporate, maybe family-owned. So she finds the most family-owned of them all, a two-location real estate company called Lund Properties.

Lund Properties is one big, happy, philandering, family-owned real estate company, where nepotism rules the day. It's owned by Will Simpson and his wife, and they employ their sons and daughters and the various spouses and ex-spouses of those sons and daughters in the business. As a matter of fact, since everyone there seems to be sleeping with everyone else, there are spouse and ex-spouse designations being formed and reformed every day. Dan Simpson, the crown prince and heir-apparent of Lund Properties, is one of those sons. My mother soon learns that no one is allowed to outperform Dan Simpson. Yet she does.

When my mom gets the real estate job with the Simpsons, she is absorbed into their strange, sexually charged world of affairs, counter affairs, office intrigues and peccadilloes. She is oblivious to this all. Circumspect and businesslike, she doesn't notice the sexual undercurrents at work, at their house, at their company parties – because it turns out that when a person works for Lund Properties, they must go to all of these places. Every agent is instantly a part of their giant, sprawling, codependent real estate family.

She is incapable of seeing the ugliness of this place. She can't perceive that the leisure-suited men are lecherously stalking the women in lowlier positions than themselves. Even though she is so American by 1977, sleeping and dreaming in English even, she understands none of this with her European shtetl sensibilities. She's not very playful overall, and if she was, it wouldn't be with sex. To her, playful is a pack of cards, poker, maybe Kalookie. To my mother, work is work.

Once she understands what the definition of work is in her new career – that she needs to match up those wanting to buy houses with those wanting to sell houses and, conversely, match up those wanting to sell houses with those wanting to buy houses, she is an automaton. She works floor, answering the office phone calls, a job the other agents dread, and picks up dozens of new clients on her assigned days, a job the other agents dread. She doesn't exactly understand – this is work? This pleasurable activity, this yakking on the phone, is work?

Since she starts this job with no expectation of what is possible and what is impossible, she achieves the impossible, selling nonstop. She lists nonstop. She sells her own listings and lists her own sellings. She is unstoppable. She doesn't quite get that this can't be done. She's a trainee, of course, and as a trainee she has to answer the phone a lot. But they don't know my mother. In her hands a phone is magic. She can reach through a handset and envelope the person at the other end in warmth and understanding, completely unfeigned. She could have a conversation with a wall, she is so friendly. And the wall would talk back. She becomes a one-woman real estate office within the real estate office. She trains new women agents helpfully, thrilled to have new friends. Dan Simpson plots against her but she just keeps on moving.

She wins every monthly Lund Properties sales award, and our house, now cleared of stacks of Slender Now canisters, fills up with golden real estate lady trophies marching on all the shelves, carrying their little golden briefcases everywhere and engraved with her name. This new career, more than anything, marks her name change, from Helen the housewife to Helene the real estate agent.

My mother uses no high-pressure sales tactics. She just honestly falls in love with every house she looks at, even if it is a clapboard shack. She sees it filled with a happy family and imagines how that house could change a family's life, how home ownership will transform them. She is able to put herself into the eye of the beholder for each buyer. She becomes one with them, oohing and aahing over stained carpeting, over worn, pressed wood cabinets, over chipped laminate countertops, over bathrooms with rusty pipes, that just "need a little work." She is the queen of sweat equity.

As she stands there, she imagines each place her home, honestly assessing just how the furniture schlepped from Chicago would fit in each tiny living room, how her magnificent chandelier would attach to the popcorn ceiling in the dining rooms, how her car would fit perfectly in the one-car carports.

My mother doesn't follow the assumed-desirable course of a real estate career – pursuing ever richer clients and ever greater commissions. My mother is the opposite – she doesn't like rich people, finding them disloyal and demanding. She almost spits and snaps when she talks about the *chazer* rich clients she had one time, how she took them everywhere, spent all her time with them, became their best friends, and then they casually let it drop in conversation that they thought they were going to go with a house their other realtor had shown them. *Other realtor?* This was like a husband suddenly mentioning his other wife.

She prefers working her fingers to the bone for the poorest of the poor, people with no down payment, bad credit, no job, living off the occasional rabbit that strays into their backyard. She likes a challenge, and she likes to change their lives by changing their addresses. She is convinced that homeownership can fix any problem. These clients become as loyal to her as she is to them, become lifelong family members. I marvel at the cards that arrive at the house – bushels of Christmas cards from all the people to whom she's sold homes.

I say, "But Mom, don't they know you're Jewish?"

She says, "No, it never came up."

She's still using camouflage. Christmas cards run in both directions, from her house to theirs as well.

She identifies with the underdog. Like a creation story, she recites her immigration story. Once she, too, was a stranger in this country. Once she was poor.

When my mother becomes a realtor, suddenly there's a new language spoken in our house. There are listings and escrows and lenders and commissions and title companies. The phone is her livelihood, and the car is her livelihood. She is born for this job. She has a built-in calculator in her head on which she can do real estate math – interest and taxes and down payments, closing costs, points, amortization, and equity. There are her phone calls to clients, to sellers, to other agents, to banks, to escrow officers. The tedium of it, the nonstop pre-approval of it, the interest rate of it, the qualifying of it, all get to me. I shut my ears, determined to never understand real estate.

There are home tours, when the real estate agents in her office must visit each other's listings – quite an event, a convoy of Mercedes Benzes and BMWs swarming down a street, like a fancy funeral procession. The problem is that my mother's listings are dumps, part of her master plan to corner the market on the lowest priced housing in Phoenix, the ramshackle, weather-beaten, condemned home market – one step away from the wrecking ball – the cash cow that, somehow, all her colleagues were ignoring. The other agents seem to have a problem visiting these, yet they couldn't doubt her success.

My mother thrives in real estate. She's thrilled each week when the multi-page, multi-volume Multiple Listing Service books get delivered to her office. She digs right in. This is her favorite reading.

The MLS book contains thousands of pages of all the houses for sale, volume by volume, in each area of town. In the 1970s, the book contains a small box for each house listed, with details and some abbreviations, along with the addresses. There are no pictures of the homes in the books at the time. Sometimes, at wit's end for some reading material while eating, I thumb through these monstrosities because they are always on the kitchen table and I'm always at the table, trapped at home with no car. I'll try to read anything, even an MLS book. It's pretty dry reading. After a few squares listing the number of bedrooms, bathrooms, whether each house has a pool, a carport, or a fireplace, I pretty much abandon the idea.

And, since it's the 70s in Phoenix, we're dealing with some pretty basic stuff. Who needs pictures of the houses anyway? They're all rectangular flat boxes like our own, with maybe an arch in front to dress themselves up. The front yards are gravel, palm trees, and cacti. They're either made out of beige or orange slump block or gray cinder block stuccoed over in various earth-toned colors. Even though the city is surrounded by mountains and there are even mountains sitting right in the middle of the city in some places, none of the descriptions mention this. Things are pretty practical here in 1970s Phoenix – there's no concern for mountain views, no concern about being on main streets. The only concern is for swimming pools.

My mother has infinite patience for this activity. These pages and pages of words, of boxes, of lists, don't bore her, they thrill her. She has an encyclopedic knowledge of zip codes and school zones and addresses, so she never has to wonder where anything is, she can zero in on properties like she has radar. She knows who built every single house and development around us, what the models were, and the elevations. She knows immediately if it's what her clients are looking for. The next step is driving to each house to preview it. Then she's ready to take the clients there.

After her game of matchmaker, when she has successfully matched the client with the house, comes the most difficult part of her job – getting them approved. Since she only takes on the poorest of the poor clients, since she can't stand the affluent, this creates quite a ruckus in our house every time. There are the incessant calls to Stewart Title, trying to hold the deal together. There's the manufacturing of some believable occupation for the buyers, something the mortgage company might believe. There are tax stubs, hand-written notes about unverifiable income, babysitting. There are other calls – to the other real estate agent, asking them to reduce their commission to hold the deal together. There's the reducing of her own commission to do the same. There is wheedling, pleading, cajoling, counterfeiting, plagiarizing, exaggerating, and, slowly, my mother's deals move towards completion. Nailed together, bandaged together, bleeding and hobbling, they arrive at a closing date. The buyer gets the keys to their new dream home, and my mother, after pocketing her now-five-hundred-dollar commission, comes home with a gift, usually a house plant, for which I have conveniently constructed many macramé hangers.

Even with selling the lowest priced houses in town to the poorest of clients, money starts rolling in. First, she pays off all the debt from the store and our phone stops ringing night and day with the sounds of collection agents. When she can afford a new car, she buys a Toyota. This purchase sends a secret message to Mickey Shapiro across the street, that she is humble and he is ostentatious, like planting a flag in the ground. They are on again and off again.

The next thing she does with her money is she builds a cabin up near Flagstaff, in northern Arizona, a lovers' getaway for her and Mickey when they're on again, since they have no peace down in Scottsdale with their teenage children. Her choice of Flagstaff is influenced by Mickey's desire to be out of the heat in the summer. So my mother takes cash and uses it to build a cabin. None of us should bother going up there – we're actually not welcome up there – as this will finally be their love nest and they can live their lives idyllically there until each one of us leaves home and then they can sneak back to town.

She builds the cabin the only way she knows how. She funnels cash into it, never considering a mortgage or a construction loan or a dime owed to anyone or anything. No, she's going to own this pile of logs and stone fireplaces all by herself, it will be her own little *Krivichi* house of her own.

It's supposed to be a cabin, but my mother is simply unable to build a cabin. The real estate agent inside of her only thinks in terms of numbers of bedrooms and bathrooms and two-car garages and resale prices, and so her cabin ends up being a three-bedroom, two-bathroom house. Inside it is cabin-like, with tongue and groove floors and walls and countertops and wood furniture and even wood toilet seats, so that walking in feels like entering a tree.

She hires a guy to build it and he works alone for months, pounding nails, wielding hammers, putting it together one tongue and groove plank at a time. It takes a long, long time to rise from its lot. Every decision requires another drive up north for my mother. River rock for the two fireplaces or some other stone? Knotty pine for the floor or unknotty pine? Wood for the countertop or wood-looking Formica?

My mom rolls eighty thousand dollars of cash into it. Mickey, being retired from whatever mysterious job he held back east, doesn't have anything to contribute. Well, only his opinions. He must have paneling. He must have a tweedy couch and a recliner big enough for a real man. He must have a real dining room table where he can hold forth on myriad topics in a loud booming voice, drowning out all others.

All of my junior year in high school she is up there,

bringing armloads of cash to the carpenter building it, supervising construction.

What could they have been doing, all those countless weekends in Flagstaff, my mom and Mickey? Now I can imagine the whole thing. Barreling up there in Mickey's shining new blue Town Car, the seats like couches, the hood of the car zooming off somewhere in the distance in front they drive two hours north. I imagine them supervising every inch of the cabin as it is built, piece by piece – the diagonal wood, the wood counter, the beamed ceilings, and the wood stove.

I imagine them finally living in the cabin, watching TV on a forlorn 17-inch Zenith, my mom directed by Mickey to constantly get up and change the channels. I imagine how disappointing Flagstaff must be for Mickey because, as far as I can tell, he prefers to be a big shot, not an anonymous nothing in a city filled with college students and intersecting highways. I imagine steak dinners and cigars.

All I knew down in Scottsdale was that the cabin was saving my life, keeping my mom and Mickey happily unmarried.

Mom had a couple standard excuses for when people would ask why she and Mickey weren't married. It was either, "my girls don't like him," like anyone on the planet could like him, or "the kids don't get along," like we're the Brady Bunch, but bad.

It was more complex than that. Certainly, our family had its share of xenophobia – we basically only like us. Our xenophobia stops some of us from making friends outside of the sisters or later may even awkwardly exclude our own husbands. But this wasn't why we didn't like Mickey. He was brash, ignorant yet opinionated, rude, and brutalized his sons. He had no use for, nor interest in, girls as human beings. He had strong opinions on how we should have been raised and would declare them without compunction.

Based on these characteristics, there must be geography and distance between the seven of us and Mickey Shapiro – a lot of space, preferably a hundred miles or more. Two hours north is perfect.

Mom's relationship with him depends on planting him in Flagstaff and keeping all of us down in Phoenix and making sure the two parts of her life never collide. Sometimes there's an awkward situation, like a sister asking for an invite to the cabin, or winter shows up and they'd have to abandon Flagstaff, returning to Scottsdale, and my mother would go back to ricocheting between our house and his. Sometimes they breakup and there's rejoicing on our side of the street. Mom makes a few forays out into the dating world, boinging around, from love interest to love interest. Boinging lower and ever lower. When none of them pan out, it leaves her inevitably and inexorably drawn to Mickey, the lowest rung on the boyfriend ladder, still ensconced in the identical house across the street, still glaring out of the front window, also identical to ours.

I ponder, does she really think Mickey is better than nothing?

I'm left alone down in Scottsdale, in charge of the house, a perfect alchemy of location, hormones, and teenage friends.

I have a parentless household, sometimes even a sisterless household. Dad dead, Mom gone, Mickey away from his prying perch across the street, my sisters off with various love interests here and there. Just me in charge and Mindy at home and I'm in charge of her.

So every day after school during my junior year of high school, the party is at my house. I am more concerned with having the house alone, with planning my after-school parties with my hippie friends lounging all over our wood paneled family room with its beehive fireplace, and weekend parties with beer cans and bottles littering the street the morning after, to really worry about the future of Mom and Mickey.

I don't really think of myself as the surly teen daughter, ready to hate all her boyfriends yet, there it is, I hate all her boyfriends. I didn't like her Jewish Singles boyfriends, like Victor, who preached at me to cook steaks in butter. I disliked Harold from Philadelphia who was too dapper and polished for us. I definitely didn't like when my desperate uncle from Chicago, single since my aunt's death six years prior, showed up at our door with a proposal, saying, "Nu, Chasia?" before she sent him packing. Yes, there's a Brady Bunch dream in my head too, that Mom will find this great professor-type husband who wears smoking jackets and comes to live in our house with his own eligible teen sons and we will all fall in love and live happily ever after.

But that doesn't happen. Apparently, with the pressure on, she must pick someone. It's the seventies and no one's allowed to be happy alone.

She picks Mickey.

Twenty-One
Jewish in Name Only

Cantor Kirshner, who seems to be in our house a lot after my father's death, asks a question of my mother one day, in worried, wheedling tones, and a Transylvanian accent.

"Why the girls aren't in BBG? They don't go to meet boys at BBYO?" I soon learn these abbreviations refer to B'nai B'rith Girls, a Jewish teen youth group, and the combined boy and girl group, B'nai B'rith Youth Organization.

My mother is caught unawares. Was there something she was supposed to do to raise us Jewish besides fill our heads with horror stories from the Holocaust?

She frowns. "I don't know. Should they be?"

My mother, who has never spent one second worrying about her daughters' involvement in anything Jewish in the world, starts wondering too, or at least she starts wondering if everyone else is wondering, and this is enough to set her to wondering. We had never been in anything formally Jewish, from Hebrew school to a synagogue, not just B'nai B'rith Girls, which is the group you'd graduate to when you'd actually had a proper Jewish education. She realizes, somewhat belatedly, that she's been remiss. We're running wild. She tries to close the fence, but the herd has already broken free.

The Cantor isn't the only one asking. My mother is inundated with this and other well-meaning advice. Much of it surrounds the exact amount of desperation with which she needs to approach her man-less state. She takes this very seriously. After all, she hasn't been single since 1951, what does she know? Could the world have changed so much? In 1951 she needed to be married. In 1975, the same.

The other advice she gets from all the *yentas* and *yachnehs* has to do with the daughters running wild like a bunch of *banshees* through town. The older ones should be married already and the married one should have had children already. Was there a problem? I hear them trying to wheedle information out of my mother. *Nu*, no *kinder*? Of course, there's no hope of any of us landing one of the advice-givers' children in marriage because we've been marked by our family reputation, but maybe, just maybe, somewhere in the local Jewish community, there could be someone stupid enough not to know we've been running wild, feral. And they may just be hoodwinked into marrying one of us.

Wendy, Denise, and I have been assured that if we go to this BBYO meeting – the teen boys' and girls' groups together – we will fit in just by the fact that we have Jewish mothers, not to mention Jewish fathers, and because our *shtetl* lineage is impeccable as far back as anyone might want to check. Wendy is American-born, but my sister and I have the bona fide of the Holocaust, which I think adds to our pedigree. We have been cajoled, nagged, and harangued into going to a gathering. We've been told we will be the most beautiful girls there, that boys will fall over themselves trying to get to us.

We walk into the meeting late since we only operate on Jewish time. All the teens are sitting in a big, loopy circle which takes up the entire area of the synagogue social hall. In the fragments of voices that fade away just before our entrance, they were introducing themselves, explaining their names and Hebrew schools, Jewish camps, and trips to Israel.

We walk in and all conversation stops, sentences fragment, break, float off in the air, little dot ellipses hanging there above the leader's head. We burst in like someone has scooped up three prostitutes from the street and hauled them in to snatch up all the little Jewish boys when the proprietary Jewish girls aren't looking. We are made up, curled up, dressed in stretchy tube tops and wooden-heeled Dr. Scholl's shoes, clunking noisily, our cheap purses flung over our shoulders. My sister and Wendy have packs of cigarettes and lighters tossed in their purses. A billowing aroma of tobacco follows them in.

The three of us look around at the circle of unfriendly faces, the girls narrow-eyed and angry and the boys looking at us like dinner has arrived, or maybe like they'd like to grasp the edges of our tube tops and pull south.

Into the dead silence and with wide-eyed disbelief, someone says, "Are you looking for the BBYO meeting?"

Denise, our spokesperson, takes the cue – we need to scram. She speaks for us, answers that question with exactly what we know they all want to hear – we know they'd never find seats for us anyway. We instinctively know that our family background isn't good enough, Skokie and the Holocaust can't cut it with this crowd. We need Bat Mitzvahs to fit in, the Wailing Wall, Camp Ramah.

She says, "Oh, no. That's not what we're looking for. I think we're in the wrong place."

Yeah, we're in the wrong place.

Wendy and I murmur our agreement and we turn around and leave the room and, as we head down the hall, we hear a little more silence in there then a lot of talk then a resumption of the single voices that we'd interrupted.

Having tried this once, there's a feeling of finality about it, that Jewish boys aren't for us, how could they be? We're done with them after this one ten-minute adventure. We head out into the cool Arizona spring evening. We cruise Central Avenue, meet some guys. I get told I'm beautiful and desirable, even if I'm not pure, even if I'm not sheltered, even if I could have been a nice girl but I've have veered off the path and don't even know how to get back on. I don't even know how to want that.

Judaism is not an option.

It turns out that being raised Jewish in name only is not enough. It was fine being a Jewish ignoramus while in Skokie, where I could be Jewish by osmosis. When we move to Arizona things are different. The population around us is overwhelmingly church-going and Christian, and we are not synagogue-attending Jews. With no hard knowledge of our religion, it is stuck being defined by what it's not – no Jesus, no Christmas trees, no churches, no crosses, no Easter, no Santa. After that it gets wiggly because my ignorance is so great. Mentions of the Bible or the Psalms results in the same judgement. These are Christian things.

I think of the what ifs, like if there'd been an amazing rabbi performing Dad's funeral maybe my family wouldn't have shrugged off our religion. If only that awful Cantor hadn't shown up with his briefcase at the shiva, selling Mom life insurance. If only the BBYO kids had flung their circle wide and welcomed us. If only this and if only that, all these things in a row, like dominoes. Maybe then we'd still be Jewish?

Instead, Judaism is all the Chicago relatives swooping in with their uncontrollable grief and mourning and the sense that they have no use for any of us once he's gone. It's the heavy thud of my aunts' bodies as they throw themselves against the casket – their grief solid, palpable, physical. It's the horrible sun-filled day in the green-grassed cemetery. It's us leaving our father there, the rabbi the first one to hop in his car and drive away.

Our Jewishness is a little nebulous when we subtract out what it isn't. It's family and uproarious laughter, and a certain *haimish* sensibility that we can't put into words because we don't know the word *haimish*. Or *mishpocheh*. It's food when we're trying to diet and it's even *that*, the eternal diet and fight with our Jewish bodies, which apparently want to gain weight Eastern European-style. All of that is Jewish. It's a fierce, unspoken pride in some kind of peoplehood, even though we're the only Jews we know or like. It's mystifying ritual and language and backwards-opening books and standing in synagogues when suddenly everyone's turned in the opposite direction and we're the only ones looking the wrong way.

Judaism is boring, interminable seders, Mickey Shapiro yelling at his sons in the middle of them. It's Mom's illegible and crookedly photocopied *Haggadot* in our hands with the names of each person's assigned reading photocopied right into them because Mom must assign the speaking parts, names crossed off as they die.

This doesn't hold, of course. It can't tie us effectively, can't hold us effectively to Judaism. A few cracks appear right away in the seventies, the string binding us wears through. Once that string is unwound, unraveled, broken, our religion falls to pieces.

The truth is that we went spinning off years before, a thousand Holocaust stories before, a thousand Yiddish accents before, dead babies, marked arms, unmarked graves, armed soldiers. A thousand forests.

I draw the curtains closed over the little *mechitzah* in my mind and I am gone.

It's late afternoon on a weekday and my sister Mindy and I are sitting on the floor of my bedroom, a Ouija Board between us, something we now do so frequently that it's actually eclipsed all the regular parts of my life. What a treat, being able to just ask all these friendly spirits all of my angst-filled teenage questions any time I want!

My fingertips resting lightly on the cursor, I ask my usual question, the same one I've asked about ten thousand times. Whoever is up there answering these questions must be very tired of this question. It's some form of "When will Greg and I be together? Does Greg love me? How many lives have Greg and I lived together? Will I marry Greg?" A big jumble catapulted at the Ouija board every day because I'm still desperate to marry myself off, still raised on fairy tales, still waiting for the happy ending, even for a life that's barely begun.

I am thrilled to get my answers. Just as I suspected, Greg and I are true loves, bound together across centuries and time. Nine centuries, to be exact. Yes, it does strain my imagination to hear this, and kind of exhausting to ponder, since just this one lifetime is frightening and terrifying enough but, by then, I'm held in the Ouija Board's thrall.

The Ouija Board experience gives me such a long view on Greg that I become beatifically patient. Suddenly there is no problem. I can outwait him dating all the school tramps. I can outwait his drop-outs, his drop ins, his all-consuming interest in where the next party is. I can outwait all the things he has to get out of his system, because I believe we are bound together over time and are meant to be together.

I imagine us through our many lifetimes together. Nine hundred years, which takes us back to William the Conqueror. Were we a Norman couple or Anglo-Saxon? Later were we British or American Colonists? Maybe one of us loses our head in the French Revolution.

The Ouija Board curser continues to lead me on a few merry dances. Answers get muddled, contradictory. Suddenly, Greg and I aren't destined to be together. The nine centuries disappear in a flash, no longer a number provided by the board. I get frightened wondering who or what is providing these answers – what's making the curser move? It becomes obvious that whatever it is, it isn't a force for good. A force for good would tell me Greg and I were meant to be together.

Mindy and I decide simultaneously that we're done. We carry the board and the cursor gingerly out to the garbage can like it just may explode in our arms and we throw it away.

Now that I no longer have the Ouija board to believe in, I'm empty and seeking again. I need to start shopping for a new religion. I'll always be Jewish, of course, but there's some idea that being Jewish is just the foundation we build upon, not a belief system. It doesn't seem contradictory to continue searching.

Just like I look for diets, I look for answers, for gods, for something that will make this all click. I believe in horoscopes and am constantly parsing out the ones in the newspaper and the ones in the astrology booklets that I buy in the checkout line in grocery stores, trying to discover my future. I buy *Linda Goodman's Sun Signs* and pore over it in minute detail. One time I take an astrology class with a high school friend to finally learn about all of this in great detail, but we quit after one or two sessions, finding it too detailed. Rising signs, this in the house of that, planetary movements. I don't care about any of that, I just want to predict my future.

I go to Eckankar meetings and am told that the secret to the universe is soul travel. I must master this, leave my teen body at home every night in bed and go zooming off among the planets, maybe into the deep sea. I find this a little troubling, and I'm not happy with the idea of hovering at my ceiling and seeing my body lying in bed. Luckily, this doesn't work for me. Anyway, I'm stuck in my body, stuck on the bed, a failure at soul traveling and joining the Great Eck.

My friends at school seem to have something I'm

missing, some inner peace. Turns out that these friends of mine, who all seem so cool and hip at school, have a secret life the whole time I know them – they've been attending church. There is a complete subset of my high school that I don't even know exists, the Young Life part of school, the Christian part of school, the church-attending part of school, where people know each other from their churches, from Sunday School, from Catechism class. They know each other deeply from a completely separate world to which I can never belong.

I'm tirelessly looking everywhere for something that is most likely right inside of me.

It's not good that I'm missing a belief system, because soon I almost die. I'm riding in the back of an ambulance, the driver and attendant arguing over where Tempe St. Luke's Hospital is located.

This illness starts unremarkably. For a week I am sick with some run of the mill asthma infection and so I sit in my bedroom missing school, and suffering silently, with a Primatene Mist inhaler clutched in one hand and a little black and white TV on a rickety TV cart in front of me. Occasionally I fall into a fitful, hallucinatory sleep, during which I imagine that the very next puff of Primatene is finally going to work and restore the air to my breathing passages. I come awake, lift the inhaler to my mouth, and take a puff. No change. Then I think maybe I didn't inhale that one deeply enough, or maybe I should have exhaled fully before I inhaled, or maybe there was some other error in my Primatene-misting, and so I take another puff and another and another, emptying a whole inhaler in a week. I'm distressed when I run out. I sleep and hallucinate that I have a new one and that the next puff will work.

A thought bubble floats into my head – am I imagining it or am I getting worse?

I sit in the bedroom behind the closed door as the week goes by, my breathing more and more shallow. Who will check on me? Will anyone pop their head in the room and see me dying on the bed? Sometimes the twins dash in the house right after school, knocking a hello as they walk by. Me being sick is not news of any type. But one day Sherry pops her head in. She's alarmed. Am I blue? Green? Blacked out with Xs for eyes? All I know is that's when the ambulance is called.

There are rules about ambulances and the first one is that it's essential that an ambulance act like an ambulance. It's supposed to arrive at your house in a mad dash. There should be the sudden flurry of the paramedics carrying a stretcher in the door, the neighbors peering out of their front windows wondering what will be carried out. A body under a sheet? Someone in a straitjacket? Or covered in blood? Then the ambulance should careen away down the street and zoom through the city on its way to the nearest hospital, where medical personnel are just waiting there at the door for the ambulance to pull up, ready to triage, stat.

I somehow don't get an ambulance like that.

I get an ambulance that shows up at our door after aimlessly meandering through our neighborhood trying to find the house and which is loaded with a couple of Neanderthal paramedics who aren't able to assess my medical status. I get an ambulance that is driven very, very slowly, first on its way

249

to my house, then on its way away from my house. Slowly, like it's a Sunday drive. The driver, instead of using the blue and red lights attached to the ambulance's roof, which would allow me to be sped on my way, instead doesn't use them. Hey, let's take Scottsdale Road all the way down to Tempe, stopping at all the traffic signals on the planet, past all the little shops and all the big shops and all the pedestrians who can peer in the back windows and see this apparent non-emergency in the back, and wonder, *why's she in there?*

I'm in the back sitting up, mainly because I can't lie down when I'm gasping for breath. The paramedic in back with me tries to make small talk and I want to be friendly because he's cute, but I can't talk. I try to express myself through pantomimes that maybe they should hurry.

When we get to the hospital, after the usual drama between my mother, who was following, and the nurses, I am put into intensive care, there to be watched very carefully, and not allowed to sleep. Apparently, using that much Primatene Mist was not the best idea. Dr. Levin theorizes that once my original infection resolved sometime during the week, the Primatene Mist had then moved into my lungs. There would be no sleep for me, and no more Primatene Mist, my good friend. My sisters are forced to my bedside in intensive care, to glue themselves there in shifts, to keep me awake all day and all night to keep me from falling asleep and my lungs collapsing.

A few days later, I'm released into a shared room. I have not died. I am sleep-deprived, hallucinatory, a little delirious. I find that my roommate is the next youngest female in the hospital, a twenty-two-year-old Mormon housewife and mother, skinny and pale and wasting away, though she positively lights up when she finds out that she has a Jewish roommate. I already know from our Mormon customers that they held a special place in their faith for Jews, but even I'm a little surprised at how happy she is that I'm her roommate.

Her eyes light up. "You're Jewish? Like the Hebrews from the Bible?" she says.

She takes it upon herself to save me. Is it too great an opportunity to pass by, saving a real Hebrew from the bible? I can't deny her insistence that I had almost died. And that I'm not dead. I agree with her, I almost died but I am clearly not dead. It's just a short leap from that concept to the next concept – that, not having died, "I had been saved." Okay, ignoramus that I am, fine, I can agree with that. I have been saved. When she takes the final leap, to the idea that I've been saved by Jesus, I balk.

Luckily for her and unluckily for my thousands of years of Jewish forbearers, I know nothing about Jewish theology, I don't even know what the word "theology" means. I have no answer to her question of why Jews don't believe in Jesus, or how to answer the question of why we don't believe when even Jesus himself was Jewish? I sort through my mental filing cabinet of tidbits I've caught here and there but find nothing in my head but the Holocaust, the Forest, Shiva, and BBYO. I don't know the answer to this question.

I put up some kind of faintly admirable fight. I sit there in my hospital gown, roped by my IV to the bed, to the room, and to her proselytizing. I say, "Jews don't believe in Jesus." I don't know why. "Jews don't have Christmas." I don't know why. "Jews don't celebrate Easter." Again, I don't know why. Not only has she been trained meticulously to this task, I have also been trained meticulously in my ignorance, trained by the steamroller of the Holocaust that rolled through my family, smashing its Judaism out of existence.

I am clearly overwhelmed. My roommate plays the Mormon Tabernacle Choir on her 8-track player nonstop and I'm pretty sure it's entering my brain subliminally while I'm sleeping. There are Bishops from her church coming and going, praying over her, maybe praying over me, her children showing up here and there, climbing on her. But in between all that, she talks theology.

What is the chance, after all, that after almost dying and then, released from intensive care, I'm put in room with a Mormon housewife who appears to be dying and takes it as her final task to convert me?

I decide she is right; I've been saved for a reason. Even if I choose not to go all the way, careening straight out of the Hebrew Bible, past the New Testament, and into the Book of Mormon, but rather to make a screeching halt and end up in the middle, at least she's saved me halfway.

I get discharged from the hospital and decide to test out my new religion. I get awkwardly down on my knees beside my bed, first locking my bedroom door because in my house, prayer of any type is definitely contraband. I make up something that I think sounds like a prayer to Jesus and I think it, but I don't say it. I'm not sure what this prayer should entail so I use everything I'd learned about Christianity as a child in the 60s, basically a stew of movies with nuns and priests, Bing Crosby in a collar, Julie Andrews as a novitiate, and, of course, Sally Field as the Flying Nun.

With no formal training but some proselytizing in a hospital, I take on what I think is Christianity. I've already given up my fledgling sex life as being too excruciatingly bad to continue, so celibacy is already part of my new religious order. I'm not planning to give up pot, so I decide that, rather than me conforming to it, Christianity would just have to conform to me, bend and wrap itself around me a little, rather than the other way around.

Finally I know the truth – there is no longer any doubt. I know everything about life and death and afterlife – every unknown outcome is suddenly solved. What a relief! I am lit up, suddenly seeing the magnificent hand of God in everything that's happened to me. Maybe even seeing the littler, more filial, hand of Jesus in all this. I can rest upon this bed of sureness rather than stumbling along blind, crashing head on into the unknown and the unknowable every day.

I get a copy of a "Good News" bible somewhere and begin reading it, get bored immediately and fall asleep, my head in the book. The one thing that sinks in by osmosis is that I now have an obligation to preach to others, just like the Mormon hospital lady, who has now assumed mythic proportions, had preached to me. Now that I was saved, I need to save everyone else. I float in a fog of good will, like an extension of being high. Other people need this, I think. I've got to bottle it up and take it to them.

I balk at knocking on doors but converting my friend Rina is another story. She's over at my house all the time and is Jewish, like me, making her ripe for conversion. So I convert her, my one proselytizing success story, and then we set out on our two-girl ministry of meeting in the center of the golf course in between our houses and smoking pot there amid the lovely manmade landscape, the carefully manicured lawns of tiff, the trimmed trees, the carefully placed homes, and the watchful employees who track us around the golf course in a relentless battle to prune us from the sight of the golfers.

On one side of the golf course is Rina's house, with her mother, a young, pot-smoking Jewish New Yorker, bewilderingly married to a cowboy second husband, the creepy, molesting pervert, Cam, and Rina's two younger brothers, both permanently dressed in striped baseball uniforms. On the other side of the golf course is my mother's house, long, low, and flat, lying on its street in the middle of a nearly uninhabited piece of North Scottsdale desert. We meet in the middle.

Whenever I go over to Rina's we have to wait for Cam to stop fawning over us and touching us inappropriately before we can escape to her room. We're supposed to laugh – ha ha ha – about how funny Cam is. He's not funny, more frightening than funny.

The pot tells us that we no longer have to wonder about the meaning of existence. Everything is under control. We want everyone to feel this way, so we soon set out to convert our mothers, both of whom don't think much of this new phase of ours. Rina immediately hits a wall of resistance, her mother laughs at the idea. My mother, the Holocaust Survivor, is, of course, appalled. She is willing to put up with a lot and has proven that she's tolerant with seeking, with searching, with Ouija-boarding, tolerant of forays into EST and meditation, and never bewildered by finding any of us concentrating on our third eye, stuck in a cross-legged yogi pose. She's fine with intermarriage, with disaffection, with affectation, with disconnection, but she draws the line here, right here, her size 8 ½ narrow foot with her extra elongated hammer toe firmly drawing a line in the gravel of our front yard. Not Christianity. She spews forth stories from her town in Lithuania, how the Christians had hated the Jews, had been happy to see them die at the hands of the Nazis. Nothing penetrates my fog and certainly not this story, which, along with her Holocaust story, I'd listened to every day of my life, my mind shying away from the horrors.

I don't convert, I don't get baptized, I don't go near the Young Life group at my high school. I have a private faith, I figure, inextricably tied up with almost dying in the hospital. I tell myself I can't just ignore that. Something big has to mark such a pivotal event.

Having hit a brick wall on our conversion activities, Rina and I are laying low, waiting for our next opportunities to testify about our faith to some hapless, unsuspecting, non-Christian, when, one afternoon after winding our way through the golf course towards my house, we pop in for a munchie. We float into the kitchen, at peace with ourselves and with our world. Our high is wearing off but, luckily, we are still high on Jesus. There we run headlong into Gary Jackson, one of my sister Sherry's friends. He sits in one of our black wetlook vinyl kitchen chairs and leans way, way back until he almost falls right onto the tile floor. But he doesn't fall because he has balance, both in his mind and in his body. Gary has somehow heard of our professed Christianity, obviously through my sister, and he has some questions for us. I light up. Oh yes, here's a potential target for conversion. Rina and I sit down amiably, ready to answer any apostacy he wants to throw at us.

"So, you guys are Christians?"

We nod eagerly.

He proceeds to question us about our great faith, about our observance of that faith, about how many times we've been to church, about how much we've read and understand the bible, how much we know about Christianity, and about what we are doing to build these precepts into our lives. He goes on and on and on – it's like a Papal Summit, a Christian Synod. Seasons change while Gary is talking, leaves fall from trees, animals become extinct, while Gary is talking.

Rina and I just sit there with our mouths hanging open. We have no answers, no justifications, no knowledge. We've done no studying, no church attending, no bible reading, no precepting. Our faith, a shimmering chimera before us, crumbles and falls, smashed into little glass fragments all around us. All we've done is said "Jesus this" and "Jesus that," then went out and smoked pot on the golf course and admired God's great creation – the man-chiseled perfection of the putting greens.

Gary finally lowers the two front legs of the chair to the kitchen floor, having done what he set out to do – destroy our faith. Mission accomplished. Rina and I decide later that he must be the devil, there's no other way to make sense out of this. He stands up and walks out, my sister nowhere to be seen, like he was just planted there for us.

And just as suddenly as I became a Christian, I become whatever I had been before, just an ignorant, unschooled Jew, born into my parents' own particular denomination – not

Reform, not Conservative, not Orthodox – just something they created when God looked the other way during the war, "Holocaust Jewish." It's a denomination that offers no peace of mind, no tranquility, and certainly no bubble of glorious numbness to control my reactions to the world.

I start feeling things again. It isn't pretty because there were a lot of things that my nascent faith had insulated me from, all the hurts and bumps and bruises of life, for a while all of this had miraculously been God's will, but now I'm alone out here, just me, standing, throbbing, with no shield, no bubble. I have to live through each thing that happens, learn through each thing that happens. My rubber bumper has come off.

I realize that maybe Jews are not meant to live an anesthetized existence, maybe knocking around through the pleasure and pain of life is part of it.

After I'm stripped of the Christianity, after I've failed to lift off and soul travel with Eckankar, after the Ouija board has been pitched into the garbage can, after my friend and I bomb out of our Astrology class, I am distressed, still looking for something to fill up my spiritual void. Why can't I seem to find it?

One day I wander into a spiritual bookstore to go shopping for a new religion to join, anything that catches my eye, because that's where it will be, of course. A new religion on a shelf where I can easily pluck it off.

I'm in there and idly twirling a book rack, spinning between the books on reincarnation and those by L. Ron Hubbard, when the rack comes to a stop with a book facing

257

me. It's called, "The Wit and Wisdom of the Talmud." I pick it up and thumb through it and at that exact moment a thought flashes through my brain, a thought that is similar to a voice, yet not my own. Such a distinct voice, so clear, that I never forget the sound of it. It says, "It's no accident that you were born a Jew."

I buy the book.

My *pintele yid*, the teeny bud of a Jewish heart inside me, that is just the merest whisper, a flicker, and about to go out, ignites right back into existence then and there. Like the Grinch's heart in the Seuss tale, my little Jewish heart grows many times its original size until, eventually, I burst back into Judaism.

And I never have to go looking for a new religion again.

Twenty-Two
Chicago Summer

Once our store is gone and I'm freed from servitude, I can do whatever I want in the summer as long as it costs almost no money. I can lay around and sleep all day. I can read slim, serialized romance novels in my bed half the day and then the other half of the day move to the couch to do the same. Since it's looking like this level of activity might last forever, I take matters into my own hands. I decide I will go back and visit my friends in Chicago.

On a boiling hot Arizona day in July 1977, I find myself on an American Airlines flight bound for Chicago, my first flight ever, dressed in elephant baggy jeans and my favorite orange gauze shirt. I am courageously flying alone my first time on a plane, and stunned by the thought that Skokie, after all, is really so close. I'm amazed – can I really step onto the plane in Phoenix and step off the plane in Chicago three or four hours later, right back into my childhood? I decide to go even though I know I'm not the Linda who left. I've lost a few things in my four years away, my virginity, my youthful figure, my living father. I have a weight problem that started that moment in the foyer when I heard my dad had died. I don't look like the girl who left in 1973, yet I get on the plane with aplomb.

Everything on the plane is a marvel to me. The *occupado* sign from the rest room, the barf bag, my ticket stub. All these people trusting that this gigantic floating living room will stay aloft. Despite the sheer impossibility of it, I turn out to be a natural flier – I love the flight.

Living in Arizona for four years straight I've gotten used to bright sunlight, burn-your-eyeballs-out-of-your-head sunlight, mirages-shimmering-in-the-roadway sunlight. I've gotten used to cacti marching up hills like an army, and mountains that are brown and covered with scrub bushes. Because my parents bought a house in the middle of nowhere, I've even gotten used to nothingness. Arizona had seemed so foreign when we moved, so I'm surprised that when I get back to Chicago everything seems foreign there too, like my eyes have changed. I'm something in between. I'm an Arizonan in Chicago and a Chicagoan in Arizona.

No one could be more astonished than me at the look and feel of Chicago. It's like I've been holding my breath for four years and, when I suddenly see the brownstones, the tree-canopied streets, the jumbled businesses, the green lawns, the inky tar down the cracks in the concrete streets, curbs and sidewalks, grass and flowers and little birds up in the trees, I exhale.

Was it really that easy all this time, just a flight, like a magic carpet I could have been back there, back where my dreams all were, back where the "what ifs" all lived – the what ifs of the boys I was supposed to marry, the high school I was supposed to attend, the house I was supposed to still be living in? Back with the boy I had loved for six straight years of childhood, from first grade to seventh, Larry Aronson? And here's my past, still extant, just standing here, waiting for me to fly in on a plane and scoop it back up any time I want?

I've been invited to stay with a Chicago friend I met when she'd come visit family in Arizona, Missy Roth. I think this will be a good idea because Missy and I have a few things in common. We're both from Skokie, both children of Holocaust Survivors, and we both lost our fathers at an early age. From there we diverge. I have a gaggle of sisters, but she is an only child, living alone with her mother in an apartment in downtown Skokie.

"It'll be great!" she says.

I ask if her mother's okay with this – probably because I can't imagine anyone being okay with this.

But she says, "No really! My mom is thrilled to have you
stay with us!"

Missy is magnanimous, welcoming, reassuring, optimistic. I am reassured.

She picks me up at the airport and we drive into Skokie, the familiar street names tumbling one after the other as we get closer and closer to where my heart still beats, then we veer away towards her apartment. I get silent, watching the streets roll by. She masterfully parallel parks on the street in front of the building.

She doesn't mention it before I fly in, but, just as we're

driving out of the airport, she tells me that her mother is deaf. Just so I know. It's never come up before and she seems a little nervous about this disclosure, assuring me that it shouldn't cause any problems because she'll communicate for me. She knows sign language and her mother can read her lips.

I don't plan to be much of a bother at the apartment. Missy will be busy with her boyfriend and says I should feel free to use it as a base to visit my friends and family.

I settle in and look at the tiny phone book I've brought with me, its indexed alphabetical tabs outlined in gold. I start calling and, sure enough, my Chicago family discovers me sunk away in Missy's quiet apartment.

The first time I see my cousins Marky and Louie, sons of my mother's deceased sister, they come get me together in a rumbling Firebird. They are eager to see me. Extremely eager. And I'm eager to see them – at least I'm eager to see the Marky and Louie I remember from my childhood with our endless games of dreidel, none of us knowing how to play. With our never-ending family get togethers at our grandmother's West Rogers Park apartment, all of us zooming in and out of the front door, weaving to the back door, down a thousand wooden steps to play in the tiny back yard and then back up again. My cousins of the endless flirtations, my mother insisting that Jewish Law allowed first cousins to marry.

But this is not the Marky and Louie who show up. Their great height has diminished. They have grown rotund, and their brains have dimmed. They unwittingly regale me with endless Laurel and Hardy routines, Marky making nonstop fun of the heavier Louie, painful to listen to now. This was pretty good stuff when I was nine, ten. Now, not so much. They fight over me, want to take me here, there, am I free for this, for that, can they have all of me?

We drive out of Skokie to their dad's house in a suburb of Chicago that didn't exist in 1973. There I am given a lavish meal by their stepmother, my step-aunt Margaret, the former nun, and my Uncle Barney, his concentration camp numbers peeping out from under his work shirt. The younger sisters, twins, are overly-developed 12-year-olds now, already wearing the heavy training bras on which their stepmother insists since that's what the nuns wore. They stare at me with starry-eyed gazes, worshiping me – as the Arizona cousin I am automatically glamorous.

When Marky later comes alone to get me for a Cubs game at Wrigley Field, he's driving another muscle car. He's proud of the car, proud of the job that got him that car, proud of the wheels and the tires and the rims and the hubcaps. He's proud of the paint job and pin striping. And have I noticed the dash cover? And for whatever is not immediately visible, he has a sheaf of pictures I can look through.

We go on a twisting, winding, serpentine crawl through the beige, tar-lined streets of Chicago. I reevaluate my opinion of Marky – he can't possibly be dimwitted because only a genius could master these roads. Each intersection contains a test and requires a decision. Is this road leading off to points unknown, will you end up on a highway to Wisconsin? Is this one suddenly turning one way – a police officer stationed at the head of it – or does the speed limit slow precariously?

263

Does our left-most through lane become an impromptu left turn lane, causing us to swerve to the right, or should we avoid the right lane at all costs, since it has become an equally impromptu double-parking lane? There's the easy way he swings into turns, the way he owns the road, the way he remains my gregarious host here in this moving living room. He is at one with the car, filling up the front seat, one giant arm looped around its back, like he was born in it, or it grew around him.

The car ticks at stop lights as we slowly make our way to Wrigley Field, slithering around the building until, suddenly, miraculously, a parking spot opens up for us, only eight, ten, twelve, blocks away from it. We huff and puff our way over to the stadium in the Chicago summer humidity, Marky regaling me with an encyclopedic fountain of information about the Cubbies as we walk, as we sit, as we cheer, as we lose, as we walk back, as we drive back, ditching workmen popping their heads out of manholes, a runaway stroller careening down city streets, and elderly women walking at glacial speed pulling their wheeled grocery baskets, finally pulling up back in Skokie.

It's kind of exciting in a weird way to be this popular with anyone. He and Louie book me for a night one week and then they book me for another night the next. They seem amazed by the specter of my month-long vacation floating in front of them.

I press the button for my grandmother's apartment. I'm in the vestibule of her apartment building, which is musty and smells like mothballs and Ben-Gay moisturizing rub. I wait. I get an answering buzz that allows me to yank open the door to the stairwell. The stairs are carpeted and as I start up silently, I hear my grandmother's door open a level above and then see her orangey head over the top of the staircase.

"Who is it?" she says. I say, "It's Linda," and clomp up the carpeted stairs in full seventeen-year-old oblivion. I'm unable in that moment to appreciate how amazing it is to have a grandmother. I've always had a grandmother. I'm unable to appreciate how insistently her life is marching on towards its inevitable end, that in ten years she won't be on her feet anymore, and in twelve years she'll give up the orangey/red hair dye and go to a shocking pure white, her body shrinking away to the size of a child. In thirteen years she'll be gone. Can I even appreciate my grandmother, standing, orange-haired, alert, watching me clomp up the stairs, her eyes made gigantic by her thick glasses?

Her apartment is the same and I'm not sure a piece of dust has landed that was not there in 1973. There is the smell of an ever-present pot of soup simmering on the stove. There's her living room with its plastic-wrapped turquoise sofa, the tiny kitchen, the rickety back staircase down to the yard, all the wooden railings of the building buttressing up the back. She shows me where my grandfather fell the very last time right before he died, showing me with a crash of her hands, with her heavily accented English, how hard it was for her when he fell on her, how she struggled to get the phone and then, instead of calling an ambulance she called my mother in Arizona. Of course.

I fail to understand how strange it must be for her, being unable to communicate with her grandchild in Yiddish.

When I'm done with my first go-round with my mom's side of the family, I have a decision to make. I know the rules of my family. We are a monolithic block in thought and deed, so I know what my attitude should be about visiting Dad's side of the family, what my sisters would do. We have disconnected from him and his memory, therefore we are disconnected from his side of the family.

We've inherited our mother's hatred for her problematic marriage to our father, her paranoia about what his family is thinking. This hatred ranges far and wide – it extends into the past and the future, even anticipating future resentments ("Oh! They don't think my daughters will amount to anything, do they?"). She resents anyone she thinks is judging her, who thinks they're better than her, and, specifically regarding the Chicago aunts, anyone who didn't help her out after our father died. I wonder, did they even know we were poor, wowed by my father's claim of riches, the swimming pool, by his phone calls to them from the outside extension in the dead of winter?

At the throbbing center of this maelstrom are my aunts Ida, Rose, and Etta, with a fourth one off in Florida. There are childhood memories of the seven of us lined up in birth order, the aunts standing before us and pronouncing judgement. Who was the prettiest, the thinnest, the fattest, the ugliest? Who will get married first, and who will never get married at all?

For me even to go to Chicago is somewhat bewildering to my family. Officially, we have left all that behind us, every bit of it, that entire region of the country, the family and all, except for whomever visits Arizona and then we'll happily socialize with our guest travelers from a world which has ceased to exist for us. So I know the answer. If I have to go to Chicago at all, I am to stick to Mom's side of the family. They'll make one allowance, to visit Aunt Rose, married to one of our dad's brothers. The aunt who has always loved us.

But I have my tiny phonebook with all their phone numbers in there and I'm nothing if not paranoid. I know the relatives talk to each other. How can I see one set and hide from the others? I recognize my odd role as the seventeen-year-old who is the Burt family representative from Arizona, who's in charge of calling all these family members. I'm intimidated by the task.

I start with the outlying aunts and uncles. I visit my dad's sister Etta and then I visit the sweetly-tempered Aunt Rose. Finally I turn my phone book to the page for my dad's other brother and his wife. It's time to visit my aunt Ida, to fly into the eye of the hurricane.

At Missy's apartment in downtown Skokie the situation is rapidly deteriorating.

Missy's mother roams the house each day in a blue bathrobe, never getting dressed. After a while it becomes obvious to me that she isn't welcoming or oblivious, as Missy had said. But she is crazy, and crazy has attached onto me like there's vermin living in the house which must be exterminated. I, unfortunately, am the vermin.

A lot of sounds come out of Mrs. Roth's mouth when I eat breakfast, lunch, and dinner, and a lot when Missy talks to her about how long I'll be staying. I only understand Missy's side of the conversations, but I can make out enough of what her mother is saying to get the message. After all, I'm fluent in the language of the European Jewish mother.

Who is this girl eating us out of house and home?

What is she to us?

She has no family, this one?

Let her go stay with her own family!

You invited her to stay with us for how long?

How much is she paying us?

She eats and eats and eats! Let her eat her own family out of house and home!

She and Missy fight furiously in sign language, but the translations spill over into Missy's verbal answers. After one week, she tells me I must go.

When my aunt Ida comes to get me for a family dinner that week, her car pants in the street, loaded up with my now-grown cousins. I'm not expecting to like them. I don't expect much from this meeting at all since I expect to be close to Mom's family and estranged from Dad's. It's my guilty secret that I even called them.

But they come pick me up and bring me to their house near our old Skokie house, right across the street from my elementary school. Their house is a right triangle from the front, one big slash of window, with a curtain charging up that 45-degree angle. In this house you walk right into the living room when you walk in the front door. There's one staircase up with bedrooms, and one staircase down to a subterranean family room where WGN plays night and day, my cousin Jeffrey stretched out on the sofa, young, with teeth too big for his head, watching.

There's my cousin Barry, whom I was raised with, babies at the same time, now a nervous, pale teenager wearing a baseball cap over his yarmulke. We take walks around the neighborhood, pushing the stroller with his baby brother in it. People admire us as a young married couple.

In this tiny house, in its matching tiny kitchen, I am welcomed and honored and treated like an honored guest, like a piece of Dad just floated right inside their home and sat down at their table. Aunt Ida asks me who I'm staying with, conveying clearly that it's an affront not to be with family.

"Why should you be a stranger?" she asks. It's the opposite side of everything Missy's mother had expressed.

I admit to my aunt that there are problems at my friend's apartment and with her mother, that Missy had withdrawn her offer for me to stay with them for the rest of the month. My aunt – with four kids in the house including a new baby – doesn't hesitate, not one second.

She says, "You will stay here."

And everyone is simply shoved over a few inches from the top of the house to the bottom, carving out space for me, and I settle in. I am home.

I fit in my aunt and uncle's household surprisingly well. Somehow, they like me, better than my sisters like me, I'm sure. Even more odd, my cousin Laurie adores me. Why she does is a mystery to me for all the years of our friendship. I recognize that I've been a little beaten by the world since moving to Arizona, searching for friends true to my heart. Yet here I find my heart. In my world, someone as amazing as my cousin Laurie shouldn't like me at all. I figure she should probably just like other thin people who exercise, like she is and does. She doesn't seem to understand that my outward flawed appearance is clear evidence of an inward disorderliness. That, basically, I'm a mess.

Laurie and I share a room, yet she immediately gives me the bed. She has a mod, funky, wet look-cushioned loveseat in her room at the time and she sleeps there, crunched into various contortions to fit.

Unlike my aunt, who can't stand to stay on a phone call, who's all business, who says what she needs to say and then gets off the phone, glaring at the caller through the receiver, my cousin Laurie sits on the phone every night while doing chores for her mother, the phone glued to her ear, switching back and forth – line one, line two, back to line one, back to line two – chopping, shucking peas, peeling vegetables. She has a lot of friends and boyfriends. She is not afraid of any of our aunts, living or dead, which I am, and she is not afraid of my sisters, though I am.

She has endless amused tolerance for my crush on John Travolta, for the fact that I've seen *Saturday Night Fever* seven times and, the next year, will see *Grease* four times. I'm somewhat consumed with parsing out deeper meaning from the plots.

She says, "It's fine – I'm not mocking you! Tell me again how it's so deep! You're not my only friend who's madly in love with John Travolta." We have rabbinic-level discussions about this.

She somehow sees inside the mess of me, my *ongeblozen*

outfits, my sheer nightgown, inappropriate for a household with males, my rapid weight gains, my shaggy outgrown haircut, and she is instantly my best friend. She's the sister I never had, and I have six.

Though I'm wild, running around with my Skokie friends till all hours of the night, my aunt gives me a key and ignores my comings and goings. Different household rules apply to my cousin and no rules apply to me. I get an impression that there are low expectations for me as a wild Burt girl, so what's the use? I'm aware there's an impression that I've been raised like a wolf, all of us a ragtag litter where any survival is a miracle. So no rules for me.

Cousin Laurie shares freely with me. We can't share clothes, but with anything else, she throws open the doors of her closet. I end up borrowing her clogs for one wild night out that I only remember in flashes. The windy Lake Michigan shore, a prematurely balding eighteen-year-old Jewish boy trying unsuccessfully to wheedle me into sex. Making out heavily in the eerie small hours of the night, one of my friends over a hill, around a bend, doing the same thing with a different boy. The tide comes in suddenly causing us to abandon our spots quickly. My clothes float away.

I show up back at my cousin's house in a bewildering state of disarray. I have clothes but no shoes and no underwear, no bra, and no key. Laurie opens the door for me silently and I follow her up the wooden stairs, avoiding all the creaking spots.

Twenty-Three
The Historical Grudge

Yes, I've had my experience in the spiritual bookstore in Phoenix, the voice of God or a guardian angel calling to me, my purchase of *The Wit and Wisdom of the Talmud*. That doesn't mean I've done anything about it. I'm still Judaism-shy, waiting for it to roll out a red carpet for me, or to throw a net over my head and drag me into a synagogue. I both want it, yearn for it, and vastly don't want anything to change at all.

Luckily, Judaism can grab a toehold on me at my aunt and uncle's home in Skokie. Their house has a different tempo than my house in Scottsdale. My house has the constant hum of my mother on a thousand phone calls, my sisters yanking our telephone around corners, down hallways, the cord smashed flat. Our house has a lot of activity all headed towards the door – it's a high school party night, a boondocker night, a barhopping night. There are no organized meals going on, more like grab and go, or grab before another sister gets it, and go.

At my aunt and uncle's house in Skokie things are

different.

First there is the kitchen. The kosher kitchen. My cousins take me on a tour of the *milchig* side of the kitchen, the *fleishig* side of the kitchen, and the *parve* area, three words that mean nothing to me. The dishwasher and the oven are both designated for meat. There are different shelves of the refrigerator designated *milchig* and *fleishig*, alternating, and each has different sides of the sink. There are pots and pans for each, knives and forks for each.

I'm bewildered. I have no idea how I'm supposed to remember all this – like does every Jewish person in every Jewish family but my own just automatically know this stuff? Can anyone even comprehend what I come from? That in my house in Arizona there would have to be not just a milk side and meat side, but a pork side?

The kitchen is my ticking time bomb. I walk in there and automatically mess up the *kashrut*. Whole sets of silverware must be *kashered* – immersed in *mikvehs* or buried for seven years – after I touch them.

In the kitchen there is a tiny kitchen table with a rickety highchair pulled up to it and that's where we eat – my aunt, my uncle, my cousins Laurie, Barry and Jeffrey, and the baby, Joshua, all squeezed in there at mealtime, passing food like they're really a family, not like mine in Arizona where, after Dad dies, we never sit down to a real meal again.

I don't actually know Shabbat is coming that first weekend at my aunt's house. To me, it's just Friday night and Friday night in Arizona doesn't mean anything to me except the weekend and parties. My Mom is too busy to cook and too busy to shop and too busy to teach me to drive and too busy to do anything, really, but work in real estate. On Friday nights if need be.

But my aunt appears to have several core beliefs, one being family dinner and that is amplified for the Sabbath. The things that are normal in their house on other nights is normal this night too – the shucking of the peas, the cooking of the dinner, kitchen prep out of the *fleishig* portion of the kitchen. There are dishes being clinked around, food cooking. Then there's the unusual – the setting of the table in the dining room.

Aunt Ida prepares for Shabbat by buying fish from the fish store, challah from the bakery, meat at the kosher butcher, and everything else at the kosher grocery – all a series of tiny Chicago mom and pop stores with watchful owners inside and impossible parking outside, just like my aunt and uncle's own store. This is just how you get Jewish food in the 70s in Chicago. You get the good stuff by going from store to store.

She doesn't do this because she's friendly with the owners. On the contrary, she's unfriendly with the owners, keeps to herself, doesn't chit chat, responds to gossip or inquiries with a little sniff, and doesn't encourage intimacies. No one said you had to be best friends.

On Shabbat, I am shooed away from the preparations. I figure they don't have time to deal with me destroying the *kashrut*. There's the elegance of the dining room table, the fancy china. We're called down to dinner. I realize later this is good and means I'm not the *Shabbos goy*, a non-Jew who could run errands on Shabbat that were impossible for an observant Jew. I run down the stairs barefoot and then I run right back up again. Apparently, shoes are required. There are dishes being clinked around, food cooking.

My cousin Barry, his baseball cap now off, only a *kippah* on, is lighting candles and making *Kiddush* in a proprietary type of way – ignoring everyone at the table. Is he self-conscious about trotting out the Judaism in front of me, trying to rush through it? Does he think that I'll think this is strange and weird? Perhaps he has no idea of how I long for this, my little Jewish soul mesmerized by the sight of the two candles, flames wavering, the three waves of the hands over them, a prayer, and Shabbat arrives.

There's some quiet right after the candle lighting and, since I'm a Burt girl who dreads silence of any type, I have to fill it up. I start talking.

"The dining room looks beautiful," I say to my aunt. "My mom has china just like this."

My cousin looks at me and shakes her head. No one responds to me. They leave the room, all marching over to the sink. I'm abashed, ashamed because I'm doing everything wrong, I don't know what I'm supposed to do so I follow them to the sink, line up. There they say a prayer as they wash their hands from a two-handled cup. I copy them, I wash my hands with water from the two-handled cup, mumbling some gibberish. I have no prayer to recite. Suddenly talking resumes. I exhale.

Then there's talking, eating. When we're done, when it's Friday night again, my friends come by to get me, honk the car horn, and I run out into the night.

The next day, much to my surprise, it's still Shabbat. There's a lull in the house along with a separate, opposing reality that the family discount store must be run, people have to work, my uncle works. Barry, the oldest of the cousins, however, is observant. This causes some friction when my uncle comes home in the evening.

"Ida, he should be working in the store on Saturday, not schlepping off to shul like some mama's boy!" I hear Sid when he gets home. Ida shushes him, soothes him, coaxes him into his recliner with his paper, his slippers, a glass of beer, followed by a warm supper. My uncle complains about Barry turning into Orthodox *schlemiel* studying Torah all day. His complaints change nothing. Barry is his mother's son, and Ida runs the Judaism in the house, not my uncle. Barry hangs onto his *kippah* and observes Shabbat.

Just as I seem to represent Sid's dead brother Harry to him, he represents my father right back at me. He arrives home each night sweating from working at the family business. My dad did that. He wears working men's khakis and short sleeve button down shirts, undershirts beneath them. My dad did that. He swears and uses foul language, forgetting to clean it up around the kids. My dad did that. My aunt runs the house and raises the children, with Sid maybe under the belief that it all just gets magically done. My dad did that.

I am a little afraid of Aunt Ida, though by the end of the summer I think that she genuinely likes me, but it is hard to tell. I think, at least I am providing her a perfect opportunity to extend some Jewish influence. She seems ecstatic when I manage to date a Jewish guy totally by accident. She is supportive of him, positively beaming when he comes to pick me up. She greets non-Jewish dates with dead silence. I am stunned that a parent has an opinion, since at home there is a feeling that we should bring home any guy we can find out there - push, tug or pull them home – there's no litmus test for the guys we date, no bar to leap over. Anything goes.

In Chicago, my aunt drives us to their tiny store down narrow traffic-clogged streets, buses ahead us and behind us, filling the air with diesel fumes. There are no universal turn lanes and no left turn lanes, so if you decide to drive in the left lane, guess what – you are just plain going to get stuck. The drivers patiently sit, stuck like this, through multiple lights, like sheep. I'm aware that in Arizona, guns would be drawn.

Each time we screech to a halt at a red light, Aunt Ida grabs the gear shift sticking out of the steering column and slams the gear up, from drive into park, like it is just too exhausting to sit there with her shoe pressing down upon the brake pedal for one extra second, the car should do the braking for her. She is willing to watch the light, wait for it to cycle to green, slam the gear shift back from park into drive, jerk away from her dead stop, perhaps when the drivers behind her begin to honk, but that's about it. She seems to want to sit on that front bench seat like it's a living room couch, relax for a minute before she has to continue tackling the exhausting task of driving.

Since I'm the visiting cousin from Arizona, I ride permanently in the back seat, able to get a good view of exactly what's going on up there in the front. The first year I come to visit, my cousin Barry, who's four months older than me, is a driver, but not yet a trusted driver, so he's relegated to the front passenger side. He's only allowed to take the wheel when my aunt can't even be bothered with the gear shifting, when she has no more energy at all and is okay just flopping over in the passenger seat waiting for Barry to crash into someone.

Along with me in the low status tundra of the back seat is my younger cousin, Jeffrey, who's only twelve. Jeffrey is permanently tanned, with streaky blonde hair, a Greek god of a Jew, so to speak. At that time he is a typical twelve-year-old, playing with yoyos, reading the Guinness Book of World Records, and playing Monopoly for hours on end to become a rich real estate tycoon.

When my aunt takes me and my cousin Laurie shopping, she checks the labels on everything before she'll consider buying, pursing her lips, and refusing to buy from anti-Semitic countries or any countries that evoke a negative feeling in her.

I hear her muttering, "China! Communist junk!" She's had enough of Communism, and the whole eastern bloc is problematic for quality. Anything Russian is excluded because they hate Jews, and, if something happens to be made in Hungary, where she was born, forget about it. I wonder what she's looking for – are any countries good? Armed with a historical prejudice, we walk away from the clothing racks empty handed.

"How is your sister Denise? Brenda? And Lauren. Why she isn't married yet?"

I'm at a family party, my Aunt Etta quizzing me, everyone turns to listen. This is dad's side of the family only, and the spotlight is on me. This get together proves what I'd always thought – that my aunts have a sixth sense about my family in Arizona. They're preternaturally interested in our lives out in Arizona, and they somehow know how to get every bit of information out of me.

This is a red alarm zone for me. I know I'm not supposed to blab about my family, and I know this without anyone needing warn me. But everyone seems to sense that there's something screwy going on out there with us. First there was the evidence of the complete madhouse my parents ran in Skokie, with police cars pulling up to disgorge random sisters here and there, even me, the pre-teen shoplifter. Gallivanting around teen bars in Evanston, one sister a runaway quickly caught, another one hanging out with the hotrodders in front of our house until all hours of the night, a downward sliding scale of behavior. So the expectations for my family are already low.

There are things going on in Arizona that have wafted their way over to Chicago, the cause of the relatives chortling gleefully over. There's one sister's sudden and predicted teenage pregnancy, her wedding, and the birth of her first daughter ("Half Jewish!" they exclaim, apparently the first in the millennia of our family's existence) and the birth of a second daughter the next year. There's my sister Brenda's upcoming wedding to "our second non-Jew," everyone tsk-tsking in unison. This is when I find out that our weddings will be boycotted if they are intermarriages. Not even a check, that serious. They can read between the lines of Mom's prevarication on their phone calls. The aunts know there's some monkey business going on.

Then there's the topic of my mother.

"And your mother?" Aunt Etta asks. She asks this like she's expecting the worse.

My mother's life since we moved from Chicago can be

neatly summarized into a few categories. There was Dad dying and her comatose widow's stupor, which was aunt-approved as of sufficient severity. There was her sudden awakening and the fervor with which she joins Jewish Singles. The aunts nod their heads sagely. Searching for a new spouse is looked on with general approval – a panicked, desperate widow in the mid-Seventies is understandable. What's a woman without a man? They shrug. There's also this great pronouncement made by each one of my aunts when they hear of my mother dating, the universally agreed-upon statement that "she's not getting any younger." This means that she'd better chase some man down now rather than wait, because only she is aging, not the men.

My aunts are part of the invisible network of voluntary *shadchans*, matchmakers, out searching for a match for my mother, coming up with a man here, a man there, some widower she shouldn't overlook, some eligible man living under a rock someplace, maybe under a bridge. No one is so bad that my mother should overlook him. She should be so picky? She's got baggage. The age thing, certainly. Being forty-five when you're married is bad enough but being forty-five when you're single is a disaster.

And the seven of us are certainly no asset. We are generally viewed as a ball and chain in their attempts to match our mother up. How will she focus her life completely on a man with us in and out of the house?

They search their minds for a man. Frugal, miserly, angry, obnoxious – none of that matters. More importantly, will she move to wherever the man is, leaving us in Arizona? Will she move to Pennsylvania? To Israel? Back to Chicago?

To civilization?

There's Mom's ongoing troublesome relationship with Mickey Shapiro. The aunts approve of this relationship for one reason and one reason only, because Mickey is Jewish. They wave away such paltry concerns as Mickey's cruelty to his sons and his hatred of us, casting this information off with a flick of their wrists. All men are inferior creatures to the all-knowing Jewish woman and must naturally be honed into something new. You take what you get and then you fix them. Cruelty, *shmuelty*. All the ironing out a man's flaws can come later. Most important is that my mother seal the deal and get married – to a Jew. And for that, Mickey's as good as anyone.

They want the scoop on Mom's careers, hopefully bad news to tsk over. First, the failed store, then the *farkoktah* diet program she was selling, and finally, reluctantly, about her success in real estate, which is not as exciting as failures and looming disaster. They get bored and look away as I describe my mother's career in glowing terms. The only happy ending to this story is remarriage, not career success. Somewhere there is the inkling that she was supposed to come crawling back to Chicago after my dad died. There is a continuing and permanent astonishment that my mother didn't immediately pack us all up and leave Arizona the minute that happened. After all, hadn't Arizona killed him? My mother was supposed to skulk home to Chicago and do what she was supposed to do – be a miserable widow. She wasn't supposed to bounce back, and she certainly wasn't supposed to thrive.

There's the stuff no one knows but that I reveal because I am a gullible open book, unable to stop myself from blabbering nonstop from their first questions. I can't resist my precipitous fall into the open-ended questions. I tell them about my loser boyfriends, "no, they're not Jewish," I admit. I somehow reveal details about our family by not knowing the simplest answers to questions about synagogues and the local Jewish community. I tell them too much about Mom and Mickey, about money, about school. I'm in the spotlight at the family party, trying desperately to give them the answers they want, to get nodding heads.

To be honest, I'm not used to anyone being interested in me at all or asking me questions. I'm thrilled to talk. But at the end of each family party, having revealed everything that was asked and more, instead of feeling close to them, I don't. I feel exposed, like I lifted the roof off our house in Scottsdale and let them all peer in.

Twenty-Four
Past Imperfect

When I'd left Chicago four years earlier, my three best friends and I were a gang of four virginal thirteen-year-olds. There were the two Lindas – Linda Winkler and me – our friend Dina, who wasn't afraid of anyone, and Jill, the one German Aryan living in Skokie, her mother's German accent ringing through the streets when she called for Jill to come in each night. We were innocents, other than a little random shoplifting, maybe some cigarette smoking done only in front of mirrors to see how cool we looked, no inhaling.

But I get back four years later and now they're in disarray, the friendships broken apart in the intervening years. Jill gossips about Dina, Dina gossips about Jill, and Linda Winkler pretends the two of them don't exist. The only thing that unifies Jill and Dina is actually their mutual hatred of Linda. Since they are not college-bound and Linda is, she apparently dumped the two of them. She hangs out with me because I apparently satisfy this litmus test.

I balance on the tightrope stretched tautly between

them. Peace must be maintained at all costs. I see each of them separately, like they've gotten a divorce in my absence. I'm aware I've come back to the wrong future.

We are seventeen but Jill is somehow married and has a baby. I'm to pretend this is normal. She has a nineteen-year-old husband, though the marriage is fragmenting and she's back in her mother's house. My days with Jill are spent pushing the baby around Skokie in his baby carriage, all the neighbors gossiping behind their curtains as Jill tries to hide her bruised black eye from her most recent fight with her husband. I'm not allowed to talk about anything important. I sometimes think it would kill Jill to have a serious conversation. The black eye looms between us, unmentioned.

I've lost a lot of things in the intervening years in Arizona, but it doesn't occur to me right away that I've even lost my friends – these friends. It's something I didn't expect – that my family's moving would change everything – both the world we left behind and the world we were driving towards. It will take a few more summers – half Skokie, half Scottsdale, half Scottsdale, half Skokie, to figure it out. I'm nowhere and nothing, trapped between the two sides of myself, not fitting in completely in either place. Though we hang out every summer, we can't ever completely recapture what's lost.

My days with Linda are relatively genteel – movies, bike riding, shopping.

One day, we're out riding bicycles even though we're clearly past prime bike riding age. We've headed out on our way nowhere, down Skokie's tar-lined streets.

Linda's dressed in a jaunty bike riding costume. Her

weight is meticulously maintained so she looks good in the shorts that are in style that summer, runner's shorts with contrast white piping and our mutual name running vertically down the side. She also has on a bright shirt with a V-neck and big fake pearl earrings. Her hair is red for some reason, or eggplant-colored anyway, with a side part and meticulously styled. This is a polished look for 1977 bike riding.

I, on the other hand, am not jaunty. I'm wearing the requisite shorts, my name also written vertically down the leg, but they're busting tight on me, pulling across my hips. They are too short, showing legs that I think would be best left to the imagination. A year earlier I'd sprouted spider veins on my right leg, which I blamed on my mother. This leg needs to be covered. This leg doesn't wear shorts or short skirts. This leg would prefer to never wear a bathing suit. My hair is bad, in some pre-college, winged hairdo, brown and non-descript. My makeup has sweated off. I have no jaunty bandana.

We're not really out for exercise, we're out in some distorted image of our thirteen-year-old selves – four years later – still looking for boys. Eagerly scanning the landscape for boys. And, since I'm with Linda, they must be college-bound boys. We're still using our bodies, our faces, as fishing nets, to scoop down into the neighborhood and see what we come up with. Will it be a "hey" shouted from a house? A friendly wave here or there? A honk from a passing car? Because we will take that in lieu of everything else.

Then, suddenly we hear a yell.

"Hey you there! Girls, stop, wait up!"

We stop, turn around. Finally we are going to meet someone. We smile like fashion models.

But what's behind us isn't a potential boyfriend, it's a huffing and puffing police officer sans squad car, trying to catch up to us on his own ten-speed, using his voice as siren, as flashing lights, as a mobile PA system.

Linda says, "He's cute!"

I say, "He's a bicycle cop."

We stop. He stops. He wipes his forehead off in the sweaty Chicago summer day.

"Girls, are you aware you ran a stop sign back there?"

Linda and I look dumbly at each other. Ran a stop sign? On our bikes?

We say that to him.

"Ran a stop sign? On our bikes?"

He says, yes, that bicyclists in the road are required to obey all the road signs as if they were cars, and are we aware that we can get a ticket for this?

I'm from out of state, and unlicensed besides, so I'm not worried about a *bike ticket*. Even though I look a little flippant and unconcerned and Linda looks flippant, unconcerned and, yes, jaunty, the officer decides against it.

"I'm going to let you off with a warning this time," he tells us. He gives us both a warning from the Skokie Police. I take this back to my aunt's house and tape it in my scrapbook.

"Ronny, you prick! You suck!"

Dina leans out the window of her car, yelling at Ronny Mandelbaum, who's pumping gas at a station in Skokie. She looks over at me on the passenger side. I'm pretty sure she's having the time of her life. I understand that in this world, negative attention is trotted out to get a reaction, to get positive attention. Nothing really seems to make Dina happier than zooming around the gas station where Ronny Mandelbaum works, around and around and around again on a Saturday night, yelling out obscenities, exhortations, profanities and, finally, sexual come-ons, which he, after much screaming back, much ribbing by his coworkers at the gas station, will take her up on.

My time with Dina is spent this way, in her AMC Pacer, out looking for guys.

So Ronny yells back, in a moment of rare wit, "No you suck! Really good!"

Dina seems to love that. She says, "Can you believe he said that?"

Our revolutions around the gas station increase, the scenery whirring by, all the other drivers on Skokie Boulevard listening, all the guys at the gas station listening, all of Skokie, their ears straining at doors.

Finally, we pull up at the gas station. She has filled my head with descriptions, lurid descriptions, not of Ronny, but of the car he drives. The car is part of the attraction. A Trans Am with a spoiler, an engine hump in the hood, a loud motor, and an expensive paint job. He spends hours working on it each weekend, lying beneath it on his quiet tree-lined suburban street, the neighbors all counting the days until he moves out with the loud car, his loud friends, and their loud cars.

We pull up, get out, and he walks up. We're introduced but I can't shake his hand because it is black with motor oil. The rest of him is shiny with sweat like his clothes might just slide off and, indeed, his pants *are* sliding off, barely hanging on by a belt on its last loop, slung low under his belly. His hair is dirty blonde and untrimmed. He's slovenly and unkempt, wearing the pinstriped shirt mandated by the service station. This is not a fashion statement, this is slob. An oval name badge proclaims him "Ronny."

I'm having some difficulty understanding Dina's attraction here. I mean, I am obviously the queen of low standards, but this is a whole new scale.

He barely glances at me and immediately starts bantering with Dina, a continuation of the fighting, flirtatious, sexual innuendo, transferred now from the moving car to the parking lot. I imagine in a few years this bantering could easily descend into wife-battering violence.

"You look hot, Dina."

"Oh, I know it, Ronny."

"Where you think you're goin' like that?"

"We're goin' where we're goin'!"

"I'll tell you where you're goin'"

"Oh yeah? Where am I goin'?"

This goes on for a full ten minutes. My eyes glaze over, but I keep a polite smile firmly on my face like I think this is very witty repartee. I give appropriate ha ha laughs when Dina looks at me, to show I appreciate her witty comebacks. It's not that I don't find a lot of teenage stuff boring, but this Skokie stuff, this driving and yelling, this double entendre-ing with sub-standard Jewish oafs, this does get to me.

Finally we leave and then I'm in for it good because then I have to reel back the tape and recount every second of Dina's conversation with Ronny Mandelbaum for her and, with her, chortle at his comeuppances, crow at her victories, until, finally, we are tooling down the road, safely away from the gas station, wild and free, zooming along in the Pacer.

Before my family had moved to Arizona, I had maintained a determined crush on one boy for six years, Larry Aronson. My sheer determination to marry myself off to Larry Aronson – at eight-years-old, at twelve-years-old – was the stuff of legend. Early on, I'd chased him maniacally and daily around the playground. I'd jumped on him and kissed him whenever one of my classmates asked me to do that. One day when he was riding past my house, my sisters pulled him off his bike and performed a fake wedding ceremony that involved a cigar band ring. I had pined for him when he transferred schools for three years, then exulted when he returned for seventh grade. But that last year before we moved, in the depths of adolescence, I found myself incapable of speech. I sat behind Larry in our home room, seated alphabetically, he an "A" and me a "B," unable to utter a word to him all year.

Despite my ongoing crush on Greg in Scottsdale, despite my other meanderings, there is still a part of me that thinks I'm going to marry Larry Aronson. I believe it enough so that I need to see him during this trip. I nag Dina's *kishkes* out until she figures out a way to make this happen.

It's another summer night. Dina has reluctantly agreed to take me to a high school party where she thinks I'll be able to find Larry along with all the other people I knew from seventh grade. I've been waiting for this during my entire month-long visit. As I walk in my old neighborhood, I almost expect the child-Larry to ride by on his bicycle. As I walk past my old elementary school, I almost expect him to be there, nine-years-old and swinging on monkey bars, responding to my written proposal of marriage with an elusive, "maybe." A "maybe" that I'm just about ready to cash in.

"Listen, Linda, I really don't want to stay long. I hate these people!" Dina glares at me so I'll take her seriously. I do. I know we've got a busy night ahead of us, needing to stalk Ronny Mandelbaum again at the gas station in downtown Skokie.

We're at a high school party filled with people who have somehow flashed forward and aged four years. I remember them all, but they float past me like I'm not there, ignoring me, like maybe I'm still in Arizona and just imagining this, imagining Carol and Abby, the two most popular girls, still irritable, still petulant, still with a string of followers marching in lock step formation around them. Can it be possible that no one remembers Linda Burt who went to school with them from kindergarten to 7th grade? I remember them all like it's a movie strip that plays over and over in my mind.

It turns out they're not so much ignoring me as talking about me behind my back and pretty much in front of my back, and exclaiming their surprise, just loudly enough and with enough horror in their voices for me to overhear.

"That's Linda Burt? OH MY GOD! She used to be so cute!"

And so, since I'm definitely worth more to talk about than to talk to, they pretend they don't know me.

It might have been a little different if I had come back looking anything like I had when I left, but I hadn't. I had gotten heavy, distorted. I didn't look like the gangly seventh grader who had moved away.

Dina hovers in front of me like an Israeli commando, watching them warily. She looks at her watch every couple of minutes and says, "Have you had enough? These people are un-fucking-believable, Linda."

Then suddenly she pushes me in front of her and says, "You gotta be shittin' me! He's coming over here! Aronson is coming over here!" And, sure enough, Larry Aronson is walking toward me. I say, "What?" and she says, "Larry is walking right towards us! He's going to talk to you!"

I come face to face with Larry but just as I'm distorted, he is distorted too. He doesn't look like I had imagined in all the daydreams these years away. I expected the cute, boyish thirteen-year-old, his dark hair flopping over his forehead, maybe still wearing his signature look from 1973, jeans and lumberjack shirts, or a baseball cap and jersey. Not this person. This is a man. Thicker and wider than I expected, the boy gone.

He says hi and then he makes polite small talk, maybe about Arizona and why I'm so pale, a topic of unending interest to Chicagoans. I say something about not being able to talk to him the entire year I sat behind him in seventh grade, and he looks at me quizzically, like he doesn't remember us even being in the same class. Or at the same school, or in the same universe.

Someone calls to him from the other side of the party. He looks over and smiles and I see the boy inside of him for one short second. Then he walks away.

The days glide along, with me hanging out with Linda Winkler while she badmouths Dina and Jill, and me hanging out with

Dina and Jill and listening to them badmouth Linda. I'm balancing on a delicate fence. I'm supposed to agree with everyone, though mostly I see what they became and what I became in the four-year gap since I moved.

I sit in Jill's kitchen for hours on end with Dina and some new friends they've managed to corral in the intervening years. The hours spent in Jill's kitchen are rough. Jill is now the center of the universe and she's ignorant and selfish and bad-tempered. Even her good moods hit me wrong, the constant repetitive recounting of a funny episode from our day, told and retold to everyone ad nauseum and I am to laugh and laugh each time, laugh like I just heard it my first time, laugh like my face isn't frozen in a fake laugh, in a painted-on laugh.

How did everything fragment? I want to believe it was me suddenly moving that set the whole thing awry, that I could have saved them had I been here, that we'd still be best friends, a gang of four innocent girls, flinging our hair, running from boys, older, but still ourselves. But who am I fooling? I couldn't even save myself.

When I return to Arizona, my sisters are agog with disbelief. Aunt Ida – our arch enemy – is the one relative with whom I chose to stay? I couldn't find a home with anyone else? Herbie? Uncle Barney? Aunt Rose? A Friend? On the street?

It seems I've betrayed my family. Among all the other beliefs we hold dear is the fact that, of all the relatives we fear and whom we fear are judging us, this is the apex. When we imagine Chicago as an anthropomorphic being, God-like, wagging its finger at us for all of our profligacy, it's Aunt Ida's image that comes to mind. And I had become best friends with Cousin Laurie? Who? That little mouse of a cousin of ours to whom we paid no attention growing up? The one who was afraid of dogs? Surely, I'm joking? I've gone too far.

Could they possibly understand? Legions of relatives were so happy to invite me for dinner, but it was this aunt, this uncle, who opened their house warmly, without question, insisting I stay there. Opened up their family to God-knows-what crazy thoughts and ideas I was bringing from our household in Arizona. Who else could have given me exactly the thing I didn't even know I was looking for? A sign, an arrow, just coming into view, just appearing out of the mist, pointing my way back to Judaism?

Back in my room writing, I find a surprise in my journal. My cousin has written a three-page entry entreating me to return. I begin to plan my trip there for the next summer, and the next and the next, one foot planted in Skokie and one in Scottsdale.

Twenty-Five
The Couch

I
t's a Saturday night after I've returned from Chicago. I'm spending my senior year sitting in our family room, and hanging out with my mother, who has temporarily broken up with Mickey Shapiro. Only this could transplant her from his family room to ours. From my critical position of observation, I can imagine there must be many obvious reasons for them to break up, but my mother summarizes it as one thing only. He hates us, she loves us, and she always picks her daughters.

My mom and I are a couple in so many words, TV buddies. We are obsessed with various miniseries – *Roots*, *North and South*, *Holocaust*, *Rich Man, Poor Man*, and *The Thorn Birds*. We will watch anything as long as it takes up a lot of time, a multi-day commitment. Saturday nights are devoted to watching *Love Boat* and *Fantasy Island*. I guess we're both waiting for our love boats to float by, to pick us up. Her love life has stopped and mine hasn't begun. She's aging backwards and I'm aging forward, meeting somewhere in the middle on the couch.

It's a necessary interlude, this sitting quietly, reorganizing the past in my brain while planted on the couch, evaluating, and waiting and fantasizing about what great things will happen to me that aren't happening now. So I sit and wait for my life to start. Again. My senior year stretches out before me at my high school, waiting for graduation, my friends all mysteriously gone, disappearing into jobs, dance schools, vocational schools, and community colleges.

I have no interest in graduating early, no interest in getting to college early. I'm not so eager to move away from the familiar, from my sisters, from our seven hearts that beat as one. I know deep in my heart that the most distance I can handle is going to a state university in Arizona. I can go no farther than Tucson in one direction or Flagstaff in the other. I don't want to change too much. I don't want to be unrecognizable as one of us.

Being one or two generations behind other American Jews, bred on the side of the Holocaust which hoists our parents into this country as immigrants, we seem to have different goals than regular American Jewish families. First and foremost, we must all stay alive. Then, having been established as alive, we should get good jobs, work hard, and earn a living. Not a fancy living, and not necessarily a prestigious living, just a living. We should obtain a middle-class lifestyle like our parents, not below and not above.

Eventually, with these goals as our hallmark, we burn up the vocational technical curriculum, including beauty college, dog grooming institute, secretarial school, medical assistant training, title clerk licensing, notary public training. Almost everyone gets a real estate license.

On the couch, my mother only stirs to life when a Hollywood star her approximate age suddenly shows up on the screen. A commercial, a guest appearance, a fluke, it doesn't matter. What a wonderful coincidence that it just happens to be 1977 and Elizabeth Taylor has just married Senator John Warner and has gained a bunch of weight. This is true enjoyment for my mother. She is almost licking her chops.

My mother, safely ensconced on her Naugahyde sofa in her house in Scottsdale on the other side of the TV set, gets to be judge and jury for the appearance of all women ever and their body sizes. In this, she is not unusual for her generation and the time period. She also considers herself somewhat of a weight loss expert due to the whole Slender Now episode. She doesn't even need such an egregious example as Elizabeth Taylor in order to come alive. My mother can perceive weight changes of anyone, up and down, at a glance. In grams.

Her greatest critiques are for how all the women on the planet are aging, with the automatic assumption, again, safely from the couch, that she is not. The grudging phrase, "She looks good," is the best any aging female who appears before us on the TV set can get from my mom. Jacqueline Onassis, Doris Day, Florence Henderson, Shirley Jones – they all pass muster. If they are fat, they are ruled out. If they look old, they get a muttered Yiddish imprecation like *"Oy gavult!"* or, on a quick intake of breath, normally reserved just for the accidental viewing of horrific car accidents, maybe an *"Oy!"*

If it's bad enough – think Rosemary Clooney – it can even require a call to the aunts in Chicago to discuss this insult to humanity – a woman letting herself go. This will be fun to chortle over.

This is a great time for me, a necessary time. I think of it like I'm in a cocoon before the butterfly bursts forth. I am literally larva or pupa, or whatever. I've grown out of all my bad behaviors, and I am a fit companion for my mom. After all, I'm almost an adult, appalled right along with her by the weight gains of all the world's women, even though my own body can't bear this type of scrutiny. We've gotten close through the vagaries of her relationship with Mickey and my non-relationship with Greg, and because of my future that looms brightly in front of me. I'm taking college entrance exams, applying to college. She's always believed in me, in all of us, and here I am, going off like a rocket. What fun to also mention this to the aunts in Chicago! She has endless optimism for my future.

It's especially fun being planted on the couch with my mother when my sisters who have moved out come to visit a few times a week. There is a pilgrimage to the couch because where there is a couch is our mother and our umbilical cords only stretch so far. The married and the soon-to-be married come by, dragging their husbands and boyfriends, all of us squishing together in a big pile. The men sit apart because who cares where the men sit? They're not us, not Burt girls, a litter of cats piled around our mother like this, contented. The piling rejuvenates us with its intimacy, our mutual agreement on every topic in the world. When it gets late, each sister untangles herself from the rest of us, pries herself off the couch, grabs her significant other, and heads home.

Life unfolds before us on the TV screen. In spring 1977, my mother and I witness the unthinkable, the Neo-

Nazis' attempt to demonstrate in Skokie, our hometown. We cannot look away. This fulfills every prediction ever made by my mother about the Nazis rising again. She sits mesmerized watching the news coverage. She can't turn it off.

Sometime midway through high school I'd suddenly realized that, while I'd end up graduating, I just may not get into college. Apparently, the requirements were not the same. Up until then, I'd gotten all my high school guidance counseling from various burned-out hippie friends, all older than me. Whatever they believed, I believed.

Chaparral is an "open" high school, kind of like a Montessori preschool, but for teenagers. I could wander in and out of the classrooms since most of them conveniently didn't have doors, sign into my classes – which basically means I will learn the material on my own – and then then disappear to the hippie hangouts, on the field or under a spaceship-like ramp that extends out of the second story of the building onto the field.

But when I finally realize that I am getting no education at all and may not get into college, I take control of the situation. I am determined to somehow wrest an education out of nothing, to homeschool myself, or at least supplement the education I'm getting. My basic theory is that I need to be much better read than I am, so I begin devouring books, anything we have at home, which just happens to be the entire Harold Robbins oeuvre, some R.F. Delderfield, and some Jacqueline Susann. I don't care. I am going to learn and become well-read no matter what, even if it is from *Valley of the Dolls*. I learn American History from reading John Jakes. Art

History comes from a book of Magritte's work that I find hidden under a sister's bed. I turn the pages, each one more troubling, more horrifying, than the next. I'm afraid to turn the pages. Finally, when I come upon an image of a lower body topped by a jar, that's it. I slam the book shut.

There is a part of me that is still the book-obsessed and diary-obsessed Skokie girl. I keep a meticulous chart of all the books I read, the number of pages each has, and how long it takes me to read them. A clipboard full. Sometimes I time myself to see how many pages I can read in a set time period, faster and faster, hoping to devour whole books by glancing at them.

I have diaries – piles and piles of diaries. I write religiously, year after year, my diaries serving not only as a friend but as a psychologist. In my freshman year, they are filled psychedelic designs and pot drawings, in later years I create some 1970s version of mandalas. Filled with abbreviations, like "OTR" for on the rag and "UTR" for under the ramp, our hangout. By senior year, my entries become inundated with French. There are my yearly New Year's Resolutions, a ritualized check list, the December 31st Linda sternly admonishing the later Linda not to be a dope fiend and to lose weight for once and for all.

I know already that I have a book inside of me. I take Creative Writing for one semester. We are to write in our journals in first person but write our class pieces in third. My teacher is mystified.

My teacher meets with me. "Linda," he says, "your journal is very entertaining but none of that translates over to your fiction writing."

He sighs heavily. This is apparently an unsurmountable problem. I can't write third person fiction and we all know that first person is never allowed. It's a puzzle with no solution. How will I ever write this book that has already started burning a hole in me if I just can't write?

I don't know it ahead of time, but it turns out that the last days of my junior year are the last days of high school as I know them. The last days of fun and parties with all my friends there. I am determined to do this thing right, to go to school all four years and graduate exactly on time, to drag myself there every miserable month, but my friends apparently hadn't planned to do the same. We all walk in the graduation ceremony in June of 1978, but they either finish their credits early, or get jobs that count for credit and work each day, I don't know. Either way, they're gone.

This kind of optimistic charging off into the future early is not for me. I'm just too terrified of finding out suddenly at the end that I'm missing some critical class necessary to get in college. I trudge onward. If this is my senior year then senior year it must be, all the way to its miserable, sputtering end, its dying, gasping last breath.

The hippie friends I'd met as a freshman, the ones who had said they'd attend their four years and get out, with or without a diploma? Gone. I'd shown up high school a fourteen-year-old, worshipping the unimaginable glamor of the juniors and seniors. But as I hop up the ladder of school, they disappear. Everyone ages out eventually. My friends gone, I'm suddenly at the top of the heap alone.

As my senior year progresses, I'm aware that I'm

superfluous on campus, like I should be gone already. And worse, since I'm car-less and my friends who drove me everywhere have disappeared, I have the humiliation of being back to riding the bus. Just me and thirty freshmen, every day, there in the morning and back in the afternoon.

It's an interesting and time-consuming process, trying to get home on the bus. I live just three miles from school – it should be a quick and easy ride. But the school bus route is labyrinth, the bus ride not without its excitement. Our driver seems to be somewhat of a daredevil and may lack some internal awareness of the exact size of the bus. She tries to fit the bus, its windshield as big as an aquarium, down the narrow, cactus-strewn streets of Scottsdale. I wonder, how will she fit the bus through these screeching turns on these newly-paved roads? The bus needs to bend, to curve, to perhaps fold in on itself, to suspend the space/time continuum and fold in half to continue its journey.

The bus driver does the only thing she can. She runs over curbs, runs over whatever is on the curbs, clips parked cars, mailboxes, traffic signals, street signs. She runs over anything in the way of this giant, lumbering box, delivering me, somehow, safely home.

"Do you want to learn how to drive or not?" My sister Sherry is standing in my room, jangling keys at me.

A few minutes later I'm finally in the driver's seat of the station wagon, my Arizona driving permit in my purse, the twins in the car. They are going to teach me to drive in just this one lesson because that's all they have patience for. There are exasperated sighs, maybe an idea that I should have learned

301

from watching. I understand ahead of time that they'll tolerate no nonsense. I'd better be really good. No malarkey, like mistaking the brake pedal for the gas pedal.

I'm reasonably sure there won't be any problems. In the desert there's plenty of space to learn how to drive and not have to worry about crashing into anything, except rural mailboxes, which always seem to appear before us with no warning. Or barricades.

I understand the Burt Family credo – we don't take Driver's Education because it's not required, and we don't take any classes that aren't required. Also, in our family we have a tradition of learning by osmosis, which is how I've been learning. I've been riding as a passenger in cars for over seventeen years by this time, so I consider myself an expert. It looks easy from the passenger seat anyway.

I put the car in drive, and I freeze up.

"Press on the gas!" Sherry yells at me from the front passenger seat.

I stare down the mile-long hood of the station wagon, which I don't remember looking this long before, and we shoot forward.

"What are you doing, you idiot?" Sherry again.

"I pressed on the gas like you said!"

"Not so hard!"

So I press hard on the brakes to correct myself and she glares at me more.

I'm out on the pitch-black street, driving past its sixteen houses, and coming pretty quickly upon the end of the block where our street ends with sheared off pavement and a wooden barricade, a drop off the edge of civilization, the dark desert stretching beyond.

She says, "Stop!"

I say, "You want me to stop?" I have forgotten how to stop.

"Yes! Stop the car!"

I know the street ends there because I've walked there a million times and also because the station wagon's headlights are lighting up the barricade. But I drive right into it.

Sherry screeches at me. "Get out of the car!"

I get out, switch seats with her and she turns it around and drives back home.

That ends my only formal driving lesson.

After that I realize it's going to be up to me to teach myself. My mother is simply not built for this job. She tells me her car is off limits.

"It's my livelihood!" she says, which means that without that car she can't sell houses, or she'd be walking to open houses, or carting real estate clients around town on foot or something.

Of course, I'm not planning on giving up. I nab her extra set of car keys out of a box on her dresser and then I cunningly lock that box, so she'll think they're locked in there. Each night, when she is safely sleeping on one end of the house, I start the car up on the other end, roll out of the garage and down the driveway and teach myself to drive, zooming on the open Arizona roads. Soon, magically, I know how to drive.

There's an awkward moment much later, after I'm licensed. She hands me her real set of keys one day to go to the store and, by accident, I lock them in the running car, a big problem at the time. When I finally reach her, she, of course, can't open the box where she thinks her extra set of keys are located. I am forced to tell her where they really are – in my room.

It's late at night. I'm in my mom's car, I've snuck out of the garage, the windows down, barreling down Dreamy Draw, a mountain pass, on my way to see Greg, whom I've now loved for four years. He gets an apartment my senior year and I go there and go there and go there while my mother sleeps soundly on the other side of the house. I zoom down this mountainous road to get into Phoenix, to get to Greg's crumbling, pot-smoke and beer can-filled apartment loaded with other ne'er do wells, there to spend endless hours making out with him on his bed.

Right then, things are as good as they'll get between us. We're almost a couple, without ever having been on a proper date, without Greg ever saying anything at all, without me knowing anything about how he feels. I never have any idea how I feel.

Compared to the first three years of our relationship, things are going very well. We've long moved on from our staring days. There was the glorious boondocker during my junior year where we spent the night rolling around on top of scrub bushes for hours kissing. For a while after that there was nothing, but now there's this giant leap forward in which I drive long distances to sit in his apartment with him and some other dropouts and pretend they're interesting, just so I can end up in another roll around make out session with Greg. We never have sex, we just roll and roll and roll, until one day I pack up all my boxes, stuff them in the Lincoln, and go to college.

There are also his surprise visits at my bedroom window. He apparently can't come to the front door, there's just a knocking on my window, like I'm in the Red Light District of Amsterdam. And then there's some awkward small talk, where I pretend this is perfectly normal. Our conversation is always devoid of why he's showing up at my house out of all the other houses in the world. And we have an unspoken understanding – I'm not to interpret his coming here as interest in me and each time I see him we have not done this – he hasn't shown up at my window, we haven't madly made out. We always start back at the beginning. It's an endless Groundhog Day.

"What are you doing?" He says, outlined by the frame of my window.

I say, "Nothing. Come in!" And I'm bright-eyed and pretending this is normal, anything not to scare him away like I'm trying to tame a deer. Greg sets the tone for our relationship.

From our first make out session in the spring of 1977 until March of 1978, by which time Greg had fully dropped out again, we continue to meet up in these shady ways. Him in my window, or both of us at a party, or me at his crummy apartment, which I enter through the door, not the window. We're moving in opposite directions fast. I'm getting close to graduation, moving beyond college brochures to filling out applications, then to acceptance and rejection letters. He is doing exactly what he was doing when I met him, partying, bumming rides, getting fired from jobs, and trying to get money out of his dad.

He asks me, "What'll happen if I stay?"

He asks me this while standing with one leg in and one leg out of my bedroom window. He asks me this from my bed, at the end of a tumultuous make out session, his friend outside revving a motorcycle, ready to leave. He asks me this at his apartment after we've rolled around madly, passionately kissing for hours, with me knowing we've gone as far as we can go without more clothes coming off.

I understand his question. If he stays, if I stay, will we have sex?

It is unfortunate for Greg that when he finally decides to get together with me, I happen to be right in the middle of my three and a half years of celibacy. I am committed to this like a slightly slutty nun. I'm willing to roll around madly kissing, I'm willing to go over the shirt, over the bra, under the bra, but that's it. By then I know the sad, sad truth of teen sex. I know the equation, that teen sex means being used and dumped. Bad enough having him look through me like I'm invisible after we've rolled passionately back and forth over tumbleweeds and crashed into cacti at desert parties. Bad enough having him look at me like he's not sure who I am after we've kissed and said romantic things to each other. Bad enough having the memory of him in my bed, his hands on me, Greg mine all mine, just to know that the very next day he'll be gone like it never happened.

I know my tolerance level. I have a pretty good idea of how much pain I can take, and I can barely take this.

So, no, nothing is going to happen if he stays.

He'll just have to climb back out of my window and

onto his friend's waiting motorcycle to zoom off into the desert night. Or try another window somewhere else.

"Man, this is some bitchen pot!" One of Greg's roommates takes a deep drag off a joint, then passes it on.

At Greg's apartment I realize this is it — this is what our ilk does, this is life post-high school. We get apartments filled with our high school hippie friend-couples, now shacked up together, and it's a party every day. Over the months when I'm teaching myself to drive, I end up sitting at a lot of apartments, all rented by graduates or dropouts, and everyone's having a good time but me.

There are the couches, donated affairs, beat up things, sloped things that you fall into and from which you cannot rise. The people sitting on the ends are safe, but the people in the middle awkwardly fall together, almost into each other's laps. Furniture that has been thrown out of someone's basement or thrown out of someone's house or just thrown ends up here. Shelves are made of construction debris, with bricks for support and horizontal pieces of wood.

And there's the pot. A never-ending joint, pipe, bong, being passed around from the sloping couch to the concave chair, one mouth to another, a burning roach desperately inhaled until it's just a tiny scrap of paper in a roach clip. One last person inhales.

There's a lot of sitting. A lot of doing nothing, talking about nothing, or feigning interest in whatever they are talking about — weed, or something that happened, or weed. The topics in this apartment are firm — partying, pot, drugs, and how high we are.

I am supposed to sit here, dumb, and pretend this is all there is – this couch and this coffee table and these people and this life and pretend that I am happy happy happy. Am I college-bound or am I sloping-couch-bound? Am I moving out to go to school or am I going to sit on this couch until one day one of these guys, unscrubbed, unwashed, uncouched, crooks a finger at me to come hither and I am his?

Greg and I don't really talk, so we need to get to the make out session quickly. What on earth would we have to talk about? What could we have in common? Could he relate to my love of reading? My obsession with journaling? Would he be surprised that he's the star of so many of my diary entries?

My life is moving on, I'm growing up, I've become an aunt, and I'm preparing for college. But Greg is frozen in time and space. I ignore the coming conflict and I ignore the looming differences. I am happy just to have made the cut at all into the apartment.

My sister Francine picks me up the day I'm taking my driving test. I'm going to become a legal driver instead of the illegal driver I've been for about a year. I've carefully researched all the driver's license testing locations in greater Phoenix and have ruled out any one which requires parallel parking to pass. I'm also aware I need to take the test in the tiniest car available to me, and definitely not in my mother's gigantic car. My sister's purple AMC Gremlin will do perfectly.

I'm used to riding with the sisters who live at home, the ones who turn any car into a party mobile, music blasting, garbage shifting on the floor as we turn corners. Francine, though only eight years older than me, is made of other stuff.

Married at eighteen and of another era, her music is on as low as can possibly be detected by the human ear. I'm stunned to discover that she's never heard of Dan Fogelberg or Peter Frampton.

Greg shows up at my house on a Saturday night at the end of senior year. I'm in my bedroom at the front of the house when I hear a knock on the window. I peek out. Of course, it's him. Who else shows up like this?

I open the window. "Hi."

He says, "Hey, what's going on?" like he was just walking by and bumped into me.

I'm living two lives, of course. I've got the stoned life, being Greg's quasi-girlfriend, and then I've got the college-bound life. One life is never supposed to acknowledge the other. Somehow, I know I'm not supposed to mention this to Greg.

Yet I say, "Everything's great. I'm trying to get a job and I'm applying to colleges."

He gets a sneer on his face and says, "College? College is bullshit! What the hell do you need to go to college for? What a bunch of crap!"

I'm startled because I thought my college boundedness was obvious. That's what I am, after all, is a brain and two legs. I barely live in my body, just inhabiting my head.

He continues. "You're going to go to college and not know what you want to do but I'll be here having a really good start on my life!"

I didn't expect this forceful of an opinion, probably because our entire relationship was mostly a series of stares occurring over distance with dead silence about anything else. I just assumed he agreed about our unspoken future life. I'd be a college professor and he'd be my un-diploma'd husband, I'd be Dolly Parton to his Carl Dean, Loretta Lynn to his Doolittle Lynn. He doesn't appear to be on board for this. Not that he lives in my fantasy world, where we have a mutual future, but if he did, did he expect both of us to be uneducated?

I realize this relationship consists of two things only, the fantasy in my head and some make out sessions.

This would be a breakup-worthy disagreement if we were officially dating. I suddenly realize he's not smart and, simultaneously, that there's no wonderful hidden Greg in there like I'd imagined. It strips away the blinders on my eyes and I suddenly don't even think he's attractive. He's ugly to me, mean. I've been so willing to be compliant with all the unending stupidity of this relationship, all its ennui, all its ambiguity, all of his casual disregard, that this moment is like opening a door into all these things that I'd observed. He states his opposition to college, but I am going to college no matter what. There's nothing more to discuss. We stand there in the glare of our complete incompatibility.

In that moment I realize my relationship with Greg exists only in my imagination. In there he was Mr. Wonderful, an idealized Greg, along with an idealized version of me with Greg. Our pretend future dissolves before me, our fake marriage dissolved, our imagined children – those tiny, black-haired, mini-Gregs who would be raised right this time and not drink and drop out of high school, not rob houses, and not use girls – they disappear too. My tiny army of miniature

Gregs gone. That day in the window, I realize he isn't nice, not even nice under an outward shell of mean. There isn't anything he loves about me at all.

Part of me has been expecting Greg to charge in on a white horse and rescue me from my future, let me compromise everything away for love. None of this happens, of course. Greg disappears from my window. I wonder, will he keep showing up at the window after I move out, like he doesn't quite believe I'm gone? Like it was some kind of joke? Like I'd always be there, just waiting for him, so we could roll around on my bed and he could say, "What'll happen if I stay? Will something happen if I stay?"

It turns out my mother and I have this in common – romantic relationships that just don't work, bad choices always seeming to be good choices as we head into them. The bad choices revealing themselves later, after the relationships have left us in tatters. In other words, Mickey's back in his own house on his side of the street and Greg's on the back of a motorcycle, roaring away.

I rejoin my mother on the couch.

Twenty-Six
No One's Getting Any Younger

Towards the end of high school, my mom and I decide to take a trip together. We're zooming along on I-10 in her spacecraft-sized Lincoln Town Car driving west on our way to California heading to Van Nuys to visit Saul and Ruth Levenson, whom my mom met while living in a Displaced Persons Camp after the war.

This is a perfect vacation for my mother. She may pass for an American on an everyday basis, but there is a part of her that needs to speak Yiddish, to compare horror stories to others who lived through the war. To shake their heads at the incomprehensible nature of evil. She can do this with Ruth and Saul. They understand that they are responsible for keeping their stories alive, even if the outside world is barely interested. It's more than thirty years since the end of the war and, as my mother says, no one's getting any younger. And there's even another good reason to schlep to California. Ruth and Saul have two single sons to match me up with, Sidney and Sam. I have this one chance to marry myself off by age eighteen, another attempt to model my life on my sister Francine's.

We have a great time driving to Los Angeles. We reminisce – about me. How I've straightened up since my earlier hippie days. We plan ahead – for me. For college, for my brilliant life that, once it starts, is sure to go off like a rocket. This doesn't happen. We sing – or at least I do. I'm into a Joan Baez eight-track tape that was recorded in German. I garble all the words as I try to sing along. Why I've decided to torment my Holocaust Survivor mother with German language music as we head west is unknown. She is fine with it.

"It sounds like Yiddish," she says, nodding pleasantly.

There's so much I want to be and so much I want to do, and Mom believes in it all – my sparkling, golden future, shimmering there before us in the car, close enough to touch. Even though I sit there, overweight and wearing the one godawful pair of jeans that fit me, and a worn orange gauze pinafore top, she believes in me. I will be beautiful. I will be skinny. I will conquer the world. And I will maybe marry Sidney or Sam Levenson.

My mother has spent years ignoring all my poor behavior so she's excited for my future and amnesiac about my past. She's the eternal optimist where her daughters are concerned, ignoring anything that doesn't match with her starry-eyed view – weight gains, acne, drug use, drinking. She simply waits for us to come around again, come back into focus.

She is the perfect mother. She has endless, unending enthusiasm for every word that falls out of my mouth. She is constantly amazed by me, this creature to whom she gave birth. I just sit there reveling in her attention, on the crushed velour seats of the car, in its faded elegance, its dusty blue agedness, a blur zooming along the Interstate. Hey, Mom, let's talk about me.

We're alone on this trip. I'm used to being number six of seven, a big pile of sisters, with a type of diffuse attention paid to all of us, which lessens in intensity from the first daughter down. This is different, awkward, a little frightening, and also comforting. I don't know it at the time, but we're setting a template for our adult relationship.

We'd started with smaller forays, before this trip, with in-town trips to Park-n-Swap each weekend. She'd buy Southwestern jewelry – liquid silver necklaces, coral carved into tiny birds and strung into pointy necklaces, squash blossom necklaces, turquoise-inlaid belt buckles, and gigantic rings that cover her knuckles. She corners the market on Southwestern jewelry, despite it clashing with her fourteen-karat gold Egyptian pharaoh head pendant she wears every day.

I stand around and watch her wheel and deal with the merchants. I know how she'll work the crowd because my mother's been charming everyone she meets for years, and I've stood by and listened since I was a kid with her at the Jewel grocery store and the Singer Fabric store in Evanston. She will talk and talk and talk. In each conversation, she will manage to squeeze in the fact that she has seven daughters. This is her claim to fame and proudest accomplishment. She'll wriggle in that she's in real estate and discover whether they'd like to go shopping for a house. She'll end up with a bunch of swap meet clients, trying to figure out if there's a real, documentable income in there somewhere that will make it past a loan officer. She does not tell them she's a Holocaust Survivor. She has an instinct for what to tell and what not to tell, how to land on her feet in any situation, even in the ramshackle society of Park-n-Swap.

We get to California and then to Ruth and Saul's nondescript bungalow.

I rate my mother's Holocaust survivor friends on a scale of suffering. I know that some of these friends are sadder than others, tight-lipped, their conversations punctuated with frequent sighs and halts. I've lived a safe American suburban life with no Nazis, no growling dogs, no train rides, no yellow Stars of David, and, by age seventeen, I have spent considerable effort avoiding these stories of my mother's. I have no way to compute how many trains plus how many deaths plus how many concentration camps equals despair, insomnia, nightmares, and sadness. I can only glean a little by listening to their Yiddish conversations, which I do imperfectly, detecting the cadence as the words start off happy and then stretch out, tangled in the web of the war. What's this person or that person they knew in the DP camp doing now? Or how are these others who were flung by post-war immigration policies to the four corners of the earth? More importantly, how many children has each Survivor had in order to spit on Hitler's grave?

Ruth has the deepest sadness of all my mother's friends. When they talk, my mother and Ruth are not so much filled with the joy of their survival as aware of the precariousness instability of living itself. Like maybe they're waiting for another shoe to drop, an anvil to fall upon their heads with no warning. They shake their heads mournfully at the idea that there is no rhyme or reason for their survival out of all the millions who did not survive, out of all those whom they considered better than them, more deserving of life. What could God have been thinking? Was he busy somewhere else, so He didn't have time for them?

I have memorized the punctuations of my mother's war years in my mind, avoiding the subject so consistently that I just think of it in summary only. Her village, Krivich. The Nazis marching in, dividing the Jews. One group marched into a barn – I think she said a barn – and a grenade tossed in. Her small family running away into the forest, my mother talks endlessly of the forest, and, finally, the Displaced Persons Camp. My mother's family miraculously survived intact, the only one to do so from her village.

I don't know it at the time, but Ruth was the sole survivor of her family, losing each sibling, each parent, one by one. She and my mother meet in the Hess-Lichtenau Displaced Persons camp postwar. Since I've memorized the tempo of this story, I've decided that it has a happy ending. Isn't having seven daughters the evidence of a happy ending? Aren't Ruth's children evidence of a happy ending? I wonder why my mother can be a Holocaust Survivor and be happy, but Ruth can't.

I'm an American girl who has known nothing but safety, and I judge all epochs by my own idyllic, sprawling childhood. I don't understand that Ruth's story doesn't have the same ending as my mother's, an intact family. Ruth's sadness is bewildering to me. The dark kitchen, the low hung head, the bathrobe all day long, the eyes.

I ask her no questions. I want no answers.

"We're here!" Saul says, pulling the car off a road.

He's a custom home builder and has taken us out to see his newest project. We zoom along a precarious winding road on a side of a steep canyon until he proudly proclaims that we've arrived. Ruth sighs.

I look around, bewildered because I don't see a house. We climb down a slope and there it is, perched on a postage stamp-sized piece of land – land that he was lucky to buy and then lucky to get a building permit for, then lucky enough to find an architect who was able to design this teetering white tower on the rocks that looks as though it may fall over at any second, leaving nothing behind but that postage stamp-sized piece of land. Saul has created something out of nothing.

I ooh and I aah. I marvel at how he's trapped the outside inside this white box, at how the windows capture the view that would otherwise be unseen except through the windows of a car zooming by on the canyon road, or to birds. My mother is stumped. Trained on the homes built in Phoenix, on her knowledge as a real estate agent, she's never seen such a thing. To her, a house is essentially a box containing an assortment of bedrooms, bathrooms, a family room, a dining room, a living room, and a kitchen. Hopefully, a hallway. She's sure the secret to the desirability of any home is a swimming pool. This geometric structure catapulting out into space – this she's never seen before

The house is modern, modular, cutting edge, built with the best of everything. Leon declares ambitiously that it will sell for a million dollars with an investment of four hundred thousand. I think of our house, the fake wood paneling in the family room, the smoked glass mirror in the wet bar, shaped and sized like a closet, at the shiny, floral wallpaper, at the coiled cooktop, at the antiqued brass hardware on all the cabinets, at the patterned metal mini blinds blotting out the light from the windows. Our windows ignore the mountain views behind us, staring instead blankly at our beige stucco fence. The idea that our house is a house, and this thing is a house is impossible to believe. Therefore, this cannot be a house, it's a sculpture.

The luckier Saul declares himself the deeper the sighs from Ruth. She mutters, "He's so lucky, losing all his family in the war?"

I meet my two marriage prospects. There's the younger son, the active, attractive Sam, who takes me for a spin in his car, my first time ever not filling a car with nervous chitter chatter, and there's the awkward Sidney, suspiciously unmarried at thirty, the older son. Sidney and I have long, interesting, somber talks in their dark little kitchen, he even calls me when I'm back in Arizona, but nothing ever comes of it.

Months later, my mother whispers to me furtively, "Maybe he likes men?" like there could be no other reason in the world why someone wouldn't like me. But right then I hear her and Ruth talking in Yiddish at the kitchen table - what would be more wonderful than a marriage of the next generation?

We head back – steaming down the LA freeways, rounding the mountains, chugging through the desert, zooming along the straight and narrow I-10 as it approaches Phoenix. And then we are home, back on the couch.

Later I find out that Ruth and Saul's tragic stories didn't end with the war. Saul develops an inoperable tumor on his spine, is confined to a wheelchair by the next year, then dies in a car accident years later. Ruth survives this, then the disaster of Sidney's death from cancer in 2008. She dies later that same year from cancer as well.

When I hear of this, I think about the gloom over the kitchen table, the shadows in the house, my mother and Ruth huddled over the table, lamenting the fickleness of life.

Twenty-Seven

Into the Blank Pages

I'm standing in the kitchen hoping our blender manages to survive the duration of my diet, which I start after our return from California. I pull out my stale can of Slender Now and diet hard. One week, two weeks, three weeks and beyond. I start getting compliments, which I'm aware is the true joy of losing weight. But after the losing phase comes maintenance and I have no plan for maintenance. I can't wait to start eating again. The compliments abruptly stop.

My diets have an inherent problem. They have a beginning, a middle, and an end, and then nowhere to go but to bounce automatically back up to the beginning again to do the same thing all over. I have no control over the pacing of this. Yes, I lose weight each time. It's just that the weight has a funny way of reappearing, as if it was inside me all along and starts bubbling to the surface.

My diet had started when we returned from California in January. By March, I look good. By the end of April, I am boomeranging back up. There's some fitful starting and stopping over the next two month. The diet just doesn't seem to stick, like my natural state is overeating interspersed with periodic dieting failures.

We have two family events in early June 1978. I'm graduating high school on June 1st, and my sister Brenda is getting married on June 3rd.

In my family, a wedding means a dress. It also means a diet to fit in the dress. An Event Diet. This is familiar territory. It doesn't matter if it's a wedding at the Pick Congress in Chicago with two hundred people and a sit-down dinner, like my sister Francine's, or a backyard wedding at our house in Scottsdale, like this one, a plastic runner set up alongside our swimming pool – my mother insists we must all shop for dresses. Even if I had ten appropriate dresses swinging in my closet, we would go shopping. Nothing will do but new.

My mother is accepting of the various weight issues in the family, including mine. But, if I lose even a microscopic fraction of one pound, she is all over it like a wolf. So much so that I think that maybe she has some kind of surveillance camera set up above the scale in her bathroom.

"How'd you do?" she asks. She's alert to the clunking sound of anyone anywhere getting on and off the scale.

It's the beginning of my event diet. I gleefully admit that, based on all appearances, like hopping on and off the scale ten times dressed and undressed, I have lost a pound.

She pulls out her real estate amortization calculator, clicking and clacking while she does the complicated math.

"If I average your gains with your losses and amortize

that out over the eight weeks till the wedding, you'll be down ten pounds. Can you imagine?"

I get a little caught up in the fantasy.

"Ten pounds?" The world could be mine in ten pounds. Surely the amortization calculator doesn't lie.

"Just in time for the wedding!" my mom says. "We should buy a dress right now. Loehmann's is having a sale. You don't want to wait till the last minute."

And then, caught up in the excitement of that one-pound weight loss, I buy a dress that never really fits me, ever.

I'm at Loehmann's with my mother when I spot it, a damask dress with giant purple cabbage roses on it and buttons all the way down the front. I have been trained by her to spot good fabrics at a glance, to know a raw silk from a chiffon and a chiffon from, yes, a damask. The fact that this dress doesn't button all the way down the front doesn't bother me because my mother and I have already figured out my future weight, apparently mine for the having. I will diet for that dress, and I will succeed, I decide. My mother and I nod our heads in unison, both of us seeing the vision of Imaginary Thin Linda standing right there before us – slim, tall, curvy, and wearing this dress. The real image? Slightly frumpy eighteen-year-old with a dress that looks like lovely purple upholstery, the buttons pulling apart straight down the middle. The store has no larger size. My mother, once a seamstress and now a realtor, assures me she can add some material here and there or get it to close by moving the buttons and sewing it around me so I can squeeze in it like a sausage casing.

At some point I am led into the Loehmann's dressing

room, surely one of Dante's nine circles of hell. There are mirrors on all the walls surrounding bench seating, the better for all the women in there to watch this parade of shame, the whole experience an incubator for eating disorders. Somehow, there are only Jewish customers all sitting in their foundation garments on the benches. My body becomes the subject of a conversation between some of them and the Jewish saleswomen. They tsk tsk at my hip size and there's an audible gasp when the buttons on the dress pull. Some revert to Yiddish to embellish their critique, and, while I can't speak Yiddish, I am fluent in the Yiddish used for insults. I hear the word *zaftig*, I hear the commentary – what kind of bra will she wear with such small straps? Such a pretty face, but those hips!

Despite the obvious problems, we buy the dress. It's hard to explain just how much I love it. It reminds me of something I've seen before and recognize, maybe in a dream. Then again, maybe I *have* seen it. Our living room couches are upholstered in purple damask flowers.

On the day of the wedding, I realize that my mother, caught up in all the turmoil, has forgotten to alter the dress and just as predicted by the Loehmann shoppers, I never figured out the bra problem. I think, well, maybe I don't need to wear a bra. I contend with the dress myself, putting safety pins in the gaping spaces between the buttons so I don't bust right out of it or give someone a view of my bra-less chest. This doesn't work. It gapes. My male cousins from my mother's side of the family, in from Chicago for the wedding, lurk suspiciously around me all night, maybe waiting for an accident to happen.

As far as weddings go, we had started off the 1970s very elegantly with my oldest sister's wedding in 1971. No cost was spared, the wedding an extravaganza meant to convey my parents' primary message to all attendees, that Hitler didn't win. Look at this wedding! Look at these porcelain place cards! Everything is pink! We have enough money to waste!

We know this is our template, Francine's fabled marriage. A Jewish boy, a virgin bride, a father to give us away, centerpieces, a sit-down dinner, custom tablecloths, a big fancy hotel, and, yes, porcelain place cards. Dad's death disrupts all that. By 1978, there is no Chicago, no Jewish boys, no centerpieces, no tables, no money, no tablecloths, no father. No porcelain place cards.

In 1978 we actually have two weddings in our family. There's Denise's in a Justice of the Peace office to Mike, and then Brenda's, poolside at our house. No one who comes to Brenda's wedding mentions our vastly reduced circumstances. The aunts most likely to comment on this have ignored both weddings, mostly because both are intermarriages, but also because there's a cost/benefit issue – a wedding must be extravagant enough to justify schlepping from Chicago. A fancy shmancy ceremony and sit-down dinner? Yes. Poolside at our house? No.

But Brenda's Chicago friends all show up, and my mom's real estate friends, the neighbors, and various family stragglers who are okay with this untethered Arizona Jewish thing we have become. There is the wedding procession arcing around the swimming pool, my uncle standing in for our missing father, there are my sister's friends, drunk and jumping in the pool after the ceremony.

We have a family picture taken on the far side of the pool, the desert and mountains stretching out behind us. The bride and the groom in his white suit are in the middle, the seven sisters surrounding them, but we're out of order, jumbled. Number six is next to number four, number five is next to number seven, not like at Francine's wedding, where we all lined up perfectly from oldest to youngest and wearing matching pink bridesmaids' dresses. The men in the picture sport either 1970s porn-stashes or muttonchop sideburns, with clothes ranging from corduroy pants and a western shirt to my uncle's ruffle-shirted tuxedo. There's me in my dream Loehmann's dress, no bra, the dress gaping between each button.

There's my newborn three-month-old niece, Denise's baby, sleeping on my bed in the front bedroom and I go in there and fall in love with her. This child that is something new for us – Irish and Jewish, blonde, and blue-eyed.

We get to plan a lot of weddings. It turns out we are over-married rather than under-married, matching up and marching off, sister by sister.

Of course, my graduation ceremony gets lost in the shuffle. I'm fine with this. A wedding in my family is, of course, vastly more important than a graduation. Puffed up on my dreams of the future, I'm sure this will simply be the first of the gazillion diplomas I'll earn, fanning out like a deck of cards. Anyway, my mother comes through for me, buying me an opal ring for a graduation gift, just like the one my sister Francine had received years before.

The night of the graduation, a friend picks me up in her family car and we drive to our high school, head out to the stadium, and make our way to our seats. Do we know as we walk past the rows of chairs on the field how our lives will bend and sway and diverge? That we'll barely know each other from this point forward, just a dim recognition at reunions?

There are two hundred fifty students graduating, all of us gathered in the broiling June dusk in our gold robes, like a gigantic flock of canaries has descended on the football field. There were four hundred people in our class, but the week before graduation I started hearing alarming tales that our senior class of four hundred wasn't graduating four hundred. I hear there will be three hundred fifty, then three hundred, and finally I hear two hundred fifty. Failed classes and missed requirements, we dwindle. It turns out that four years isn't always the right four years.

We stand, we sit. There's a standing ovation for our class superhero football player who, early in our senior year, fell off a mountain and lived. He accepts his diploma, rolling his way from one side of the stage to the other in a wheelchair. Stunned and tearful, we rise. We acknowledge that something is ending and something beginning.

We throw our gold Chaparral High School mortars into the air and then search frantically, trying to figure out which one is our own. And we disperse, moving off into the rest of our lives.

In the fall of 1978, with the car filled with my stereo, my record albums, my fledgling beauty products, and one stale can of Slender Now, my mother drives me the two hours south to

326

Tucson. The trip somehow mirrors our original trip to Arizona when we'd moved five years before, my father at the wheel of our station wagon, heading off from Chicago optimistically, sure he was driving towards the pot of gold at the end of the rainbow. His left arm rested on the open window, his right arm shot out like a beam on top of the steering wheel. Exultant, triumphant, jubilant. I remember being in the back of that car, dreaming of all the great things to come, my optimism a familiar chirp in my head.

In my diaries I have a habit of paging forward randomly to pose a question from Present Linda to Future Linda about whether love had finally arrived. Did I have a boyfriend? What great things had happened? What was the future like in those blank pages? For a while, there is the wonder of the pages in between.

When I come to these pages, they're always a shock. My answer is, invariably, that love has not come, and that the future so anticipated had somehow morphed back into the present as the pages flipped by.

Heading to college, we drive straight into those blank pages.

"Mom, I'm worried about going to college. I say this as we barrel down I-10, rounding Picacho Peak. We're pretty close to Tucson.

She is ready for this. She regales me with tales of her friends' daughters who also were afraid of going to college, now apparently all doctors and lawyers, like Cindy Schwartz and Debbie Berger, and I suddenly know that I'm supposed to be her Cindy, her Debbie, through me she can claim her rightful spot *kvelling* among the Jewish ladies.

"And anyway," she says, "you'll come home every weekend!" She nods her head definitively, like I'm going to just magically fly up there each weekend, owning no car.

I'm leaving my home, my sisters, and my baby niece and nephew. The thought of life moving on without me at home is gut-wrenching. I want nothing to change while I'm gone. I want the world to stand still until I'm back in it.

We exit the Interstate at Speedway, then we make a right turn at Park. I recoil. I'm completely unprepared to memorize new street names, new stores, new maps in my head, new TV stations, new broadcasters. It was bad enough when we moved from Chicago to Arizona.

The campus is a madhouse as we pull up at the dorm. My mom manages to park the gigantic Lincoln somewhere, but the car is really just wedged in, sticking out. We only have a minute to rush my things up to my dorm room, everything packed in banana boxes and orange boxes left over from our store, the banana boxes to double as stereo shelving. She enlists some burly fraternity guys to help carry the boxes and I flush with shame when they look me over. They're wearing topsider loafers and no socks, yacht clothes. It's 1978 but it's not really the 70s anymore. We've somehow arrived in the 1980s.

My mom says, "I have to go before I get a ticket."

I'd expected a long, leisurely goodbye, something meaningful to bridge my old home to my new one. Maybe lunch. I'd definitely hoped that she'd unpack with me and warm up these roommates for me with her oft-repeated narrative about being a real estate agent with seven daughters and about how I was number six. I need her to make my way for me.

Instead, I am left alone in the dorm with my three roommates, all strangers, my boxes all around me. I notice that we've each brought a stereo and mine is the worst of them all.

I suddenly want to grab those banana boxes, tell my mom I've changed my mind, and hightail it back to Phoenix. What on earth was I thinking, leaving home?

But I stay in the room and move to the window. I watch as the speck of my mother walks towards the parking lot and gets in her car. I watch the blue rectangle of the car as she drives away, back up Park towards Speedway. Then she's out of my view.

I stay right there, on my own personal fork in the road, Present Linda colliding with all those Future Lindas in all those blank pages in my diary, right on the spot that is supposed to be my glorious future. The slump-blocked dorm, three strangers for roommates, an upcoming war over stereos, and my mother driving away.

Acknowledgements

I've been fortunate in my writing teachers. I don't know how I could have written anything at all without their generous sharing of their knowledge and craft. My first, without whom I probably never would have written a word, Dr. Lois Roma-Deeley, and so many others: Theo Nestor, Susan Shapiro, Samantha Dunn, Steven Wolfson, Barbara Abercrombie, Steve Almond, Dr. Barbara Starikoff, Paul Morris, Amy Silverman, Deborah Sussman, and more. I can only hope that the wisdom and insight I've learned from them is conveyed in the classes I now teach.

I'm grateful to my fellow writing students in the workshops I've attended for the last twenty years who were supportive and enthusiastic when, alone, I might have faltered. I'm reminded that in the magical alchemy of writing workshops my stories are born, and that I am held up by a thousand hands.

I'm grateful to the readers of my first book, *Looking Up: A Memoir of Sisters, Survivors, and Skokie*, many of whom wrote to me to tell me how the book had touched them and evoked similar memories of their childhoods. These letters buoyed me up when I faltered. They reassured me of the importance of telling the next part of the story, to answer the question of what happened to the seven sisters after we drove away from Skokie.

I'm grateful to my family in Chicago, and grateful for being able to tell my stories of those times, filtered through my then-teenaged brain, making it onto the page so many years later, even if my perceptions differ from their own. I'm especially grateful to my aunt and uncle who allowed me to spend a portion of my teen years in their home, to be able to straddle my two worlds, Skokie and Scottsdale. I appreciate their tolerance in allowing me to bring wildness in and take some Judaism out with me when I left.

I'm grateful for receiving unending love, support, and encouragement from my husband, Howard, an astute editing assistant, and my children, Daniel, my source of Hebrew knowledge, and Ray, to whom I owe some distinctive chapter titles and a last-minute critical eye.

I'm so grateful to be one of seven sisters, and grateful for the encouragement to write this story, to let our past come alive and let our parents live again on the page. I hope by writing I allow my parents and the millions who were lost to be remembered.

It's often said that the story picks the writer. For me and this history, that is especially true.

Yiddish/Hebrew Terminology

Amerikanish – all things American, American-like

Banshees – a wailing female spirit

Bashert – meant to be, destined

Bimah – podium in a synagogue

Bissel klug – a little slow

Bubbe – grandmother

Chai – A pendant with the Hebrew letters *chet* and *yud*, which form the word "life" and the numerical equivalent of eighteen.

Chazer – pig

Chops and klops – acting impulsively

Chuppah – wedding canopy

Dummkopf – dummy, stupid

Farkoktah – screwed up, crappy

Fleishig – meats and meat-related products normally associated with a kosher kitchen

Goniff – thieves or crooks

Goyische – Christian, non-Jewish

Haggadahs/Haggadot - the text recited at the Seder on the first two nights of Passover

Haimish – friendly or homey

Hora – a circle dance found at Jewish celebrations such as weddings and B'nai Mitzvahs

Kaddish – Mourner's Prayer

Kalookie – card game

Kashered – to make kosher, to purify

Kashrut – the body of dietary laws prescribed for Jews.

Kinder - children

Kishke – as food a mixture of flour or matzoh meal, sugar and fat, stuffed in an animal intestine, or derma. As expression – "nagging her kishkes out" – churning guts

Krivich/Krivichi/Krywiec – a village in now-Belarus

Kvelling – bursting with pride or satisfaction

Litvak – a Jew of Lithuanian origin

Mamaleh – little mother or mother's little one

Mechitza – a divider in Orthodox Jewish worship separating men from women

Mikveh – ritual bathing for cleanliness in Orthodox Judaism; a ritual bath which can return physical items to cleanliness

Milchig – milk-related products, normally in a kosher kitchen

Minyan – quorum of ten needed to for traditional public worship

Mishpocha – family, people

Nu – So?

Ongeblozen – full of him/herself, conceited, overdone

Oy – an expression of dismay

Oy gevalt – used to express shock or amazement

Parve – Neutral foods in a kosher kitchen, neither milk nor meat

Pintele yid – a Jewish spark deep within, waiting to be ignited when the time is right

Pisher – little big shot

Schervas – whore, prostitute (Polish – "kurva")

Schlemiels – a stupid, awkward, or unlucky person

Schlepping – haul or carry, moving with effort

Schlimazel – an extremely unlucky person, a habitual failure

Schmendricks – ineffectual, foolish, or contemptible person

Schnorring – one who habitually takes advantage of the generosity of others

Shabbos/Shabbat – the Jewish Sabbath

Shabbos goy – A non-Jew who is able to do tasks a Shabbat-observant Jew cannot

Shadchan - Matchmaker

Shpiel/spiel – a fast speech often repeated and intended to persuade

Shtetl – a small Jewish town or village

Shul – Jewish house of worship, synagogue

Tref – non-kosher

Yentas – Gossip or busybody

Yachnehs – loud-mouthed woman, a gossip

Zaftig – overweight, plump

Zayda – grandfather

All pronunciations and transliterations by the author. More information can be obtained at YIVO Institute for Jewish Research www.yivo.org, and through the Yiddish Book Center www.yiddishbookcenter.org.

About the Author

Linda Pressman is a freelance writer, editor, speaker, and author. She has a bachelor's degree in History, a Master's in English, and completed all but thesis towards a Master's in Medieval History. She currently teaches Life Stories through the city of Scottsdale and in the local Jewish community.

Her first book, *Looking Up: A Memoir of Sisters, Survivors and Skokie*, won the Grand Prize in the Writer's Digest 20th Annual Book Contest. It is housed in the permanent collections at Yad Vashem, the U.S. Holocaust Museum, and the National Library of Israel.

She can be reached on her Facebook page at Linda Pressman, Author, by email at lindajpressman@gmail.com and linda@lindajpressman.com, on Twitter at @barmitzvahzilla, and on her website, lindajpressman.com.

Made in the USA
Coppell, TX
06 February 2022